The Midnight Disease

The Midnight Disease

THE DRIVE TO WRITE,
WRITER'S BLOCK,
AND THE
CREATIVE BRAIN

Alice W. Flaherty

HOUGHTON MIFFLIN COMPANY
BOSTON · NEW YORK
2004

For information about permission to reproduce selections
from this book, write to Permissions, Houghton Mifflin Company,
215 Park Avenue South, New York, New York 10003.

Visit our Web site: www.houghtonmifflinbooks.com.

Library of Congress Cataloging-in-Publication Data
Flaherty, Alice W.
The midnight disease : the drive to write, writer's block,
and the creative brain / Alice W. Flaherty.
p. cm.
Includes index.
ISBN 0-618-23065-3
1. Writer's block. 2. Authorship — Psychological aspects.
3. Authors — Mental health. 4. Creation (Literary,
artistic, etc.) I. Title.
PN171.W74F58 2004
808'.001'9 — dc21   2003051143

Printed in the United States of America

Book design by Victoria Hartman

MP 10 9 8 7 6 5 4 3 2 1

The excerpt on page 183 from "My Muse" by Stevie Smith is from *Collected
Poems of Stevie Smith,* copyright © 1972 by Stevie Smith. Reprinted by per-
mission of the Executors of the Estate of James MacGibbon and New Di-
rections Publishing Corp. The excerpt on page 237 from "The Telephone
Number of the Muse" by Donald Justice is from *New and Selected Poems of
Donald Justice,* copyright © 1995 by Donald Justice. Used by permission of
Alfred A. Knopf, a division of Random House.

To Andrew Hrycyna

CONTENTS

ACKNOWLEDGMENTS   I most want to thank my husband and closest friend, Andrew Hrycyna — also my strictest editor — with whom I had many happily violent arguments about everything from Aristotle to Alice in Wonderland. Katharina Trede's influence permeates the book, with her knowledge (all that European stuff), her nuanced readings, and her ability to keep from categorizing the world too rigidly. Deanne Urmy, my editor at Houghton Mifflin, contributed her literary sensibilities and tolerance, as did my wonderful, warm agent, Mary Evans — as sharp a critic as a negotiator.

I am also grateful to Benjamin Davis, Rachel DeWoskin, Nancy Etcoff, C. Miller Fisher (for good advice, "Don't tell anyone about it," that I couldn't follow), Ben Greenberg, Alison Hickey (who gave me an Aeolian harp both literarily and literally), Jonathan Rosand (for all things B.C.E.), Adina Gerver, Patty Gibbons, Ann Graybiel, Esteban Gonzalez, John Herman (knows all the right people, among many other things), Stephen King, Walter Koroshetz (walks on water as a neurologist), Dimitri Krainc, Paul Kafka-Gibbons (great novelists make great critics), Claire LaZebnik (ditto), Kay Redfield Jamison, Scott Liebert (tried to keep me legal), Mia MacCollin, David Perkins, Bruce Quinn, Graham Ramsay (photographer and composer), Mike Rose (remarkable intellectual generosity), Oliver Sacks, Katrin Sadigh, Elaine Scarry, Lee Schwamm, Andrei Shleifer, Ted Stroll (for the most thorough of readings), Janet Taylor, Mike Wiecek, Shirley Wray, and especially Anne Young (who gave me at once freedom and a role model).

Finally, I'd like to thank my parents and my sisters, Franklin, Sarah, and Margaret Flaherty (for, among many other things, letting me write at the kitchen table while they washed the Christmas dishes), and my daughters, Katerina and Elizabeth Hrycyna (for providing all the cute twin anecdotes. I hope when they're teenagers they'll forgive me for having used them).

The Midnight Disease

Introduction

Poets teach us to use words with special force. We may need their help in finding new ways to talk about brains.
—— J. Z. Young, *Programs of the Brain*

A creative writer is one for whom writing is a problem.
—— Roland Barthes, *Writing Degree Zero*

WRITING IS ONE of the supreme human achievements. No, why should I be reasonable? Writing is *the* supreme achievement. It is by turns exhilarating and arduous, and trying to write obsesses and distresses students, professional writers, and diarists alike. Writers explain why they write (and have trouble writing) one way; freshman composition teachers, another; literary critics and psychiatrists and neurologists have increasingly foreign explanations. These modes of thinking about the emotions that surround writing do not easily translate into one another. But one fact is always true: the mind that writes is also the brain that writes. And the existence of brain states that affect our creativity raises questions that make us uneasy. What is the relation between mind and body? What are the sources of imagination?

How can both neuroscience and literature bear on the question of what makes writers not only able to, but want to, even need to, write? How can we understand the outpouring of authors such as Joyce Carol Oates or Stephen King? Why does John Updike see a blank sheet of paper as radiant, the sun rising in the morning? (As William Pritchard said of him, "He must have had an unpublished thought, but you couldn't tell it.") This compulsion seems — and is — an unbelievably complex psychological trait.

Yet it is not so complex that it cannot be studied. Neurologists have found that changes in a specific area of the brain can produce hypergraphia — the medical term for an overpowering desire to write. Thinking in a counterintuitive, neurological way about what drives and frustrates literary creation can suggest new treatments for hypergraphia's more common and tormenting opposite, writer's block. Both conditions arise from complicated abnormalities of the basic biological drive to communicate. Whereas linguists and most scientists have focused primarily on writing's cognitive aspects, this book spends more time exploring the complex relationship between writing and emotion. It draws examples from literature, from my patients, and from some of my own experiences.

Evidence that ranges from Nabokov to neurochemistry, Faulkner to functional brain imaging, shows that thinking about excesses and dearths of writing can also clarify normal literary output and the mechanisms of creativity. The few current books on creativity that include a neuroscientific perspective have neglected crucial brain regions such as the temporal lobe and limbic system in favor of a still-popular — but arguably oversimplified — emphasis on the role of the right side of the brain.

Focusing on the importance of the brain in the drive to write helps suggest treatments for disorders of creativity that are sometimes medical. It should do so, though, without ignoring the fact that most innovative people, and most people struggling with blocks, are not mentally ill. Concentrating on the brain structures underlying creativity provides surprising answers to such diverse questions as how we learn to write, the nature of metaphor, and even what causes the strange sensation of being visited by the muse.

Although *The Midnight Disease* attempts to be a scientifically accurate book, it is far from a dispassionate one. How could I speak

Figure 1. This plate from Max Ernst's *Maximiliana* (1964) graphically illustrates the strange vitality of letters. The zoomorphic script comes alive and wanders off into the margins — except for the character fighting the Elizabethan figure, perhaps to test whether the pen is mightier than the sword.

dryly on a subject as charged as the origin of literature? I am infatuated with writing, and this emotional engagement shapes the book. Writing can do extraordinary things. One night when I was a child, I read a passage in C. S. Lewis's autobiography, *Surprised by Joy*, which described one of his own reading experiences as a child. He had been reading Longfellow's poem "Tegner's Drapa," when a line jumped out at him: "I heard a voice that cried / Balder the beautiful / Is dead, is dead. . . ." The beauty of that line, the way it tore at him, drove him to become permanently addicted to reading and writing. Strangely, even out of context, the line stirred me as well. Something swept me out of his book high into the cold air above the northern wastes. What was it that was transmitted from the writer of "Tegner's Drapa" to the writer of *The Allegory of Love* to me, possibly even to you?

In her book *On Beauty and Being Just*, Elaine Scarry imagines Leonardo da Vinci seeing a woman with a face so beautiful that he tries over and over to capture it in different drawings. Later artists are moved by his copies, which they then try to copy themselves. Eventually the critic Walter Pater writes his famous essay on Leonardo, and the copies of the woman's face spread from one art form into another. Beauty drives copies of itself, whether in art, or when we want to make children with someone we love. Great scientific ideas drive their own transmission in the same way — it is not a metaphor when researchers refer to an elegant theorem as beautiful.

In another sense, though, it is the brain, not beauty, that drives those copies. Many parts of the brain play a role: Leonardo's exquisite motor cortical control of his pen, the way his visual cortex perceived shape from shadow, his face recognition area. Yet some parts of the brain may be more crucial than others for the emotional aspect of the drive toward beauty or meaning.

One of these regions is the pair of temporal lobes, located in the cerebral cortex roughly behind the ears. The temporal lobes have been somewhat neglected by neurologists, in part because damage to them does not produce glaring motor or cognitive problems. Still, the temporal lobes are important for producing literature, in part because they are necessary for understanding word meaning — and also Meaning in its philosophical senses. In addition, changes in the temporal lobes can produce hypergraphia.

A second region of the brain that is surprisingly relevant to creative writing is the limbic system, the seat of emotion and drive and, I'll argue, some aspects of the feeling of being inspired (a feeling, alas, that does not always coincide with producing great work). It gets its name from the fact that it forms a limbus, or ring, deep under the cortex. The limbic system connects more strongly to the temporal lobes than to any other region of the cortex. This strong link underlies the importance of emotion and drive to creativity — factors that are anatomically as well as conceptually distinct from the cognitive contributions of the rest of the cerebral cortex. The limbic system also reflects the way mood swings can drive creativity.

The temporal lobes and the limbic system appear to underlie the drive to seek beauty and meaning in nonliterary forms of artistic achievement as well. The temporal lobes' role in hypergraphia, for instance, may parallel their role in intense drives to paint and to compose music. The same brain changes that drove Vincent van Gogh's frenzied painting (at his peak he produced a new canvas every thirty-six hours) seem to have driven his hypergraphic letters to his brother, Theo. Further, to the extent that hypergraphia and frenetic artistic achievement are special cases of the more general phenomenon of a sense of vocation, or of workaholism, they can shed light on how or whether to control these double-edged states. Nearly all of us, artists or not, feel the terror of work as well as the joy of work.

Along with my fascination with writing, my work as a physician shapes the book. I am obsessed with illness and how it changes my patients. Moreover, like many doctors, I have acquired the occupational illness of seeing disease everywhere. During dull conferences, my colleagues and I amuse ourselves by diagnosing one another: Horner's syndrome, swan-neck deformity, congenital toe-walking, frontal release signs.

Can any good come from casting such a medicalized eye on the world of writing? Medicalization tends to lead to pathographies of artists: El Greco's elongated figures are explained away as mere astigmatism, Dostoevsky's writing as nothing but epilepsy. Pathologizing the process of writing could make us see creativity as abnormal or even dangerous. Yet affliction is everywhere, perhaps especially in writing. Suffering has driven great writing, and problems with writing, notably writer's block, have caused great suffering.

One of the most moving, and most readily helped, groups of patients I see is college students admitted for their first psychiatric break. Often what finally brings them to their university's attention is that they can no longer write and are beginning to get incompletes in their courses. These are students with biologically based psychiatric problems that affect their creativity and their ability to express themselves. Their treatment often underestimates their problems with work as side effects of family issues. Indeed, the two are hard to separate. But work — how we make things of and do things to the external world — is nearly as basic, and primeval, a factor in human happiness as family relations. The inability to write reflects the sufferer's feeling that he or she cannot contribute to the world, cannot communicate with others in any meaningful way.

The medical model for fighting suffering, although it has distinct limitations, is also immensely powerful. Bringing a doctor's eye to writers' own accounts of their creative process can lead to startling and useful conclusions — ones that don't necessarily involve prescribing pills. To give a simple instance, many writers who hate themselves every winter for their sluggishness and lack of productivity could be aided not by "more motivation," but by bright full-spectrum light for a half an hour every morning to treat their brain's seasonal response to the shortened days.

Problems of motivation are not, of course, restricted to writers. Some of my patients have severe movement disorders and, despite the best intentions, from day to day their willpower is no longer enough to drive their limbs. Yet someone with, say, Parkinson's disease who has spent months in a wheelchair will, if there is a fire, be able to leap from her chair and run. This confusing inconsistency often convinces family members that their mother or husband isn't ill, but simply isn't trying hard enough. Sometimes not even the patient wants to give up that belief. To admit that your will is sometimes ineffective is terrifying.

In place of the will, what do I offer my Parkinsonian patients? Pills, of course, or permanently implanted electrodes in their brains to stimulate them to move. I began to wonder if similar medical treatments might help people with disorders of motivation not just in movement initiation abilities, but also in cognitive skills such as writing. Motor-cognitive tasks are not perfectly analogous. In simple movements, stronger motivation — the fire under the wheelchair — is generally better. But in complicated tasks, if the motivation is too strong, the adrenaline that usually helps movements can cause the performer to freeze. This "stage fright" aspect to writer's block is often neglected. Another difference between "psychological states" such as block and "neurological" states such as Parkinson's disease is that relatively subtle behavioral interventions (psychotherapy, for instance) can be immensely helpful in the former, but not in the latter. Because of my biology-based training, and because so many others have described the ways that therapy can help writing problems, I sometimes neglect therapy and other behavioral interventions in this book. Yet they are important, ultimately biological, treatments. They work, in the end, by altering one's brain chemistry and neuroanatomy.

As a doctor, I hope I do not simply see normal problems as illness; I want also to see that illness is often nearly normal. If we are all a little bit sick, it is not all that sick to be sick. Illness is even sometimes useful. It is easy to forget that whether a behavior is a disease or a gift may depend on its context. The fallow periods that some writers call block are, for others, a fermentation stage in the creative process.

Take the famous "little man with a perfect memory" so movingly described by the Russian psychologist A. R. Luria in *The Mind of a Mnemonist*. Although the man Luria studied had a photographic memory, he was cursed rather than blessed by it. Reading and writing were among the many activities his too-good memory made hard for him. Every word, even every letter within a word, called up so many associations that it was nearly impossible for him to concentrate on a chain of thought. His distracting memory ended his writing career as a journalist, and he finished his life as a circus performer doing memory tricks. (Or would only a writer say that this career change was unfortunate?)

Other people who have near-perfect memories, but different social and intellectual resources, have used them to great advantage in successful writing careers. One instance is the prodigious memory of the prolific literary scholar Harold Bloom, who has reportedly recited *Paradise Lost* backward.

The Midnight Disease is shaped not only by my work as a doctor with people, but also by my work as a neuroscientist with brain imaging to study neural activity. Is it therefore my goal to reduce the composition of marvels like Dante's *Inferno* to nothing more than electrical and neurochemical patterns? Emphatically not. Do I want to say that talking of the chemical states of our brains is more important than talking of experience or the will? Emphatically not. We will always be talking about mental states, too, because they are powerful, subtle, indispensable concepts. But when Dante describes his writer's block ("It seemed to me that I had undertaken too lofty a theme for my powers, so much so that I was afraid to enter upon it; and so I remained for several days desiring to write and afraid to begin"), he is describing a brain state as well as a mental state.

Many readers, while granting that our minds are the products of our brains, believe that there are some aspects of our thoughts — especially during creative inspiration — that come from outside us. It would be a mistake to dismiss this emotionally resonant position. In fact, I will show in the last chapter that this position supports current scientific hypotheses of how our brains handle creative, moral, and religious impulses.

While doctors care about disease because they want to cure it, many neuroscientists care about disease as a scalpel with which to dissect health. When something falls apart, you can see its pieces more clearly. In this way, for instance, researchers learned about the role of the left and right sides of the brain from split-brain patients.

As a neuroscientist, I am fascinated by hypergraphia and writer's block because of what they tell us about normal creativity. Most writing about creativity squares its shoulders pluckily and stares the phenomenon in the face. The result is countless biographies of uniquely Great Men, or statistical studies of one hundred Nobel laureates. But staring creativity in the face has turned many writers to stone. *The Midnight Disease* sneaks up on creativity from behind, by considering its disorders.

As a researcher, I am obsessed with the powerful notion of testability, which is the foundation of the scientific method. Single examples often mislead ("A friend of a friend lost sixty pounds on this new diet!"); most explanations and treatments for writing problems still need rigorous testing by what scientists consider the gold-standard method: the double-blind, prospective, randomized clinical trial. Indeed, neuroscientists have been squeamish about the difficulty of testing theories about creativity and its problems and sometimes dismiss the field as intellectually unhygienic. Nonetheless, despite the complexity of problems such as writer's block and treatments such as psychotherapy, despite the fact that every individual is different, the effectiveness of these techniques is still ultimately testable. In this book I try to spell out some ways to evaluate their worth. Fascinating new techniques will in the near future make such tests easier. In the interest of keeping the text readable, I have exiled much information about research methodology, replication, and contradictory studies to the notes at the back of the book; readers who are interested in pursuing a topic further can do so there.

The application of science and medicine to problems such as writing well disturbs many people specifically *because* of the notion of testability, of cold human experimentation. Experimentation is not necessarily something that is done to you, however. Cautious self-experimentation can be crucial to taking control of your own problem. If writing at night doesn't work, try writing in the morning. If you try medications, do so with a clinician willing to help you evaluate the results and not just prescribe according to a protocol. If medications don't work, try psychotherapy, or vice versa. A new approach may be especially important in writer's block, which can stem from rigidity that makes the sufferer use the same failing approach over and over. This rigidity has some features in common with known syndromes of frontal lobe malfunction. People who do try new techniques often make readily correctable mistakes in the way they go about their self-experiments. I hope that by pointing them out I can make those mistakes easier to avoid.

Presenting my biases as a scientist might seem to be inconsistent — scientists are supposed to be objective. But I argue in this book, as many before me have done, that all scientists have biases; it is merely that most fail to admit them. Scientific diction can be as deceptive as oratory; its mind-numbing passive constructions and jargon often bring only the appearance of neutrality.

Why, if I am a scientist, have I written a book? Scientists should write scientific papers. A melancholy fact is that in the sciences, the book has become as marginal a literary form as the sestina or the villanelle. With the rise of the Internet, books may soon be obsolete even for general readers. (I should confess that often while writing this work, I would check a reference on the Internet rather than stand up and walk to the bookshelf five feet away.) Perhaps writing this book is my eulogy for the book, or a wistful hope that people will always be crazy enough to write books. In the end, though, because of an unusual personal experience, writing this book was something I could not stop myself from doing.

I always wrote a little more than was normal, but I was able to keep my tendencies discreet. When occasionally a friend would ask if I ever considered publishing what I wrote, I was puzzled; it seemed such a private pleasure that it was as if someone who thought I was good in bed asked if I had considered doing it in public. (Thus I still lacked a key aspect of being a writer. Who was it who said that an artist is someone who gets pleasure from the praise of complete strangers?) In medical school when I first heard about the existence of hypergraphia, I began to wonder whether my own writing were hypergraphic — partly because suggestible medical students tend to believe they have whatever disorder they are currently studying, and partly because my writing was indeed becoming more driven. When I wrote my first book, a handbook of neurology, I was a hospital resident working 80 to 110 hours a week. Without any plan to start a book, I found that some notes I was taking to help me on the wards crept up on me and took over. Soon I was skipping meals and waking early to work on them. As a joke, I told people that the book was an attempt to make my hypergraphia useful. Then I got pregnant and had a postpartum mood disorder during which my writing truly exploded. After that, it was no longer witty to describe my writing as a medical symptom.

My postpartum mood disorder, which had several manic as well as the more typical depressed features, came after I had given birth prematurely to twin boys who died. They were so small — one grasped my finger before he died, and his hand hardly fit around it. For ten days I was filled with sorrow. Then suddenly, as if someone had thrown a switch, I was wildly agitated, full of ideas, all of them pressing to be written down. The world was flooded with meaning. I believed I had unique access to the secrets of the Kingdom of Sorrow, about which I had an obligation to enlighten my — very tolerant — friends and colleagues through essays and letters.

While postpartum major depression occurs after one in ten deliveries, postpartum mania occurs after one in a thousand. Mania and depression can come in complicated mixtures. As I found out, one manic feature is hypergraphia. Not all mania is the textbook mania of flamboyant dressing, risk taking, and barroom fights. Its principal effect on me was to make me hole up in my office and write. Why pathologize this and call it a disease? I could still do my normal job. But my writing *felt* like a disease: I could not stop, and it sucked me away from family and friends. Sensations outside of language dried up: music became irritating discord, the visual world grew faint. Cramming the inclinations of a writer into a skull already filled with many years of training as a scientist created extraordinary pressure. While my hypergraphia felt like a disease, it also felt like one of the best things that has ever happened to me. It still does.

For the next four months I ricocheted daily between euphoria and terror. On good days, ideas would wake me at four in the morning, tendrils of words coiling around me like some heady perfume. It was as if a door had opened onto a hot wind from the tropics, the sort of wind that propels ships carrying peacock feathers and rubies and apes and incense. On bad days, the words were like a charnel house through which I had to search for the bodies of people I loved. In either case, the desire to write was overpowering. I wrote during department meetings, when I should have been doing experiments, when I could have been with friends. The sight of a computer keyboard or a blank page gave me the same rush that drug addicts get from seeing their freebasing paraphernalia.

Although the inevitable depression followed, it lasted only a month or so and its apathy was in some ways almost a relief. When the world went dead, words lost their meaning; there was no pressure to write. I was not really a blocked writer, I was no longer a writer at all. It was peaceful — unless I tried to speak or write. Then it was as if my lungs were full of water, suffocating.

I became pregnant again. In a strange symmetry I delivered premature but healthy twin girls, Katerina and Elizabeth. A similar excited postpartum state started eleven days after delivery, eventually followed by a similar torpor. This time, though, I tried a mood stabilizer. Although the drug slightly decreased my periods of agitation, it gave me an excruciating writer's block. My head again filled with ideas, but this time I could not articulate them. The pressure in my head continued to build until it was a throbbing abscess that I was frantic to drain.

Before I started taking the mood stabilizer, I had never experienced what I would have called writer's block. Although it is still hard for me to believe that a pill could cause block, I know I felt that mute pressure only while on that drug, and that the block increased as the dose did. I tried several other medications — doctors' faith in pills dies hard. Eventually I found ones that helped. Would they help everyone with writing problems? Probably not. But general rules pointed out drugs that were likely to help.

As my writing calmed, the world and the words oscillated less violently between supreme Meaning and nonsense, and my hypergraphia turned back into normal writing. More or less. Some researchers believe one's brain is never quite the same after a manic episode, however mild. Even now, when I am writing well, my pulse speeds up, I feel gripped by something stronger than my will, and I have some of the delicious feeling I had at my most hypergraphic. When I can't find an idea, I now much more quickly begin to think that I am blocked.

The sudden change in my writing was in one respect a "natural response to bereavement," as my friends kept reassuring me when I started throwing around words like "hypergraphia." Nonetheless, it was also an unusual brain state. It wasn't just bereavement: not only my first, unhappy pregnancy, but my second, happy one triggered the change. It is likely that pregnancy-induced mood disorders and hypergraphia are linked to the wild hormonal fluctuations that happen at birth (a similar change may explain premenstrual syndrome, and estrogen can treat depression even in men).

Hormones are not the only way, or even a major way, to induce hypergraphia. But it disturbed me that writing, which seems one of the most refined, even transcendent talents, should be so influenced by biology. I wanted to understand how my brain was different when it started writing obsessively and when it became blocked. Like many patients with a problem, I began reading everything I could find on the subject — ranging from Hippocrates' descriptions of the "sacred disease" through what Edgar Allan Poe and later Michael Chabon have called the "midnight disease" that causes writing. I wrote this book to try to explain to myself what had erupted in (or into) my brain to turn me, almost against my will, into a writer.

You may well ask what my experience has to do with the writing of normal people. The answer is that although my brain may have a screw loose, everyone has the same screw. (That is *not* to say that drugs are necessarily the way to treat most writing problems.) Mental illness is not completely separable from sanity. There is a sense in which mental illness is awfully like sanity — only much, much more so.

Because my drive to write has been so magnified and altered by illness, I think I see more clearly how important are the emotions that underlie periods of writing well and periods of block. The pleasure of writing and the pain of its absence tells something crucial about the motivation to write and the way it springs from our instinct to communicate. It is a feeling that is essential both for our ability as writers and for our potential to interact as human beings.

This book lays out what neuroscience is beginning to tell us about the drive to write and to create, about creative block and its treatment, about the cortical and limbic underpinnings of these drives and blocks, and finally about neurological aspects of the relation between metaphor, the inner voice, and inspiration. Many of these ideas are preliminary — not meant to be the final word on these complex subjects, but to spur further debate.

Chapter 1 describes several relatively well defined brain conditions that increase the desire to write. Some patients with temporal lobe epilepsy, manic-depression (bipolar disorder), and other disorders experience florid hypergraphia. Yet their hypergraphia is usually a trait they value in themselves. It can be something others value too, for their writings can range from the simple (one epileptic patient's copious journal was endless repetition of "Thank GOD, no seizures" in variously colored inks) to the sublime (the novels of Gustave Flaubert, also a temporal lobe epileptic).

The odd behavior of temporal lobe epileptics can tell us about the odd behavior of some professional creative writers. Chapter 2 describes how the temporal lobes may help drive "normal" emotionally engaged writing just as they drive "abnormal" hypergraphia. Moreover, the existence of people with temporal lobe changes who begin to paint or compose music provides evidence that the temporal lobes' role in creativity applies also to nonliterary creativity. The frontal lobes may help judge and edit the somewhat indiscriminate ideas whose generation was driven by the temporal lobes. Temporal lobe explanations of creativity shed new light on more traditional theories of creativity; for instance, the hypothesis that creativity resides primarily in the right side of the brain.

Hypergraphia is neither painful nor common. Writer's block is both. The paradoxically eloquent literature on writer's block, from famous sufferers such as Flaubert and Franz Kafka, and from clinicians, explains block as everything from an oppressed inner child to penis envy. What we know about the psychological mechanisms of writer's block, described in Chapter 3, can also help us to understand block in relation to another agonizing problem, procrastination.

A neuroscientific, as opposed to a psychological, perspective on block (Chapter 4) allows biochemical explanations and treatments of block. In the frequent case of block related to mood swings, a medical model of block can clarify why writers such as Samuel Taylor Coleridge, who were made miserable by writer's block, were also able in bursts of creativity to write hypergraphically. I explore the origins of such cycles from multiple perspectives, including behavioral, neurochemical, and evolutionary. The close relationship between productivity and mood is complex, as when mood disorders both spark and hinder the drive to write, or when alcohol abuse eases the anxiety of writer's block but decreases the ability to write well.

It turns out that the drive and the ability to write are to a significant extent controlled by different areas of the brain. The cerebral cortex has more of a role in the ability than in the drive to write. Chapter 5 describes how recent advances in neuroscience, including brain imaging technology, have made it possible to study the ability to write in normal people, as well as in language-impaired people. The advances have brought an explosion of new information. Even high-level literary phenomena, such as metaphor and metonymy, are turning out to have defined brain substrates. Writing also requires reading, as is apparent in dyslexia. The odd phenomenon of hyperlexia (compulsive reading) and the even odder experience of synesthesia or colored reading (a cortically based experience that may underlie some poets' use of metaphor) also cast new light on brain mechanisms for literature.

The limbic system, in contrast to the cortex, has a greater role in basic drives and how they are influenced by drugs such as antidepressants or opiates. One limbic drive described in Chapter 6, one almost strong enough to be an instinct, is the drive to communicate. Powerful neural and emotional changes result when the drive to communicate is blocked, as when a social monkey is made mute, when an American with limited knowledge of French moves to Paris, or — a somewhat more complicated phenomenon — when a writer's great success with a first novel makes writing the second one harder. Limbic dynamics underlie the close relationship between suffering and the drive to write, and have implications for determining who becomes a writer and why. It turns out that problems such as procrastination are usually better treated by putting the writer in the appropriate limbic or motivational state than by cognitive strategies such as making To Do lists. Most procrastinators are very aware of exactly what they are not doing.

Reading and writing give us not only an intellectual, cortical apprehension of word meaning but also an emotional or limbic sensation of meaningfulness or importance. In Chapter 7 I argue that metaphoric thinking, important for science as well as literature, can link these types of meaning. Metaphoric thinking is largely a temporal lobe function. So, it is likely, is the inner voice we hear in our heads every day. Temporal lobe changes occur during states in which the inner voice starts to feel alien, as in the auditory hallucinations of psychotics. Temporal changes may also occur during the very different processes of religious and creative inspiration. The sensation of receiving dictation from an external force or muse, felt by some writers at their most inspired, may share with psychosis a neurologically based projection of the inner voice onto the external world. Such biological origins do not strip bare the mystery of creativity. Rather, the fact that such a transcendent process could also be an embodied one shows that it is even more mysterious than we thought.

1

Hypergraphia:
The Incurable Disease of Writing

Many suffer from the incurable disease of writing, and it becomes
chronic in their sick minds.

— Juvenal, *Satires* 7.51

One night recently I woke my wife with a nudge. "*Now* what is it?"
she asked. The question I had for her, urgent though it seemed to
me, was a little anticlimactic under the circumstances. But I forged
ahead. "Darling," I said. "Do you consider me . . . prolific?" Her
response will not bear repetition in these pages.

— Jay Parini, "On Being Prolific"

CONSIDER A YOUNG MAN, twenty-five years old, who began to have
dangerous spells of altered consciousness. The episodes started with
an emotion — frequently of fear, but sometimes of ecstasy. During
the spell he would turn his head and cry out, and his limbs would
thrash so violently that he often injured himself. Afterward, he was
confused and had trouble speaking and writing. For days he was filled
with feelings of doom. There was an alarming family history: the
man's son died during a prolonged seizure, and his father had either
epileptic or alcoholic attacks. The man himself had the markedly
asymmetric facial features often seen with abnormal brain development. He had pronounced mood swings, compulsive gambling, attacks of rage, and he spent ten years in prison. At the same time he

was deeply and thoughtfully religious, brooding on the notion of guilt and on mystical issues. His sexuality too was unusual: although apparently asexual until his midthirties, he then married twice and had extramarital affairs.

His interest in writing began early in life and was intense enough to drive him, despite precarious finances, to resign his job and write full-time. Although he felt that writing worsened his medical condition, he also believed that he wrote better and more when he was sicker. In his lifetime he wrote nineteen novels and novellas, along with voluminous notebooks, diaries, and letters, many written or dictated at a furious pace. He described the drive to write in the voice of one of his characters:

> Again, what is my object precisely in writing? If it is not for the benefit of the public why should I not simply recall these incidents in my own mind without putting them on paper? Quite so; but yet it is more imposing on paper . . . Besides, I shall perhaps obtain actual relief from writing. Today, for instance, I am particularly oppressed by one memory of a distant past. It came back vividly to my mind a few days ago, and has remained haunting me like an annoying tune that one cannot get rid of. And yet I must get rid of it somehow . . . For some reason I believe that if I write it down I should get rid of it. Why not try?

Hypergraphia in Temporal Lobe Epilepsy

Neurologists believe that this complicated man's complicated traits — his spells of altered consciousness, his mood swings with their free-floating feelings of doom and ecstasy, his religious and philosophical temperament, his altered sexuality, and his overpowering desire to write — are for the most part symptoms of temporal lobe epilepsy; that is, seizures originating in the temporal lobe of the cerebral cortex. Epilepsy starting in other lobes of the cortex does not produce these traits. The young man, as you may have guessed from the quotation from *Notes from the Underground,* is Fyodor Dostoevsky.

Temporal lobe epilepsy is the best-understood cause of hypergraphia, although not the only one. It does not always, or even usually, create talented writers. What it can create is writers who are extraordinarily motivated. In the 1970s the neurologists Stephen Waxman and Norman Geschwind described a number of such patients. Their findings generated great excitement because at the time there were only a few examples of well-characterized brain changes that produced alterations in complex aspects of personality. Scientists are never happy until they can assign a number to the phenomenon they are studying, and researchers soon invented a simple way to do that with hypergraphia. They mailed a short letter to their patients with epilepsy, asking them to describe their state of health. The average answer of patients without hypergraphia was seventy-eight words. The patients thought to have hypergraphia averaged five thousand words.

One hypergraphic patient of Geschwind's, rather more typical than Dostoevsky, began having seizures several months after a head injury. They began with a rising or fluttering sensation in his stomach, sometimes with the feeling that he was falling or rising in the air. An EEG (electroencephalogram, a test of brain electrical activity) showed epileptic spikes in the right temporal lobe even between seizures. The man attended art school for some years, but also spent several years in prison for assault. He began writing extensively around the time of his first seizure, keeping a diary and writing songs and poems. Because he feared that his work would be stolen, he hid it in various places in his home. He often wrote aphorisms for hours at a time, saying "Once I start, I can't stop," and that his writing concerned "basic questions of life." Here is a typical page of his aphorisms:

- Silence is the greatest art of observing.
- If I could only see,
  What's really killing me
  I'd open my damn silly eyes
  and stop being so carefree.
- Once I had everything that I wanted. Now all I have is me, myself, and I.

- Men who can converse have more enjoyment and so do the women who can converse back.
- I once heard that whores make the best wives, but who wants to marry a whore?

Can any benefit come from lumping a writer such as Dostoevsky, whose works are in the Canon, with my second example, who, despite a fey charm, does not write well? I think so. The epilepsy of these very different people is not an illness incidental to their writing; it seems to have triggered it. And there is growing evidence that the temporal lobe is important for creativity in many driven writers without epilepsy. Dostoevsky the epileptic can give us insight into Dostoevsky the literary creator. In fact, what we know today about hypergraphic patients may give us a window into the brains of all those driven to write.

If the brain is shaped like a pair of boxing gloves, the temporal lobes are in the thumbs (see Figure 2a). Each is one of four lobes in the two cerebral hemispheres (sides of the brain), which have a wrinkly outer rim of gray matter called the cerebral cortex, over a layer of white matter (Figure 2b). Under the white matter are often other large clumps of gray matter called subcortical regions. Gray matter contains plump cell bodies, the centers of the neurons (nerve cells). White matter contains very long, thin fibers that leave the cell bodies and connect to other neurons. Although neuroscientific names are usually impenetrable, in a rare instance of scientific clarity, gray matter is actually gray, and white matter is actually white. More or less.

The lobes of the cerebral cortex are large in mammals, especially smart ones. They govern the more sophisticated stages of sensory and motor processing, control higher cognition, and make it possible to do complicated tasks such as singing lieder and embezzling. Much of human consciousness, our experience of our own minds, seems to come from the cortex.

The bulk of the temporal lobes is behind the ears. That is fitting, as parts of the temporal lobes are the site of sound processing, including language processing and music comprehension. Other areas of

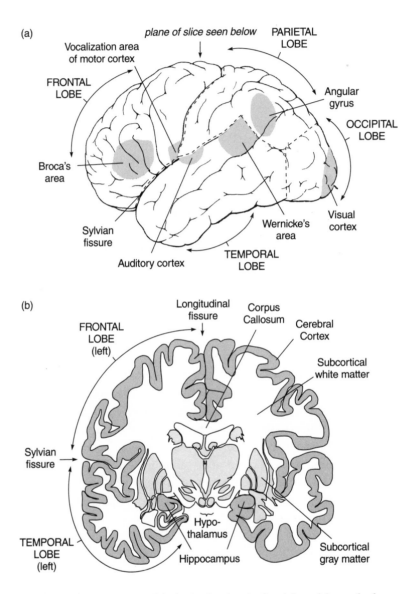

Figure 2. (a) A surface view of the brain showing the four lobes of the cerebral cortex and the two major speech areas: Broca's area and Wernicke's area. (b) A cross-sectional slice through the brain, taken in the plane of the ears at the vertical arrow in (a).

the temporal lobes are vital to memory storage, especially a region called the hippocampus; to emotional response, especially a region called the amygdala; and to the recognition of visual objects. The Dostoevsky quotation shows several of these temporal lobe phenomena simultaneously, including the involuntary memory so often described by Proust, and the annoying phenomenon of tunes stuck in one's head.

The tips of the temporal lobe can be lopped off without much changing a person's behavior. This fact is used to advantage in temporal lobectomy, a surgery that removes a diseased part of the temporal lobe to control epileptic seizures. A person can live relatively normally without much of a temporal lobe, perhaps because we have two of them, so that one lobe may compensate when the other is damaged. In fact, the temporal lobes never act alone. They are always exchanging information with the three other lobes of cortex (the frontal, parietal, and occipital lobes), as well as with the subcortical regions in each lobe and deeper in the brain.

The frontal lobe is perhaps the most intimately interconnected with the temporal lobe, at least for the functions considered in this book. The frontal lobes control judgment, initiation of action, and movement. Distinct from the temporal lobe's role in speech comprehension, the frontal lobe controls speech production. Damage to some areas of the frontal lobe can produce paralysis, as occurs after some strokes, or apathy, as after a frontal lobotomy. In other areas of the frontal lobe, damage can produce an uninhibited and rambunctious patient. The parietal lobes control the sense of touch and its integration with movement and other senses. The occipital lobe's role is primarily in visual processing.

Under the four lobes of the hemispheres, deeper in the brain, are structures less directly important for cognition but more influential in emotions and the basic functions of life. The deepest region is the brainstem, which directs vital activities such as heart rate and breathing. Just above it is the cerebellum, which coordinates movements — and also, new research shows, some cognitive and emotional behaviors. The midbrain, which joins the brainstem and the cerebral hemispheres, regulates drives. It is not visible in Figure 2a because it is buried deep under the hemispheres, but the brain slice in Figure 2b shows a part of it. The midbrain propels many functions over which we wish we had conscious control; for instance, hunger and sexual desire. It is a major component of the limbic system, a rim of interconnected cortical, subcortical, and deeper brain regions that control the ups and downs of emotion. Through the limbic system the midbrain has many connections to the cerebral cortex, especially the temporal lobe. The interaction is complicated. It is largely the limbic system that gives us the motivation to do cortical tasks, and it is the cortex that allows us to have cognitively complicated desires — not just for any woman but for, say, Marlene Dietrich as opposed to Greta Garbo. Just how the limbic and cortical systems interact, I will argue, is important for literary creativity.

Seizures — which, if chronic, are called epilepsy — arise only from the cortex, most commonly from the cortex of the temporal lobe. Temporal lobe seizures are a window on brain states that selectively affect creativity. What makes the temporal cortex particularly prone to seizures seems to be its heightened sensitivity to electrical stimulation from other neurons.

For neurons communicate with one another by firing, that is, by sending electrical impulses down their axons to synapses, which are junctions with other neurons. Firing triggers the synapses to release chemical neurotransmitters (to be described in more detail in Chapters 5 and 6). Seizures are like electrical storms in these circuits. An area of the brain becomes wildly active, the neurons firing without restraint in a chain reaction. Seizures may be triggered by a region of the brain that is damaged in some way, often a small brain scar from a birth defect or a head injury. The seizure can then spread to healthier regions. Otherwise-normal people can seize when their brains are stressed enough — every few years, a resident at my hospital seizes after being on call in the emergency room all night. Most people with epilepsy have symptoms only during a seizure (ictal symptoms), but some may have symptoms between seizures (interictal symptoms) as well. Hypergraphia is an interictal symptom.

Although the personalities of people with temporal lobe epilepsy vary, and in most cases patients are impossible to distinguish from the rest of the world, some exhibit a cluster of five personality traits often called the Geschwind syndrome: hypergraphia; a deepened emotional life sometimes described as hyperphilosophical or hyper-religious (a squishy category ranging from attending mass twice a day to believing oneself to be the Buddha); emotional volatility, including aggressive outbursts; altered sexuality (usually decreased sexual activity); and overinclusiveness, an extreme talkativeness caused by excessive attention to detail. (Most of us have a too-close relative with this trait.)

Dostoevsky's personality neatly illustrates all five traits of the Geschwind syndrome. His prolific and highly detailed writing, moral obsessions, violent rages, and unusual sexuality made him stand out from people around him. Like many others with temporal lobe epilepsy, he seems to have had a heightened sense of the meaningfulness of everyday events.

The Geschwind syndrome's constellation of personality traits is one of the clearest examples of a well-defined brain state causing high-level personality changes. It may also have implications for the personalities of some people without epilepsy. Those with the same set of Geschwind syndrome personality traits, but without temporal lobe epilepsy, still have altered temporal lobe activity, even though they do not have outright seizures. So there seems to be a spectrum of temporal lobe activities and of personality changes that they cause.

Hypergraphia in itself is perhaps only a neurological oddity. But because it may tell us something about the neurology of literary creativity, it is worth agreeing on a working definition. Most obviously, hypergraphics write a great deal — specifically, much more than their contemporaries. (We need to take social context into account to adjust for facts such as the greater volume of writing before telephones existed.) Second, hypergraphia comes from a strong, conscious, internal drive — say, pleasure — rather than from an external influence. (People who write a great deal simply because they are paid per word are not hypergraphic.) Third, the writing usually has themes that are highly meaningful for the author, often philosophical, religious, or autobiographical. (The gibberish of some brain-damaged patients doesn't count.) Fourth, apart from the loose constraint that the writing be meaningful at least to the author, the writing need not be any good. (Maudlin diarists can be hypergraphic.) Finally, I will try to reserve true "clinical" hypergraphia to describe neurological or psychiatric patients with known or likely temporal lobe changes. But otherwise-normal people who meet the first four criteria are similar enough that they are worth discussing together with the hypergraphics. In fact, they are the main reason for discussing hypergraphics at all.

Not all writers meet the first four criteria. Most notably excluded are those who write solely to make money, to get tenure, to please their father, to meet boys. Of course, even the most hypergraphic writer likes getting paid, so secondary gain almost always has some influence. The exclusion of people writing primarily for secondary gain is important, however, because, as Teresa Amabile has shown, work driven by intrinsic motives tends to be more creative than that triggered extrinsically. When two people are given a project, one paid to do it and the other not, the former's creativity seems to be inhibited by the reward. Surprisingly, at least when studied in schoolchildren, the inhibiting effect of external reward seems to be greater on girls than on boys. If this is true, we should perhaps be ruthlessly pleased that so many female writers were spared this inhibition by being essentially ignored in their lifetimes. And we should also be pleased that male writers are relatively able to withstand the corrupting effects of both fame and bad reviews.

The criteria for hypergraphia also exclude unconscious trance writing, or "automatic writing." Although few people today take trance writing seriously, at the turn of the twentieth century, writers such as James Joyce and W. B. Yeats often sought aid from it. Yeats's wife, Georgie Hyde-Lees, whose trance writing inspired much of his later poetry, used it as well to provide him with some rather pointed marital advice.

I could perhaps have defined hypergraphia with fewer criteria (for instance, just in terms of the amount written) or with more (requiring that what is written be well written). But hypergraphia on the present definition picks out something relatively primary in the brain, a function that depends heavily on temporal lobe activity and may link closely to what the neuropsychologist Steven Pinker calls the language instinct, the biological drive to communicate.

Hypergraphic handwriting tends to have distinctive physical characteristics. Hypergraphics often use highly elaborate or stylized scripts, even mirror writing like that used by Leonardo da Vinci. For emphasis, they frequently write in all capitals or in colored inks. They may not confine themselves to the main text, but may add exuberant annotations, drawings in the margins, and illuminated initials. Lewis Carroll, who most likely had temporal lobe epilepsy, exhibited several of these peculiarities — including what he called looking-glass writing and an exclusive reliance on purple ink — in the 98,721 letters he wrote from his late twenties until his death at age sixty-five. When I was at my most hypergraphic, I loved the physical feel of ink on paper so much that I would copy out dozens of poems in my most ornate handwriting. As a too-symbolic side effect, the mood stabilizer that gave me writer's block also made my penmanship as tremulous as that of an eighty-year-old. Afterward I only typed. Luckily, computers have added thousands of fonts, dingbats, and animated clips to the repertoire available to the modern hypergraphic.

Does all hypergraphia arise from altered temporal lobe activity? Increased writing behavior does sometimes follow injury to brain regions outside the temporal lobe, most commonly injury to the right frontal cortex. However, the resulting texts are very different from the organized and meaningful prose seen in temporal lobe hypergraphic writing. Damage to the frontal cortex produces merely a primitive form of "orthographic compulsion," such as repeatedly writing single letters. This activity probably reflects not a drive to write, but a very different and even odder phenomenon called utilization behavior, in which a patient with frontal lobe damage will reflexively use a tool, such as a pencil or hammer, simply because it is there.

Utilization behavior can occasionally go to remarkable extremes.

The eminent neurologist who first described it, François Lhermitte, himself went to remarkable extremes to demonstrate just how far his patients would go. For instance, he silently presented them with a syringe on a tray and his own naked flank; they did not hesitate to placidly inject him. His first paper on the syndrome included a photograph of this behavior — including the naked flank — proof that it is not only psychiatrists who are often more unusual than their patients.

While personality characteristics between seizures of people with temporal lobe epilepsy reveal some of the temporal lobes' effects, the characteristics of the seizures themselves are revealing too. Seizures stemming from the visual cortex of the occipital lobe start with predominantly visual symptoms; motor cortex seizures in the frontal lobe often start with repetitive jerking; temporal lobe seizures typically begin with an emotion or emotionally charged sensation such as an evocative smell. The emotional symptoms vary widely and may include fear, a rising thrill that some patients have called a Christmas morning feeling, sexual excitement, or a profound religious experience. As the seizure spreads, it can cause motor symptoms — not just the simple jerks seen in motor cortex seizures, but complicated behaviors such as undressing in public. During a seizure, one patient treated at my hospital took off all his clothes, walked through a bramble patch for ten minutes, and did so much damage to his skin that he had to be treated in the burn unit.

Temporal lobe seizures can also produce sensory symptoms — less often basic symptoms than higher-order alterations of perception, such as those in which objects seem to contract or expand. These size changes are often called Alice in Wonderland phenomena, for the way Alice's body would telescope after her various ingestions. In fact, many aspects of *Alice in Wonderland* probably drew on Carroll's own experiences of seizures. When Alice fell down the rabbit hole, for instance, her sensations reflected a common seizure aura of hurtling through space. ("'Well!' thought Alice to herself, 'after such a fall as this, I shall think nothing of tumbling down stairs!'") Researchers, who can reproduce these sensations with electrical stimulation of the temporal lobe, can also induce "out-of-body" sensations in which the subject feels he is viewing himself from outside. The parallel between this phenomenon and the writer's necessary sense of distance from his own life is evocative — if perhaps only metaphoric.

When sensory changes become more intense, they turn into hallucinations in which the subject no longer knows that the sensation is not real. The most common hallucination in temporal lobe epilepsy, as in schizophrenia, is not visual or tactile but auditory — usually hearing voices. Immediately after the seizure, when the patient's temporal lobe is essentially stunned, he or she may have severe language difficulties. Temporal lobe seizures also produce phenomena that while not strictly sensory are called experiential because of their alterations of consciousness. These include feelings of unreality, déjà vu, jamais vu (the feeling of never having seen something which is in fact familiar — a phenomenon perhaps linked to the freshness of perception that creative writers need), and the illusion of a presence only partly distinct from the patient or writer — whether of a doppelgänger, as Dostoevsky described in his novel *The Double,* or of the muse. Overall, the strong changes in emotion, higher-order perception, and the relatively common occurrences of hearing voices and of postseizure language problems all pick out functions that share related brain systems.

One of the most famously epileptic writers was Gustave Flaubert, and his descriptions of his seizures are classic for temporal lobe epilepsy. They tended to start with a sense of doom, followed by a feeling that the boundaries of his self were dissolving. He wrote that his seizures arrived as "a whirlpool of ideas and images in my poor brain, during which it seemed that my consciousness, that my me sank like a vessel in a storm." He would moan, have a rush of memories, see fiery hallucinations, foam at the mouth, move his right arm automatically, fall into a trance of about ten minutes, and vomit.

Other writers who scholars have argued had temporal lobe epilepsy include Tennyson, Lear, Poe, Swinburne, Byron, de Maupassant, Molière, Pascal, Petrarch, Dante, Teresa of Avila, and Saint Paul. Edward Lear, for instance, began having seizures around the age of five.

He was exquisitely ashamed of his epilepsy and feared that it might lead to progressive mental decay. Acute attacks of painful nostalgia — "the Morbids" — came in close association with his seizures. He had a childhood memory of a twilit performance by clowns in Highgate, and of "crying half the night after all the small gaiety broke up." The suffering associated with his epilepsy may paradoxically have driven his attempts to distract himself by writing comical nonsense verse.

Because all the writers I have mentioned were born before EEGs — the current best tool for diagnosing epilepsy — the accuracy of their diagnoses is not certain. The diagnoses are based on descriptions of fits that sound like seizures; but not all fits are seizures, as anyone who has seen a toddler in a tantrum knows. Biographers and doctors sometimes also based a diagnosis of epilepsy on the degree to which the writer's personality fit the classic Geschwind syndrome, yet nonepileptics can have the same traits. Unfortunately, the more ancient the writer, the less evidence available, and the less certain the diagnosis.

Other Illnesses That Cause Hypergraphia

Epilepsy is not the only illness that can cause hypergraphia. Indeed, psychiatrists disagree with neurologists about whether it is even the major cause, pointing out that the great German psychiatrist Emil Kraepelin described hypergraphia in manic-depressive (bipolar) patients fifty years before Geschwind described it in people with temporal lobe epilepsy. Although at first glance manic-depression and epilepsy are widely different disorders — one a psychiatric disorder with mood swings, the other a neurological disease with seizures — on closer look a great deal of overlap is apparent in both the symptoms and the treatment. Manic-depression is a genetically transmitted syndrome that shares many mood and personality characteristics with temporal lobe epilepsy. Even modern clinicians, let alone biographers of those long dead, sometimes have to struggle to decide between diagnosing temporal lobe epilepsy and manic-depression. Poe and Byron, for instance, have been diagnosed both ways, as biographers try to explain their mercurial temperaments and prolific writing. The similarity of the diseases may reflect the fact that temporal lobe abnormalities are present in manic-depressive illness as well as in temporal lobe epilepsy, even if less well defined.

Besides hypergraphia, manic-depressives often share with temporal lobe epileptics unusual religiosity and altered sexuality. A manic patient's loose cognitive associations are similar to a hypergraphic's overinclusiveness, and the classic "pressured speech" of mania is in many ways the oral form of hypergraphia. (What makes one person speak and another write? In part, temperament; shy people are less likely to collar others at parties. I'll discuss some other reasons in Chapter 5.) Temporal lobe epileptics often have emotional outbursts and depressions that are similar to, if milder than, those in manic-depressive illness. Even the handwriting of manic people and those with Geschwind's syndrome is similar — manic handwriting usually gets larger and more flowery as the mania intensifies. The manic handwriting in Figure 3 shows these characteristics, as well as the hypergraphic need to fill all the available space by writing in the margins. Finally, the anticonvulsant drugs used to treat epilepsy can also help manic-depression, strongly arguing for a psychopharmacological link between the two diseases. (A caveat: lithium, which helps manic-depression, can worsen seizures.)

A surprising proportion of writers are manic-depressive. The psychologist Kay Redfield Jamison, one of the foremost experts on manic-depression, has explored this phenomenon in depth. Even her list of just the known manic-depressives who wrote poetry, in English, and whose names began with C is impressive: Thomas Campbell, Thomas Chatterton, John Clare, Samuel Taylor Coleridge and his son Hartley Coleridge, William Collins, William Cowper, and Hart Crane. The work of Jamison and others shows that writers are ten times more likely to be manic-depressive than the rest of the population, and poets are a remarkable forty times more likely. Even student poets not diagnosed with mental illness have more manic traits than students who do not write poetry. Their mild traits, falling short

Figure 3. The writing of a hypergraphic person with mania, showing the characteristic dramatic flourishes and the pressure to fill every available space. Emil Kraepelin, who first characterized hypergraphia, wrote of these patients in 1921, "Certainly they themselves do not count on being read; the pleasure of writing itself is the only motive."

of the full-blown disease, are what John Ratey and Catherine Johnson have called shadow syndromes.

During depression, people tend to write much less (and, oddly, their handwriting often shrinks in size). In fact, writer's block is much more likely than hypergraphia to accompany depression. When depressed people do write, it is generally when the depression is agitated; that is, when it contains a mix of manic and depressed features. How, then, to explain the long tradition linking depression with the literary drive to create? This belief was written down as early as the fourth century B.C.E., when Aristotle famously asked, "Why is it that all men who have become outstanding in philosophy, statesmanship, poetry, and the arts are melancholic?" A major reason is that Aristotle, Plato, and other protopsychiatrists of that era closely linked melancholy to periods of "frenzy." That is, they did not strictly distinguish manic-depressive (bipolar) illness from depression without manic periods (unipolar illness). Nor did medieval, Enlightenment, or even most nineteenth-century writers.

Nonetheless, recent work that does try to separate people with manic-depression from those with unipolar depression has found some link between unipolar depression and literary ability or interests, if not florid hypergraphia. Writers have more unipolar depression than the rest of the population; the same studies that found a ten- to forty-fold greater incidence of manic-depressive illness in writers found an eight- to tenfold greater incidence of unipolar depression. So many writers write about their depression that it has become a genre with its own anthologies, such as the collection *Unholy Ghost.*

This link between writing and depression may stem in part from the fact that depressed people tend to be strongly introspective, a trait that may foster writing. Depression, when it does not incapacitate a person, may actually make him or her see the world more accurately than normal people do. (Of course, an accurately pessimistic view of things can also be paralyzing.)

The connection between depression and writing may also reflect the fact that many people with episodes of unipolar depression write more once their depression has worn off. In some instances they feel that their ideas were triggered by their experiences when depressed, even though at the time they lacked the energy to write. In other cases, depression may trigger rebound periods of increased energy, even "hypomania" — periods of increased energy that are not intense enough to be truly manic. As you may imagine, psychiatrists and their clients often have strongly differing opinions about whether a state should be labeled manic or hypomanic. Many people with hypomania find it an extraordinarily productive and pleasant state, even as others may find the hypomanic person irritable or irresponsible.

Many psychiatrists argue that unipolar and bipolar depressive disorders should not be thought of as completely separate entities. For clinicians such as Emil Kraepelin, Hagop Akiskal, and Katharina Trede, the two conditions are opposite ends of a spectrum, with substantial overlap in symptoms, treatment, and even inheritability. On such a view, writers with unipolar depression are simply those whose manic periods are quite mild. They do not write much during (because of) their depression, but they do write during hypomanic periods between depressions. Writers with only moderate manic symptoms often write more publishable material than writers who, like Coleridge, had full-blown mania; their mildly high-energy periods do not cause enough disorganization or psychosis to make writing difficult.

Grouped or separated, unipolar and bipolar disorders are tightly linked in being disorders of mood. And creativity has been more closely linked to mood instability than to cognitive traits such as high IQ. Of course, you need not become manic-depressive to write, any more than you need to develop temporal lobe epilepsy. Most writers do not have either trait — at least, to the degree that they have had a diagnostic label pinned on them. Nonetheless, even in normal writers, the neurobiology of mood and the limbic drive to write may be equally or more important than the purely cognitive skills taught in most writing courses.

In the last part of the postpartum mood disorder that I described in the Introduction, I was hospitalized for depression. It started when

I changed to a mood stabilizer with riskier side effects than the previous one and had to stop nursing. My writing then dried up too. Strangely, I hardly missed it. Rather than feeling crazy, I began to feel grindingly sane. Much too sane to do anything as frivolous as write — or, eventually, do anything at all.

When so much sanity made it hard to lift my arms and legs, my psychiatrist prescribed one antidepressant, then two. These gave me back energy without changing my mood and I became unbearably agitated. That had one advantage — suddenly I was writing again. Admittedly, what I wrote was awful, but it was a relief to be able to write anything. Once more something in me was pressing to get out, if only myself escaping myself. Words fled from my head like rats from a sinking ship. Eventually, though, the rats could not get out fast enough. As the pressure in my head from the antidepressants continued to build, I stopped taking the pills I had been given, those white and lavender and yellow and blue capsules that for so many months, twice a day, had spelled cryptic messages across my palm. I continued at my job without outward difficulty, but when I came home from work, I just stopped moving. Once the antidepressants wore off, my torpor was so peaceful that I found it hard to call it depression. I wondered if I had wandered by some back door into a Zen state of enlightened indifference.

My husband and my psychiatrist, skeptical of my enlightenment and not persuaded by my notion that mental illness is sometimes preferable to sanity, eventually convinced me to go to a psychiatric hospital. I had first heard of that hospital as a half-imaginary literary institution something like F. Scott Fitzgerald's Princeton, for it appeared in several of the psychiatric memoirs I had read as an adolescent. Later, I knew it from having once worked there. I was not looking forward to being the patient of former colleagues, but it turned out to be reassuring to already know the staff on my floor, and how to get into the room with the Cap'n Crunch. By chance I was assigned the nurse whom I had always liked the best — a thoughtful woman who had features so refined and calm that she was featured on all the hospital's ads. And the mental health aide who came to search my bag for sharp objects, said happily, "You're the one who likes Proust!" remembering an animated conversation we had had a few years before.

My husband brought our daughters to visit every day. That was lovely, the most vivid events in my muffled midwinter. They would wrap their small arms around my neck and laugh, too young to realize where they were. Then they would find the box of art-therapy markers and scribble wildly, on paper, on the conveniently scribble-proof (and suicide-proof) institutional furniture, on each other. One night, after they had doodled all over their faces and arms and little potbellies, another patient looked at them and laughed, "And they say *I'm* crazy." I wondered if I were a bad influence and their scribbles were the earliest sign of hypergraphia — or, slightly more sensibly, if more of us would write wildly if school didn't teach us to dislike writing.

Psychiatric hospitals are not terrible places to write — they bear certain similarities to writers' colonies like Yaddo, except that health insurance pays. And except that if you spend too much time in your room writing, "isolative" is entered on your chart. Everything is done for you in the hospital; it is like a womb. For the first three days I gave in to my catatonic urges and spent twenty hours a day in bed. Because I had worked successfully until the day before I was admitted, I convinced myself that I was only in the hospital for a rest cure. Although that was whitewash, when the medications were restarted, I became agitated again and began badgering the staff about my discharge. That accomplished, I was soon back at work, outwardly the same. Work, in fact, generally pushed moods out of my head, as my patients were always so much more unhappy than I was.

As in Thomas Mann's *Magic Mountain*, the need to fight that seductive tug to stay ill, to fight the freedom to do nothing but daydream, was one part of what made me restless to get out of the hospital. The other part was that I physically could not leave. When I signed the standard voluntary admission papers that require a three-day review after a request for discharge, I had no idea of the claustrophobia this provision would bring. There was nothing wrong with the hospital; I was not on an especially unruly floor, and I liked most of the patients and staff there. But the locks, and the fact that expressing a desire to leave was seen as proof that I needed to stay, made me frantic. Thinking about the experience even now makes me sweat.

What do prisoners do? Write, of course; even if they have to use blood as ink, as the Marquis de Sade did. The reasons they write, the exquisitely frustrating restrictions of their autonomy and the fact that no one listens to their cries, are also the reasons that mentally ill people, and even many normal people, write. We write to escape our prisons.

To make me less "isolative," I was asked to attend group therapy. There I learned the other patients' goals for the day ("I would like to go outside," "I would like to go outside and have a cigarette," "I would like to master anger management so I can get my privileges changed and go outside"). Another thing I learned from group therapy was that all the manic-depressives were urgently writing memoirs. I really was at a crazy Yaddo.

The memoirs of the mentally ill are full of confused action, failed promise, and grinding pain; they do not tend to make good narratives. The writing of the other patients horrified me, as I struggled to suppress my own compulsion to write about myself. Sometimes I wonder whether the inability to broadcast your suffering is what separates the mentally ill from the sane. It is not a trivial difference. If I could only have hidden my depression, I would have avoided a hospitalization that was in some ways very painful. But I couldn't. If I could keep from describing my hospitalization here, I could avoid the stigmatization this book may bring (although my family and colleagues have been absolutely supportive).

The memoirs of the mentally ill and of drug addicts are often, and sometimes rightly, ridiculed by reviewers for just this obsession with the author's own suffering. But at least they let other sufferers know they aren't alone. I often treat students whose mental illnesses frighten them even more because they aren't aware of how many successful people have them too. Often I have been tempted to say to one of those students, "I know just what you're going through. No, *really*. Here's something that worked for me that you might try." But I don't.

I'm afraid they might be horrified, afraid my colleagues would see it as a "boundary violation," afraid ultimately that my firsthand knowledge of mental illness is too distorted to be useful to them.

Still, it is not primarily altruistic motives that force me, like Coleridge's ancient mariner, to tell my tale. It is something much more visceral. Perhaps the compulsive memoirism of the mentally ill can help to explain an age so memoir-mad that most young novelists present their thinly veiled autobiographies as fiction. (I, for variety, present mine as neuroscience.) Thanks to the Internet, there is even a new variety of continuously updated on-line memoir sometimes called the blog (from Web-log). Thousands of authors simply write their diaries directly onto Web pages for the rest of the world to read. Why do people want to recount their lives? What could it mean to want to share one's worldview with strangers? I have a few theories, but I'll save them until Chapter 6.

Despite the shortcomings of mentally ill writing, the hospital had a literary tradition — and a physical campus — more impressive than that of many liberal arts colleges. One day a staff member gave me a virtual tour from my window. He pointed out buildings where two famous poets had stayed. If I pressed my nose against the window's steel mesh, I could just see where a third had taught poetry to patients soon before being admitted herself. All three, manic-depressive. The scientist in me can quote the study (the single study, I must point out) that finds manic-depressive artists to be more productive when they are adequately medicated. The residual psychiatric patient in me is not convinced — it thinks I wrote better when I was at least a little bit ill.

My hospital stay reinforced my belief that manic-depressives write a great deal. It was not as much help with the question of *why* they write. One way to answer that question is in neurological terms. EEG studies show that people in manic states, like those with temporal lobe epilepsy, have selective brain-wave changes in the temporal lobes. And it is these temporal lobe changes in people with either disorder that seem to trigger hypergraphia.

A second way to answer the question of why manics write uses familiar terms such as "desire" and "need," rather than neurological ones. On this approach, which philosophers of mind call folk psychology, manics write because they want to (hypergraphia, again, is not passive automatic writing), and they want to for a host of reasons that are similar to, if perhaps more intense than, the reasons nonmanics write. Manics write because what they are writing about seems vitally important to them, worth preserving. Manics write because one topic reminds them of another, not an uncommon method of composing even for nonmanics, but one that, when taken to a manic extreme psychiatrists call flight of ideas. Manics write because the sounds and shapes of words entrance them. Hence their characteristic rhyming and puns (known as clang associations), and hence also the high frequency of manic-depressive poets.

The folk-psychological and neuropsychological descriptions of why manics write are useful in very different ways, but they are not mutually exclusive. My belief that I write because I love to is not inconsistent with my belief that I do it because my brain is in a particular state. Yet the pain of the mind-body problem — the question of how mental states such as experiences, beliefs, and desires can relate to brain states such as neuronal membrane potentials, receptor densities, and wiring diagrams — does not vanish quite as easily as the problem itself. However logically consistent it may be to believe that I write both because I choose to and because I am a chain of molecular interactions, to think them at the same time hurts — perhaps for the same reason it hurts to think that light is at once a wave and a particle. It is a sore tooth I prod over and over with my tongue. I went into neuroscience because I thought it would help me solve the mind-body problem; instead, it seems to have made me unable to forget it.

It is possible that some of manic hypergraphia is cultural. Of course, it does not occur in preliterate societies, although pressured speech and the composition of oral poetry are likely to be its close relatives. Hypergraphia might also be one of the many psychiatric syndromes that are culturally specific: running *amok* in Malaysia; *ode-ori* in Nigeria, which causes a sensation of parasites in the head;

koro, which causes some Southeast Asians to believe their genitals are retracting into their body and will kill them; and, many will argue, multiple personality disorder (dissociative identity disorder), which is much more common in the United States than elsewhere. Hypergraphia might reflect a manic distortion of that particularly Western desire to get published. Yet many hypergraphics clearly write for their own pleasure and are reluctant to show their writing to others. And what we know of non-Western psychiatry suggests that hypergraphia occurs in mania there too.

A friend of mine who grew up in China told me about her favorite aunt, who had to hide her bipolar disorder without medication in a society that at the time reviled mental illness. Whether her aunt's moods were high or low, she always lived with the tension of pretending to be sane (a problem that affects all of us to some degree). To contain it, she would shut herself in her room writing every night after she came home from work. Still a child, my friend was not allowed to read any of her aunt's writing, but her mother told her it was incandescent, brilliantly satirical, anti-Communist material. The Red Guard routinely searched houses, and the punishment for such writing would certainly have been death. As fast as her aunt wrote, she had to destroy. First she would burn her output; then she would bring the ashes to my friend's family's house, which was distinguished by having the only flush toilet in the area. My friend remembers her aunt's nocturnal visits, the way she lit up the room when she entered it. My friend still wishes she could have some of her aunt's fervor.

After my friend left China, conditions there improved and her aunt was able to write long, wonderful letters to her. Letters my friend wondered if she should burn, for by then she had romantic associations with seeing her aunt's handwriting turn red and translucent, as the flames took life from it. Despite a promising career and a passionate avocation of creative writing, my friend sometimes thinks she would be more productive if she had bipolar disorder too — a fact that makes her aunt fondly call her "my little crazy wannabe." (The existence of a Mandarin equivalent to this phrase is one of the miracles of language.) In fact, as I describe in the next chapter, close relatives of people with bipolar disorder are generally more productive than the sufferers themselves, and than the general population. So my friend may be able to have her aunt's strength without her suffering.

Besides epilepsy and mania, other temporal lobe disorders can tell us about the drive to write. The chief is Wernicke's aphasia, a problem with language comprehension caused by damage to an area of the temporal lobe called, conveniently, Wernicke's area. Because Wernicke's aphasics share some characteristics with manic-depressives and temporal lobe epileptics (notably high speech output and manic or irritable moods), Wernicke's aphasia supports the position that these traits are largely related to the temporal lobe. Wernicke's aphasics, unlike hypergraphics, speak much more than they write, probably because their brain damage makes writing too difficult. And while their language is at least partly nonsensical, it is generally delivered with a cheerful grin, since they are unaware that they are not making sense. In fact, Wernicke's aphasiacs may talk more just because they are "liberated" from the need to be coherent. A typically windy example of a Wernicke's aphasic's speech is the following:

> . . . oh hear but that was a long time ago that was when that when before I even knew that much about this place although I am a little suspicious about what the hell is the part there is one part scares, uh estate spares, OK that has a bunch of drives in it and a bunch of good googin, nothing real big but that was in the same time I coached them I said hey stay out of the spear struggle stay out of trouble so don't get and my kids, uh, except for the body the boys are pretty good although lately they have become winded or something . . . what the hell . . . kind of a platz goasted klack . . .

Because such language sounds fairly normal if you do not listen too closely, it is sometimes called politician-speak. The parallel between the "normal" logorrheic who writes contentless twenty-page office memos and the blather of Wernicke's aphasia, advanced mania, or schizophrenia should remind us that while hypergraphia is in certain ways related to creativity, the relationship is not unproblematic.

Hypergraphia can be a writing problem in its own right and can benefit from treatment. But unlike people with writer's block, hypergraphics generally think their writing style is appropriate, take pleasure in writing that way, and resist treatment.

Schizophrenia is another brain disorder that sometimes causes hypergraphia. (Like those suffering severe mania, however, severe schizophrenics are rarely able to do much meaningful writing.) A classic example of a high-functioning schizophrenic who became hypergraphic is the Unabomber, Theodore Kaczynski, with his copious manifestos and journals. Unlike the long list of manic-depressive professional writers, there is no equivalently long list of successfully published schizophrenics. In part, this may derive from the emotional distance that separates most schizophrenics from other people and makes their writing less accessible. Even a number of the few published writers who were labeled schizophrenic were probably misdiagnosed. For instance, the playwright August Strindberg and the poet Antonin Artaud, diagnosed as schizophrenic, were more probably manic-depressive or schizoaffective (having a combination of manic-depressive and schizophrenic features).

Perhaps the most famous writer whose schizophrenia was possibly misdiagnosed is the poet Ezra Pound. He had a long and consistent resumé of outspoken fascism and anti-Semitism, spending World War II in Italy making fulsome radio broadcasts in support of Mussolini and Hitler. At the end of the war he stood trial for treason, but was declared schizophrenic. One psychiatrist and historian has evidence that Pound's diagnosis was most likely a collusion between his literary supporters and his psychiatrists to help him avoid being convicted for treason. Pound instead spent his time as a psychiatric inpatient, at the center, by some accounts, of an eerie hospital literary salon.

As in the writing of epileptics and manics, the drive behind schizophrenic writing seems to stem from changes in the temporal lobes. Important abnormalities exist in other parts of schizophrenics' brains too, most notably in the frontal lobe, but the temporal lobes appear to generate their vivid inner voices, experiences that may be interpreted as hallucinations or may, in milder cases, find expression in distorted metaphors.

"Normal" Writers

Can we apply to normal (nonmanic, nonepileptic) writing what we know about these disorders? Most writers, even the most obsessed, do not fall into the clinical categories I've been exploring. And certainly most writers do not appeal to such neurological or psychiatric explanations when describing why they write. What drives most writers to write, and how do their experiences of their motives connect with the neurology we've seen so far? One place to start may be the people who write prolifically but are not writers by profession. In talking about writers we often neglect this group, which is far larger than the few people who successfully make writing a career.

Arguably the biggest group of amateur writers comprises those who are suffering from something: bereavement, illness, exile, "narcissistic injury" to self-esteem, adolescence. Suffering triggers limbic system and temporal lobe activity through their roles in emotion, and, as I describe more fully in Chapter 6, increases the desire to write and communicate. I see this in my hospital practice, where patients frequently bring me unpublished memoirs they have written about their illness. A less elaborate form of illness-induced writing, long noted by physicians, has been given the medical name *le signe du petit papier,* for the way in which anxious patients show up for appointments with a tightly folded list that unfolds to reveal dozens of questions they have been saving to ask.

The most extreme example of such illness-induced writing that I have seen was one of my patients with Parkinson's disease, who rated his troubles in four different areas, every half-hour, twenty-four hours a day. At each three-month visit, his hands trembling with his disease, he would present me with a hundred-page color printout of his findings — including transparent overlays. He did this not because he was manic-depressive or epileptic, but because he was suffering — and was doing everything in his power to gain control over it. Harold Brodkey's *This Wild Darkness* and Anatole Broyard's *Intoxicated by My Illness,* both written just before their deaths, are examples of how moving this genre can be in the hands of gifted writers. The sufferings of the strongest people can become not just battles to be won, but tools they turn to their advantage, as when blind people develop especially acute senses of hearing and touch.

What other than medical illness spurs normal people to write prolifically? The chief cause is not quite illness, but nearly: love, especially unhappy love. Other forms of suffering, including social upheaval, exile from the land of one's youth (a plight that in one sense afflicts everyone), and war, may trigger writing. At least in this country, though, they are less likely than love to do so, perhaps because they are external threats that require action, and the action takes away from the time for writing. Love of another, especially if it is unrequited, is a threat to self-esteem — and self-esteem is something we think words can fix. Writing and talking to whoever will listen to us rises especially from the anguish we feel when the beloved is absent. The words we write, the stories we tell about her to ourselves, serve us, Pygmalion-like, as our artificial Galatea until she returns. In bereavement, the need to tell these stories can become unbearable.

Little direct information is available on the neural underpinnings of how suffering drives normal people to write. Cautiously generalizing findings from pathological states to normal processes, however, has been a mainstay of modern medicine; the former so often is merely an extreme of the latter. In the case of the drive to communicate, there is solid indirect reason to believe that normals too have altered activity in their temporal lobes during such states. Love and suffering are powerfully encoded by the brain's limbic system, the network most directly responsible for the control of emotion. And the region where the limbic system interacts most directly with the language system is the temporal lobe.

One patient who had a particularly complicated interaction of forces driving her to write was fifteen-year-old Anna, sent to me for evaluation of new hypergraphia. She was an appealing, bright girl who had experimented a single time with drugs and accidentally taken a huge overdose. For months afterward she felt as if her thoughts were less organized, and she was tormented by words stuck in her head, repeating over and over. This led to secondary obsessions such as, "What if this word took over my life?"

About ten days before I saw her, she suddenly started writing constantly. She wrote in gym, on her pocketbook, and in her therapist's office; she wrote a ten-page letter to her parents while they were in the room. Since many of our patients' problems are difficulties we doctors have accidentally caused by our interventions, I asked her about new medications. It turned out that the writing began soon after her psychiatrist had tried one of the more energizing neuroleptic medications to help her disorganized thoughts. It is a drug that can stimulate a mild, nearly manic state in some people for a week or two after they start it. And in fact, Anna's hypergraphia soon faded away after we stopped the drug.

Drug-induced hypergraphia is not rare. (For instance, Robert Louis Stevenson's *The Strange Case of Dr. Jekyll and Mr. Hyde* was written during a six-day cocaine high during which he generated sixty thousand words.) Anna, however, had complicated emotional issues with language that were not just related to the drugs. For instance, her mother had speech so pressured that when she was in the exam room Anna had no chance to talk and seemed frustrated. I asked her mother to leave for a while. Anna and I sat alone in the room together, nearly mute. The words she had been trying to say to me earlier seemed to have evaporated.

Because I don't see many adolescents as patients, I had originally thought that I was more afraid of Anna than she could be of me. It turned out that I was wrong. After a few minutes away from her mother, Anna had a striking bout of conversion hysteria, of turning an emotion into a physical symptom. (This is an old-fashioned condition which, although common in Freud's Vienna, we hardly ever see anymore except in children.) She suddenly felt that her tongue was swelling up, that she could no longer talk, and she was not sure that she would even be able to breathe for much longer. She did not seem to be pretending; she looked truly panicked. It didn't help to re-assure her that her tongue looked fine, her airway was clear, and that she was speaking normally. She kept saying, whether with anxiety or relish I wasn't certain, "When my mother comes back and hears this, is she going to be mad!" Yet as soon as her mother came back and gave her a mint, the symptoms melted away and Anna was flooded with relief at being able to return to her role as a maternally squelched adolescent.

Anna's problems communicating in front of her mother or with-out her support, her fears of being taken over by or losing her words, were with her long before the drugs she took. They were the trigger for a problem that another recipient might not have had. This is one of the reasons that choosing psychiatric medications is so compli-cated. Drugs interact with brain states unique to each of us.

Besides people who are suffering, another not-completely-normal class of normal writers is professional creative writers. There seems to be a continuum stretching from the general population who do not much enjoy writing, through creative writers, to hypergraphics. The gray zone includes the Romantic writer Thomas de Quincey, who used to rent a room, write frantically on scraps of paper until the room was filled, and then move, leaving the scraps for the maid. Some of the evidence for this continuum comes from the existence of people like Dostoevsky and Flaubert, both hypergraphics and highly talented writers, and from the research that shows temporal lobe changes in certain nonepileptic people.

Several factors besides skill are more significant in professional writers than in most amateurs. One is love of the surface level of lan-guage: the sound of it; the taste of it on the tongue; what it can be made to do in virtuosic passages that exist only for their own sake, like cadenzas in baroque concerti. Writers in love with their tools are not unlike surgeons obsessed with their scalpels, or Arctic sled racers who sleep among their dogs even when they don't have to. Another difference between amateur and professional writers, almost by definition, is that the latter more successfully engage their audience. It is partly a question of skill, but more often a matter of goals. Amateur writers tend to write primarily for self-expression, whereas writers able to become professional can hide or transform their own agendas enough so that they are of interest to others. Is this position the same as Freud's famous dictum that artists take unacceptable drives and present them in an acceptable way? Perhaps, although I would make room for artists who take phenomena so acceptable that we hardly notice them and twist them into something magical, as in Nicholson Baker's delirious description of the comma.

Who counts as a prolific — if not quite hypergraphic — writer? Those often mentioned include Balzac, Burgess, King, Oates, Proust, Trollope, Updike . . . Of course, who gets on the list is influenced by factors other than output. For instance, my list contains few genre writers because of the convention that genre writing isn't quite writing. But Isaac Asimov, for instance, worked seven days a week, writing as fast as he could type, ninety words a minute, and reportedly never suffered a blocked minute. He had completed 477 books by his death at age seventy-two. Proust, on the other hand, is included on most lists of prolific writers because of those long sentences, and because he presented all his books as one giant novel — even though his lifetime output was not especially high.

There are many descriptions of driven writing by the writers themselves. James Thurber, for instance, described how his writing crept into everything: "I never know quite when I'm not writing. Sometimes my wife comes up to me at a party and says, 'Dammit, Thurber, stop writing.' She usually catches me in the middle of a paragraph. Or my daughter will look up from the dinner table and ask, 'Is he sick?' 'No,' my wife says, 'he's writing something.'"

There are also many descriptions of driven writers by other, usually less prolific, writers. Their tone tends to be more sour. Thus Martin Amis on John Updike — "a psychotic Santa of volubility" — or Shirley Jackson's husband, Stanley Edgar Hyman — "When Shirley gets in front of a typewriter it's like a pissing sow." Or this, by Victoria Nelson from a book on writer's block:

> The extraordinarily prolific writer whose output flows unchecked is of-
> ten an object of awe for the blocked writer who, envying him in the
> same way that an overweight person envies the anorexic, fails to see that
> this deluge of words often conceals an inverted case of writer's block.
> Like Hans Christian Andersen's little dancer who couldn't get the en-
> chanted red shoes off her feet, the compulsive writer cannot stop writ-
> ing. Compulsive writing is, in fact, a way of hiding from some of the
> deeper demands of literary and emotional experience.

The view reflects a general distrust of writers who are too productive. Ironically, the thought is that although art should communicate
with an audience, if the artist communicates too effortlessly or too
often, he or she runs the risk of being labeled prolix or a hack. In an
interview, Joyce Carol Oates defended the origin of her own prolific
writing:

> "Coming back to the question of your own creativity. Is there a compul-
> sive element in all this activity . . . ?"
>
> "I assure you, there is very little that is compulsive about my life, ei-
> ther in writing or otherwise. I believe that the creative impulse is natural
> in all human beings, and that it is particularly powerful in children un-
> less it is suppressed. Consequently, one is behaving normally and in-
> stinctively and healthily when one is creating — literature, art, music, or
> whatever. An excellent cook is also creative! I am disturbed that a natu-
> ral human inclination should, by some Freudian turn of phrase, be con-
> sidered compulsive — perhaps even pathological. To me this is a com-
> plete misreading of the human enterprise."

Oates's reply raises the provocative question of what is accomplished by using medicalized words like "hypergraphia" to describe
aspects of literary creation. Stylistically, giving innocent phenomena
Latin or Greek names may only reflect that, as a researcher, I am no
longer a native speaker of English. The more fundamental issue is
that of treating aspects of creativity as abnormal brain states. Is doing
so pathologizing an activity that should be praised? Some people
with temporal lobe epilepsy, for instance, object to having personal
characteristics that they value, such as their writing or their religious
impulses, attributed to a brain abnormality. Yet everything in our

personalities, sick or well, comes from our brains — modified, of course, by experience. Should we stigmatize traits simply because they have a known biological origin, or because they, like most traits, can also have negative aspects? Dostoevsky rejected this position in his description of Prince Myshkin's epilepsy:

> "What if it is disease?" he decided at last. "What does it matter that it is an abnormal intensity, if the result, if the sensation, remembered and analyzed afterwards in health, turns out to be the acme of harmony and beauty, and gives a feeling, unknown and undivined till then, of completeness, of proportion, of reconciliation, and of startled prayerful merging with the highest synthesis of life?"

As our knowledge of neuropsychology grows, there will be fewer and fewer traits without known brain origins, and more and more treatments to alter those traits. Describing creativity in neurological terms is becoming a powerful and rich way of talking about a subject that has until recently been extraordinarily resistant to anaylsis.

2

Literary Creativity and Drive

> One often hears of writers that rise and swell with their subject,
> thought it may seem but an ordinary one. How, then, with me,
> writing of this Leviathan? Unconsciously my chirography expands
> into placard capitals. Give me a condor's quill! Give me Vesuvius'
> crater for an inkstand! Friends, hold my arms!
>
> — Herman Melville, *Moby Dick*

HYPERGRAPHIA, ALTHOUGH INTRIGUING, is a neurological curiosity that when uncontrolled can lead to very bad prose indeed. What makes hypergraphia worth studying is what it can tell about a much more meaningful phenomenon, creativity. Even though many creative works are not hypergraphic but spare and tightly edited, hypergraphia can help clarify the origins of creativity in two complementary ways. On a psychological level, it draws attention to the overwhelming but often neglected importance of drive to creativity. On a neurological level, it points to where creativity comes from, physically, in the brain. Within these two discussions, I look at some complementary, more traditional theories of creativity that address its cognitive rather than motivational aspects.

The Creative Mind

What defines a creative work is usually disputable. We may doubt a work's creativity when it is too readable, as with Dickens's novels. We equally doubt a work's creativity when it is too unreadable, as with James Joyce's *Finnegans Wake*. This book is particularly interesting because it seems to deliberately imitate the language that some hypergraphic schizophrenic writers use involuntarily: the neologisms, onomatopoeia, and scrambled word salad: "Margaritomancy! Hyacinthous pervinciveness! Flowers. A cloud. But Bruto and Cassio are ware only of trifid tongues the whispered wilfulness ('tis demonal!) and shadows shadows multiplicating (il folsoletto nel falsoletto col fazzolotto dal fuzzolezzo), totients quotients, they tackle their quarrel."

Joyce's daughter Lucia was schizophrenic. He was devoted to her and refused to accept her diagnosis for years, bringing her to specialist after specialist across Europe. Carl Jung was the twentieth, and the only one not to immediately dismiss her as hopeless. Nevertheless, he eventually compared her and her father to two people going to the bottom of a river; but one was falling and would drown, while the other was diving. While Joyce's descent was not as deep, it is not clear that it was completely voluntary; his own mental health was notable for periods of severe depression and, among other oddities, a tendency to hide in cupboards during thunderstorms. Yet being able to explain *Finnegans Wake* as the result of illness would not answer the question of whether it is creative.

Although — at least in principle — everyone approves of creativity, many have been skeptical of attempts to study or enhance it. The artist's view is often that creativity should be left alone; that looking too closely could endanger it. The basic scientist's view also is often that creativity should be left alone; that it is by definition too anomalous for controlled study. That has left the study of creativity enhancement to New Age practitioners, inspirational business seminar leaders, and a few brave social scientists.

Even social scientists have been hesitant. Freud, in his essay on Dostoevsky, wrote that "before the problem of the creative artist, analysis must, alas, lay down its arms." (To be fair, psychoanalysts have struggled more valiantly with the problem than have other clinicians. Psychopharmacologists, by contrast, have had a tendency to dismiss creativity as a reason made up by patients to excuse not taking their pills.) Some social scientists believe that enterprises as diverse as scientific discovery, literature, dancing, and successful business decisions should not all be lumped under the single concept of creativity. Howard Gardner, for instance, has argued that different intelligences are needed for different domains such as language and mathematics, and that creativity in one domain does not necessarily extend into another.

Nonetheless, researchers on creativity have begun to combine information from a number of different disciplines; they argue persuasively that it is such an important phenomenon that we cannot afford not to study it. Most agree that a useful definition of creative work is that it includes a combination of novelty and value. Creativity requires novelty because tried-and-true solutions are not creative, even if they are ingenious and useful. And creative works must be valuable (useful or illuminating to at least some members of the population) because a work that is merely odd is not creative. This two-pronged definition of creativity also provides an explanation of why the creative can lie close to the insane (unusual but valueless behavior).

The definition of creative work as novel and valuable captures the societal aspect of what gets called creative work. Creativity is not the property of a work in isolation: novelty and value have to be defined in relation to a social context. When I use a lever and fulcrum to move a rock in my garden, I don't get the creativity points that I would if I were Cro-Magnon. Sometimes the social context is not clear, however. Who should judge whether a work such as *Finnegans Wake* is creative? The general public is neither skilled nor interested enough, whereas specialists in a field are sometimes so invested in the status quo that they resist innovation. The role of social context in determining value also underlies the process whereby the geniuses of one generation are the hacks of the next, whereas people dismissed as mad are rehabilitated as geniuses.

Sometimes the social context is all too clear: the notion of creative freedom becomes so rigidly codified that it is paradoxically restrictive. A close friend, a wonderfully inventive storyteller and decorator, nonetheless feels uncreative because she does not Paint or Write. Another recalls arguments with a high school art teacher who insisted that he stop "limiting" his painting to black and white and freely use color as the rest of the class did. Even at my daughters' very liberal preschool, a teacher gently expressed concern that one of them enjoyed coloring too precisely within the lines of coloring books (the other twin scribbles wildly). These examples raise the issue of whether creativity can be taught, a thorny subject that I will sidestep.

Just as creative work requires both novelty and value, the creative thinker who produces it requires both talent and drive. Although it is difficult to measure, drive palpably erupts out of some works, as in the epigraph that begins this chapter. Melville's hypergraphia is only a fragment of his literary inspiration, reflecting his drive but not his talent.

Here let me lay down my arms before the question of talent and take up a different set of weapons to shoot the easier target, drive. Hypergraphia is a window onto the nature of creative drive, and its neurological underpinnings are better understood than those of talent. Drives are largely controlled by the limbic system, a group of brain nuclei that interact strongly with the temporal lobes. Admittedly, separating drive and talent is sometimes complicated, because they are so enmeshed. When someone is highly motivated to do something, that person is likely to learn to do it well, and when someone can do something well (especially when it wins praise), the ability to do it often increases the drive to do it.

The consensus, however, seems to be that drive is surprisingly more important than talent in producing creative work. For instance, researchers find a poor correlation between general intelligence and creativity, experimentally confirming Thomas Edison's famous aphorism, "Genius is one percent inspiration and ninety-nine percent perspiration."

The psychologist Dean Simonton's "Darwinian theory of creativity" provides a surprising view of the relations among creativity, motivation, and productivity. His model proposes three stages of the development of creative ideas. First, the creator produces many different ideas. Second, the bad ideas are weeded out, either by the creator or his or her critics. Brahms, for instance, published his first string quartet only after writing and discarding twenty others. He claimed to have papered the walls and ceiling of his room with rejected pages: "I had only to lie on my back to admire my sonatas and quartets." Third, the surviving good ideas spawn the development of new ideas, and the process repeats. There is a close analogy with Darwin's three stages of individual variation, natural selection, and trait transmission.

Simonton sees a perhaps inescapable conclusion to his Darwinian theory: the great advantage of having as many ideas as possible, just as organisms such as bugs and mold benefit by having as many offspring as possible. Most of us would resist this bug analogy, arguing that having thousands of offspring works well only for simple organisms that do not need to care for their offspring. By contrast, just as complicated organisms like primates and elephants have few children whom they intensively nurture, so complicated creative ideas would seem to be rare children who need enormous care. Having thousands of children is not an evolutionary advantage if each needs nine months of gestation and four years of college.

But Simonton argues that even in complicated fields, leaders often have creativity that strongly reflects their productivity. He provocatively names this trait "the constant probability of success" and points out that of about 250 Western composers, three alone — Mozart, Beethoven, and Bach — are responsible for almost one-fifth of the standard repertoire. Simonton's argument, that the volume of a writer's or thinker's total output is one of the best predictors of the amount of his or her truly creative work, has the interesting implication that if the number of great works is directly proportional to the total number of works, then the writers with the most masterpieces will also have the greatest number of justly ignored works. As the poet W. H. Auden put it, "The chances are that, in the course of his lifetime, the major poet will write more bad poems than the minor."

There are, of course, some exceptions to Simonton's theory: highly productive would-be authors who fill file drawers with unpublishable trash, and authors such as Chidiock Tichborne who have a tiny but exquisite body of work. (Tichborne wrote his only poem, the remarkable "Elegy," while in the Tower of London on the night before he was disemboweled for treason against Queen Elizabeth I.) But statistically, these counterexamples are the exceptions. Most writers with a single, perfect work probably generated many drafts which they, like Brahms, destroyed before the public ever saw them.

The argument that creativity is proportional to total output, is 99 percent perspiration, does not completely let us escape that problem of the remaining 1 percent, the sliver that separates the workaholic genius from the merely workaholic. Without some talent, generating reams of text is not enough. As Eyler Coates put it, "We've all heard that a million monkeys banging on a million typewriters will eventually produce a masterpiece. Now, thanks to the Internet, we know this is not true."

Talent does slip back into the Darwinian model during its generation: some creators simply produce a more varied range of ideas as well as a greater number. (Later in the chapter I explore some reasons why this might be so.) Talent also influences Simonton's selection stage, in which passages or works of poor quality are weeded out. This thought highlights an aspect of writing that I have neglected so far, namely editing. The drive to write produces a first draft; it is the drive to write well that produces the second, third, twentieth. Thus editing is a stage at which we cannot avoid the notion of talent, a concept that includes, but is not limited to, everything from apt word choice to plot twists to philosophical insight to a sense of what will appeal to the audience.

Often the editing talent is not the writer's own. An outside eye and hand is usually essential, especially for writers who tend toward hypergraphia. A classic example is Max Perkins's work in turning Thomas Wolfe's *Look Homeward, Angel* into a readable book. Most writers rely on a number of reader-critics to help them, hence the almost comically long list of acknowledgments in most prefaces. I even went so far as to marry a professional editor, Andrew Hrycyna, which is something I would recommend to any writer (if Andy weren't already married, that is).

How, specifically, does motivation affect creativity — both the generation and the editing of ideas? It matters where the drive comes from. All driven writers focus on their work. But people driven by intrinsic motivations such as curiosity and enjoyment have a relationship to the product of their work different from those moved by extrinsic motivations including praise, money, and a constantly varying world of punishments. Someone who is fascinated by language attends to details and to the overall texture of a writing project more than she will if she is writing simply to satisfy the public. While strong intrinsic motivation increases creativity, surprisingly, adding extrinsic motivations — even positive ones — can actually decrease creativity. If that is true, paying a writer may paradoxically make him write less well. (As you might guess, I wouldn't say that this means writers should not be paid.) Reward may encourage the writer to stop work as soon as he or she has completed the minimal amount necessary for the reward, resulting in what the economist Herbert Simon calls satisficing. Extrinsic motivation may also have a negative effect on creativity by distracting the subject's attention from the task to thoughts of reward or punishment.

This implies that the best way to foster creative writing is to give the writer freedom to work on a subject he loves. But the motivation to write may be infectious, as Plato described in the *Ion:* "[The muse] first makes man inspired, and then through these inspired ones others share in the enthusiasm, and a chain is formed, for the epic poets, all the good ones, have their excellence, not from art, but are inspired, possessed, and thus they utter all these admirable poems." Experimental evidence for Plato's position actually exists. Children shown videos of other children enjoying their work not only enjoy their work more, but seem to escape the negative effect of extrinsic rewards: rewards made them perform even better.

A person with strong intrinsic motivation to do his or her job often thinks of it as a calling, a vocation in the semireligious sense. And secular vocations sometimes begin with a secular conversion experience just as religious ones do. (Conversion experiences are common in temporal lobe symptoms, as in the Geschwind personality syndrome of temporal lobe epilepsy, and in mania.) However irrational, such experiences can be life changing.

When I applied to medical school, I wasn't especially committed to being a doctor. I wanted to know how the brain works, and I thought an M.D. was merely a tool that would allow me access to more resources than a Ph.D. would. I suspected that I was too introverted to do well working with patients. My undergraduate advisors, all Ph.D.'s, had worked hard to convince me of what they saw as the tedious life of a physician, treating the same diseases over and over. The M.D.s' rhetoric about saving lives went right over my head.

Consequently, on the first day of medical school I daydreamed through the usual speeches promoting the program and profession. Then came a case presentation of a young man who had had a brain hemorrhage after a bike accident. To decompress the patient's brain, the surgeon had removed a piece of skull and sewn it into his abdominal cavity, for sterility and safekeeping, until it could be replaced. The patient was recovering, but was still groggy and disoriented. (Although perhaps not so disoriented as the elderly, rather deaf neurosurgeon thought he was. When the physician asked him what he did for a living, the young man said dreamily, "Shiiiiiaaaaatsuuu maaaaassaaaage." "See?" said the neurosurgeon, who did not look like someone who had massages regularly, "clearly delirious.")

That chunk of skull in the belly, the radical but simple rearrangement of someone's body to save his life, riveted me. And the fact that the someone was a specific person, with a particular girlfriend and parents who were worried sick, was a revelation after years of reading about neuroscientific abstractions. I became abruptly convinced that I was in the right profession, that I had a calling to be a doctor. The exaggerated, perhaps even pretentious, feeling of duty and joy that filled me was such that I am embarrassed to describe it. But I still feel a little of it every time I turn on a new stimulator in a Parkinson's patient and watch her go from being frozen to walking nearly normally. The feeling doesn't leave me — indeed, it is an essential aid in the instant before I walk into a new patient's room, an event that is still always faintly terrifying. But the feeling is equally a torment when I know I have betrayed it. For instance, during one of the worst days of my residency, a superior insisted that I perform a painful (and I thought unnecessary) procedure on a dying patient who begged me to leave him in peace. In the end the patient, the nurse, and I were all sobbing as I executed the procedure. Thinking of that night still fills me with shame.

So a sense of vocation doesn't guarantee happiness at work. Nor does it guarantee being good at the job. Perhaps it merely gives its possessor a subtle feeling of megalomania, a sense of being in some manner chosen for a higher goal. Sense of vocation as disease. How is vocation related to workaholism, and is hypergraphia a special case of either? To some extent "workaholism" is a term others use to describe people who prefer to describe themselves as having a vocation. The others are saying that he doesn't enjoy himself as much as he thinks, that he works to relieve anxiety, not for pleasure or a goal. Yet even those with a true vocation never feel only the joy of work without occasionally feeling its terror. When your work is part of who you are, and you feel you are working badly, you become foul to yourself. This is part of the tight link between hypergraphia and writer's block.

The distinction between avocation and vocation is fascinating and complicated. Many people who cannot enjoy their work, whether because of the anxiety that arises when so much is riding on their performance or because they were not allowed to choose their work, can throw themselves into a hobby with obsessive fervor. And many of the people who are able to get pleasure from their work do so, in part, by thinking of their work as a hobby or a game. Perhaps this explains why some writers find their first book, written on the sly during coffee breaks at their day job, easier than their second, when the success of the first has allowed them to become full-time professional writers, with all the attendant anxieties.

American popular wisdom is, in certain ways, more accepting of hobby obsession than work obsession. Friends and relatives frequently advise people who think they have vocations — whether writers, musicians, lawyers, or daytraders — not to work so hard, and pityingly dismiss the workaholics' obsessions as an escape from personal issues or an artificial way to build self-esteem. The few workaholics who follow their friends' advice to slow down often become miserable. Perhaps the classic example is the businessman who is so successful that he retires early but then is desperately unhappy. Occasionally, even people who hate their jobs respond to retirement in this way. It makes sense: if hard work is a defense mechanism against stress, then removing the work increases stress. But it also makes sense for healthier reasons. We are born to work, to make and do things. The businessman in Cancun is understandably as miserable as a Border collie trapped in a Manhattan apartment, dreaming of chasing sheep.

While a resident, I was pleased to think that I was not a workaholic, at least compared to the typical doctor at my competitive teaching hospital. I went home at a reasonable hour and I never worked at home. I remembered smugly a time when a cousin, who had lived with me for a while during medical school, asked with some disbelief if I ever studied. Healthy! Then I finished my residency, my schedule relaxed, and I suddenly found myself in work withdrawal. I couldn't be comfortable anywhere except in the emergency room, the heart of the hospital. My work outside the ER was gray and meaningless. In the ER it was warm, blood was everywhere, drunks bellowed happily in the drunk tank, I could use an ultrasound machine to sneak glimpses of what my fetal sons were up to. (Mostly they poked and kicked each other; occasionally they planted their lips on each other in a gesture halfway between a bite and a kiss.) It was probably not a coincidence that my postpartum hypergraphia followed on the heels of the end of my residency as well as the death of my first children. Writing became my vocation after both my motherhood and my absorbing work had died.

Is the recent tendency to see every heightened drive as an addiction — work addiction, sex addiction, Internet addiction — useful? Yes, in that these behaviors are often out of a person's control, and can hurt him or his family. But they can sometimes bring advantages too. The thought of a life of happy mediums depresses me; if enjoying my work passionately means that I become agitated when I can't work, that seems like a fair price. A friend was in a very close marriage; her husband suddenly died. Should she have maintained more emotional distance to spare herself the pain of his death? No. The goal should not be to protect ourselves from suffering, but to be strong enough to bear it. Writer's block, for instance, can stem either from the fear of failure or from insulating ourselves so well from the desire to succeed that we weaken our motivation to write.

Besides the theories of creativity that focus on motivation, I want now to discuss three other types of psychological explanation. I have selected theories have been widely influential, have some practical implications, and may parallel some of the neurological explanations of creativity to be discussed at the end of the chapter.

The first theory stems from the psychoanalytic model and argues that creativity resides in the unconscious. In Freud's original formulation, creative work was a way to divert, or sublimate, excess libidinal energy into a more publicly acceptable form. The notion of sublimation is still widely influential. It may help make sense of how some people can channel their efforts into projects that most of us would consider very dry — as Nietzsche described in *Thus Spake Zarathustra:*

> "Then you must be a scientist whose field is the leech," said Zarathustra; "and you must pursue the leech to its last rock-bottom, you conscientious man!"
>
> "O Zarathustra," answered the man, "that would be an enormity.

How could I take up such a huge task! What I am the master and connoisseur of is the *brain* of the leech: that is *my* field! And it is a whole universe!"

Extending the Freudian model, the analyst Ernst Kris argued that creativity requires a balance between primary and secondary process, two modes of thought originally proposed by Freud. Primary-process thought is concrete, emotion driven, visual rather than verbal, associative, and irrational. The primary process handles a desire by recalling visual images or memories so vividly that they are interpreted as if they were present experiences, even as hallucinations. Primary-process thought characteristically occurs in dreaming and in psychotic states such as schizophrenia, but also, according to Kris, in states of inspiration. For Kris the primary process is the original source of ideas, whether artistic or scientific.

Secondary-process thought, by contrast, is abstract, less emotionally charged, language based, elaborated, and logical. Kris believed the secondary process is necessary to test and winnow the ideas generated by the primary process. In his scheme, as in Simonton's, creativity needs not only a powerful source of ideas but a powerful editor to channel them.

Followers of Melanie Klein, notably Hanna Segal, have argued that artistic creation is a response to the emptiness of depression — an attempt to make up for the artist's inadequacies or to atone for the artist's aggression toward people he loves. The artist fears that his failings will hurt or destroy those loved ones, but hopes that his art will somehow preserve them. For Segal, "All creation is really a re-creation of a once-loved and once whole, but now lost and ruined object, a ruined internal world and self. It is when the world within us is destroyed, when it is dead and loveless, when our loved ones are in fragments, and we ourselves in helpless despair — it is then that we must re-create our world anew, reassemble the pieces, infuse life into dead fragments, re-create life."

Segal's ideas recall Marcel Proust, and his attempt to re-create a lost past through his art. From Proust's experiences also stemmed his despairing belief in the involuntary nature of memory. He described a life in which true, vivid images of the past could not be called up at will, but could be released only rarely, by sensory triggers such as the little madeleine:

> And as soon as I had recognized the taste of the piece of madeleine soaked in her decoction of lime-blossom which my aunt used to give me . . . immediately the old grey house upon the street, where her room was, rose up like a stage set to attach itself to the little pavilion opening on to the garden which had been built out behind it for my parents . . . and with the house the town, from morning to night and in all weathers, the Square where I used to be sent before lunch, the streets along which I used to run errands, the country roads we took when it was fine.

Memory and writing are intertwined. Writing tries to extend our memories infinitely. Conversely, writing often provides metaphors for memory: Aristotle's signet ring impressing memories in the mind, Locke's tabula rasa, Freud's "mystic writing pad" of the psyche. For Freud, Proust's lifelike memories are the vivid primary-process thought that drives creativity. For a literary theorist, as I discuss in the next chapter, regaining a lost world through writing recalls the Romantic notion that writer's block and despair precede literary creation (as they do in Wordsworth's *Prelude*). For a neurobiologist, the fact that it is a smell that triggers Proust's memory and his book reflects the fact that smell is a temporal lobe function. Temporal lobe amnesia can trigger frantic writing as its victim tries to capture the experiences slipping past. The movie *Memento* provides an intense fictional representation of this. The amnestic protagonist progressively covers himself with tattooed messages because he cannot otherwise remember where his notes are.

Even many creativity researchers who are emphatically non-Freudian rely on his two-process model, although they may use quite different terminology. For instance, some researchers call creativity a process of alternating between states of unfocused and focused attention; others say it requires alternating between states of high and low arousal, and so on. Modern researchers have found some experimental evidence that creative people have better access to primary-process thought. They fantasize more, have better memory of their dreams, are more easily hypnotized, and score higher on measures of mildly psychotic traits. Drugs licit and illicit, therapy, and everything from dream journals to "creativity exercises" have been proposed to foster primary-process thought. Secondary-process thought has traditionally been promoted through formal education. Recently, however, pills for attention deficit disorder such as Ritalin, and pills for manic thinking such as mood stabilizers or neuroleptics, have begun to take a role in shaping how both children and adults perform their work.

Cognitive psychologists offer theories of creativity that recast the primary-secondary dichotomy as being between divergent and convergent thinking. Divergent thinking, which shares much with primary-process thought, produces a number of solutions to a poorly defined problem ("Make as many useful things out of these paper clips as you can"). Convergent thinking, roughly analogous to the secondary process, uses all the information available to solve a well-defined problem ("If Huck and Jim row downstream at 3 mph but the current is 5 mph, how long will it take them to reach New Orleans, assuming they are not hit by a steamboat?"). Divergent thinking is essential for the novelty of the creative product, whereas convergent thinking is essential for testing its appropriateness. Readers with Classical tastes may prefer to think of convergent thought as Apollonian and divergent thought as Dionysian.

On the scheme of many cognitive psychologists, convergent and divergent thinking alternate in a process of roughly five stages. First, creative thinkers roughly define the problem. Second, they learn as much as they can about it. Third, when they reach an impasse, they let the problem incubate subconsciously. Fourth, in the "eureka" stage they find an idea or several ideas suddenly emerging from the incubation period. Fifth, they test the ideas. The results may help them redefine the problem and start another iteration. It is during the third and fourth stages that divergent thinking plays the greatest role.

A third set of theories of creativity argues for mental illness as its cause, especially in the arts. As the sculptor Augustus Saint-Gaudens declared, "What garlic is to salad, insanity is to art." The doctrine was already well established by the time of the ancient Greeks. For them, the disorders that were most associated with creativity seem to have been epilepsy and the linked phenomena of mania and depression. The Greeks, and many since them, emphasized not intelligence but passion and drive as the fount of creativity. Socrates and others expected poets to receive their ideas in a frenzy, possessed by the Muses. Plato even thought that the sane should not be allowed to write poetry: "He who approaches the temple of the Muses without inspiration, in the belief that craftsmanship alone suffices, will remain a bungler and his presumptuous poetry will be obscured by the songs of the maniacs."

Even before the madness-mad Romantics, throughout the Renaissance and the Enlightenment the notion of melancholy (which also included manic-depressive illness) was strongly linked to creativity. Indeed, melancholy was so valued that poems such as Milton's "Il Penseroso" were written in its honor. The eighteenth century saw a fad among the rich of hiring someone to personify melancholy in their estate parks. The person was usually instructed to dress like a hermit, to refrain from cutting his hair or nails, and to live in a picturesque grotto provided by the employer. When hermits were scarce, statuary or clockwork figures were used instead.

Of course, artistic crazes for mental illness show not only that such illness has long been perceived as creative, but also that many artists have worked within a received set of conventions that may encourage them to sound more unstable than they are. Was all the overwrought Romantic verse written by people with mental illness? Probably not. On the other hand, the writings and the lives of artists such as Blake and Coleridge and Joyce quickly convince us that their unusual thoughts and actions were not the result of genre conventions or role-playing. Even the omnipresent use of words like "mad" or "crazy" ("crazy about writing") to describe enthusiasm reflects a belief, widespread even among people without mood disorders, that a normal, stable life is not always conducive to pleasure, aesthetic or otherwise.

Most modern researchers still believe, like Plato, in the link between art and mania. But what is the rate of mental illness in creative people outside the arts? Based on the best scientific surveys available so far, rates are about 70 percent for creative musical performers, poets and prose writers, painters, and composers, but only 25 percent for creative natural scientists, politicians, and businesspeople. Should we then conclude that creativity has a different basis in business and science than it does in the arts? Or that businessmen and scientists are less creative than poets and painters?

One complication of interpreting data such as these is that they tend to group different types of mental illness together. Disorders such as schizophrenia may be more compatible with fields that allow social isolation, such as mathematics, than, say, the performing arts. Manic-depression may specifically trigger the desire to communicate, make perceptions more vivid, and loosen associations in a way that makes written creativity more likely. The alternation between the convergent thinking of mildly depressed periods and the more divergent thinking of normal or hypomanic periods may also foster creativity.

As I have mentioned, though, the people who are the most creative — or at least productive — are not the mentally ill but their close relatives. Researchers think that most mental illnesses are caused by multiple genes and that close relatives have some, but not all, of those genes. One explanation of why those genes have persisted through the ages, and do not get bred out of the population, is that they may give some advantage — perhaps creativity — to people who have a smaller number of them — even if a larger number cause the disease.

Clear examples of such genes exist outside of neuroscience. The sickle cell gene, for instance, protects its bearer against malaria but causes anemia. People who have only one copy of it have only a mild anemia and, if they live in an area where malaria is common, are at great advantage. Having two copies of the gene, however, produces a devastating anemia. A similar but more multifactorial pattern of inheritance may explain the persistence of genes that cause manic-depression and perhaps unipolar depression.

The James siblings — mildly bipolar philosopher William James, unipolar depressive novelist Henry James, career neurasthenic and bipolar Alice James, and severely bipolar Robert James — are an excellent example of how both manic-depression and writing can run in a family, with the mildly affected members being more productive than their most ill relatives and also than the general population. A more recent example is the hypergraphic novelist Danielle Steel, whose son suffered from severe manic-depression. Her book and moving testimony before Congress about his early suicide helped to increase public awareness of the plight of the mentally ill. Manic-depression, interestingly, is the only mental illness that correlates, mildly, with higher socioeconomic status. But other disorders can have adaptive features as well. For instance, obsessive-compulsive personality traits, if not the full-blown disorder, are useful in work that requires a high degree of accuracy.

Does mental illness cause creativity or does the association stem from an independent cause? A few researchers have proposed that there are more mentally ill people in the arts because the creative work is particularly stressful and drives artists over the edge. Other researchers have suggested that there are so many mentally ill people in the creative arts simply because it is difficult for them to hold other kinds of jobs. What accounting firm would hire someone like Byron, who kept a pet bear in his college rooms? (Byron did so in response to a Cambridge regulation specifying that he could not keep a dog.) What hospital would hire someone like Joseph Beuys, who regularly wrapped himself in felt and rancid fat? (Beuys explained his obsession with these substances as having started after a plane crash in the Crimea from which he was rescued by Tartars, who rubbed him with fat and wrapped him with felt to heal and warm him. His story is most likely entirely false.)

Mentally ill people may become creative artists because of the novelty of their perspective, just as Tocqueville saw things about the United States that we had not. An outsider may have startling thoughts about normal life, whereas we know all too well what the sane have to say. This advantage of disease may extend beyond mental illness. A colleague has a patient, a painter, who had a stroke that distorted his color vision. She encouraged him to continue to paint anyway. About a year later, he thanked her profusely and told her that his work had actually become more popular because of the way his colors hover intriguingly between the known and the strange.

People may be partial to theories linking creativity and mental illness for reasons other than validity. Romantic views of madness are pleasant both for the mentally ill, who can take pride in having a trait thought to be linked to creativity, and for sane people unsure of their creativity, who can be glad they lack a trait that would bring such suffering. Some people who become writers or artists may welcome a psychiatric diagnosis that would at least partially remove their responsibility for making such an unsober career choice.

Not everyone benefits from the theory that creativity and mental illness go hand in hand — it makes the many creative people who are happy and well adjusted feel that they are somehow not doing their jobs if they are not trashing their hotel rooms or wearing only mauve satin. They may be reassured by the fact that almost without exception no one is severely ill and still creative. All the theories linking creativity to mental illness are really implying mild disease — psychotic traits, for example, rather than unremitting psychosis.

Severe mental illness tends to bring with it bizarre preoccupations and inflexible thought. One study comparing the creative process of normal ("normal") poets and schizophrenic poets shows that the schizophrenics refuse to revise their initial drafts and are unable to take an objective view of their work. Even apart from such rigidity, the suffering that mental illness brings is a huge energy drain, distracting the sufferer from creative work. As the poet Sylvia Plath said: "When you are insane, you are busy being insane — all the time . . . When I was crazy, that's all I was."

The Creative Brain

The neurology of creativity is starting to catch up with the strides that neuroscientists have made in translating other mental processes such as language and memory into more biological descriptions. At least at first glance, the most obvious window onto the brain's role in creativity would seem to be the effect of psychoactive drugs. In the nineteenth century, writers such as Samuel Taylor Coleridge and Thomas de Quincey began to use opium to make their memories and imagination more vivid (and, progressively, simply to slake their addictions). De Quincey described how the "fierce chemistry" of his opium dreams gave him "a power not contented with reproduction, but which absolutely creates or transforms." Still, addictions also hampered their writing and that of other authors. Charles Baudelaire asked, "What is the sense of working, tilling the soil, writing a book, fashioning anything whatsoever, when one has immediate access to paradise?" And William S. Burroughs said that although he could not have written *Naked Lunch* without his experiences as a heroin addict, he also could not have written it if he hadn't stopped — a description that once again reflects Kris's argument that both primary- and secondary-process thought are necessary for creativity.

Writers have used many different types of drugs. In the distant past, writers generally did not distinguish between creative inspiration and religious inspiration; the same drugs were used to stimulate both. New data show that the oracle at Delphi seems to have worked in a cave over a rock fault oozing petrochemical fumes. To renew her prophetic frenzy she would go farther into the cave and inhale the fumes, the B.C.E. version of sniffing glue. Alcohol, an equally ancient technique, has had more constant popularity — despite evidence that it is counterproductive. Modern writers have many more pharmacologic options than the Delphic oracle and the Bacchantes. Hallucinogens (think Aldous Huxley and Anaïs Nin) and stimulants (think Stevenson, Freud, Sartre, Auden) are perhaps the most popular. The range of drugs used suggests that the direction in which the writer's consciousness is altered does not matter much, as long as it is altered.

Judging the effect of the drug on the work can get complicated, however. Drugs give the feeling of creativity more easily than they yield products judged creative by others — at least by others not on drugs. Oliver Wendell Holmes, Sr., the nineteenth-century Boston physician who helped popularize the use of ether anesthesia, also helped popularize its recreational use. Here he describes the truths it revealed:

> I once inhaled a pretty full dose of ether, with the determination to put on record, at the earliest moment of regaining consciousness, the thought I should find uppermost in my mind. The mighty music of the triumphal march into nothingness reverberated through my brain, and filled me with a sense of infinite possibilities, which made me an archangel for a moment. The veil of eternity was lifted. The one great truth which underlies all human experience and is the key to all the mysteries that philosophy has sought in vain to solve, flashed upon me in a sudden revelation. Henceforth all was clear: a few words had lifted my intelligence to the level of the knowledge of the cherubim. As my natural condition returned, I remembered my resolution; and, staggering to my desk, I wrote, in ill-shaped, straggling characters, the all-embracing truth still glimmering in my consciousness. The words were these (children may smile; the wise will ponder): "A strong smell of turpentine prevails throughout."

In fact, the equivocal ability of drugs to produce revelations for writers lends support to the theory that writers do not take drugs to help their writing, they take drugs because of their tendency to mood disorders, and mood disorders often trigger drug addiction.

Neuropsychologists have some evidence that creativity arises through interaction between the left and right hemispheres of the brain. The functions of the two hemispheres roughly mirror each other. In healthy people each hemisphere controls sensation and movement on the opposite side of the body. Thus damage to the left hemisphere can cause numbness and paralysis of the right arm and leg, and vice versa. But language production and comprehension are found only in the left hemisphere of most people. (The situation gets more complicated in a few left-handers.) By contrast, the right hemisphere controls the intonational and emotional aspects of speech, rather than semantic ones. Many other cognitive functions are unevenly distributed across the two cortical hemispheres. The left seems to have the more important role in logical or sequential thinking, while the right is somewhat more significant for spatial and emotional thinking, musical appreciation, and visual imagery. The specializations of the two hemispheres are relative, however, not absolute.

The two hemispheres are connected by only a few bands of white matter. The largest is the corpus callosum, shown in Figure 2b (Chapter 1). In people with very severe temporal lobe epilepsy, surgeons sometimes cut the corpus callosum to prevent seizures from spreading from one side of the brain to the other. The resulting "split-brain" patients, whose hemispheres cannot communicate with each other, have taught us a great deal about the difference between left and right hemispheres. For instance, the split-brain disconnection makes it possible to present a stimulus such as a word to one hemisphere at a time (in normal people, both hemispheres see and hear words nearly simultaneously). When a split-brain patient sees a word only with his right hemisphere he cannot understand it, whereas with his left hemisphere he can read it but can't draw a good picture of it.

At rest, most people's left hemisphere is more active than their right. In writing, the left hemisphere becomes even more active (in painting and music, there is more right hemisphere activity). But in one set of experiments where subjects were asked to invent and write down fantasy stories, subjects who did so creatively had more right hemisphere activation, as measured by EEG, than did less creative subjects. A few other groups have provided some support for a selective right hemisphere role in creativity.

Results of this sort have sometimes been interpreted as showing

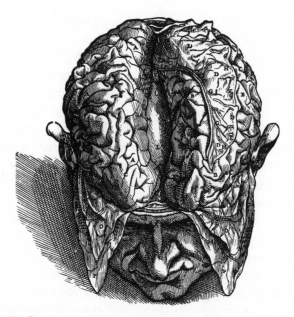

Figure 4. Vesalius in this plate from *De Humani Corporis Fabrica* (1543) has splayed the two cerebral hemispheres to show the corpus callosum connecting them. Vesalius's habit of leaving the face on his anatomical specimens argues more eloquently than any words that this brain is the center of a person, in all his curly humanity.

that the right hemisphere is the sole seat of creativity. The hypothesis, despite its slender experimental grounding, has captured the popular imagination — producing many books with titles such as *Right Brain, Write On!* Right-brain enthusiasts often conflate the distinction between right and left hemisphere activity with their other artificially dualistic enthusiasms, such as holistic versus linear thinking, or contemplative Eastern versus authoritarian Western thought. Experiments show that creativity requires not just more right hemisphere activity, but a balanced interaction between the right and left hemispheres. Split-brain patients, who lack the possibility of that interaction, show low creativity even though they have nearly normal spatial and language abilities. It may be that because resting left hemisphere activity is generally higher in creative and noncreative people alike, the relatively greater increase in right hemisphere activity among creative thinkers reflects the need for a balance between the two hemispheres, rather than for a dominant right hemisphere.

If so, the interaction between left and right brain is yet another process that is reminiscent of the interaction between Freud's primary- and secondary-process thought, and between the modern creativity coach's divergent and convergent thinking. All of these schools converge on the prediction that interaction or alternation between the two modes of thought or hemispheres fosters creativity. And the theories parallel the standard literary model in which a creative writer alternates between generating text and editing.

Split-brain patients are notably alexithymic, a word meaning "unable to read emotions." They cannot put their feelings (a somewhat more right hemisphere function) into words (a left hemisphere function). Researchers have argued that the patients' detachment from their emotional selves is a key part of their lack of creativity. This hypothesis may apply to creativity in general, because alexithymia is not a problem restricted to split-brain patients.

Within each left and right hemisphere, the various lobes of the brain contribute differently to creative thought. The frontal lobes may be most important for the structure and flexibility of creative thought, the judgment or talent part of the talent-plus-motivation mix. This theory is based on studies of people with frontal lobe damage, who tend to lack initiative and foresight. They often perseverate; that is, they continue to respond in a stereotyped way even when the situation changes and their response becomes inappropriate. If you show a pen to a patient with frontal lobe damage and ask him to name it, he may accurately do so — but will then reply "pen" to any additional objects you show him.

In mild ways, all of us can occasionally show these frontal lobe deficits, as when we repeatedly feed more money into a vending machine that has just failed to deliver our soda. Distraction or rest can often break the thinker out of his rut. In the "pen" patient, entry of a relative into the room, or even a sudden noise, can be enough to allow him to identify the next object, "watch." (Unfortunately, he will then name everything "watch" for a while.) Similarly, a healthy person solving a creative problem may need to step back from the problem, by taking a shower or a vacation, in order to solve it.

One study has looked directly at frontal lobe activity in people doing creative work. Normal subjects were asked to perform a creativity test in a positron emission tomography (PET) scanner, which uses radioactive material to measure brain activity in different regions. People who performed creatively on the test had increased frontal lobe activity during the test; those who had a lackluster performance had decreased activity.

While the frontal lobes probably have a greater role in judgment, the temporal lobes may be important for creative drive. The hypergraphia produced by temporal lobe changes is one example that directly reflects this drive. Another is a rare affliction called frontotemporal dementia. Unlike the more common Alzheimer's dementia, people with frontotemporal dementia have, as its name suggests, selective damage to only the frontal and temporal lobes of the brain. Characteristically, their personality and social behavior degenerate, but the patients show no concern. A subset of people with frontotemporal dementia have a dramatic characteristic: they actually gain artistic ability as they become ill. These patients turn out to be those whose temporal lobes are especially damaged and whose frontal lobes are relatively spared. (Such people are perhaps better described as having temporal rather than frontotemporal dementia.)

A typical example of such a patient, described by the neurologist Bruce Miller, is a fifty-one-year-old woman who, without previous artistic training, suddenly began taking art classes. She became uncomfortable socially and stopped going out. At age fifty-five she completed her first, remarkably talented paintings, which recalled scenes from her childhood. Like other artistic patients with temporal dementia, she was intensely driven by her art, and willing to repeat her work as many times as necessary to obtain her desired end. From age fifty-nine to age sixty-three her creativity slowly declined, and she restricted herself to copying the paintings of others. By age sixty-six she was incontinent and her speech had become disorganized and rude. She was expelled from her art class and stopped painting. Her last paintings were slightly distorted family portraits. She died at seventy-one. Autopsy showed damage that was severest in the temporal lobes, with little damage to the frontal lobes or elsewhere in the brain. Is it appalling that creativity could flower from such a bed of illness? Perhaps, but how much more appalling it would be if nothing, as usually happens, had flowered at all. All the works of the spirit are made with corrupt bodies.

People whose artistic activity stems from temporal dementia seem to have decreased function in their temporal lobe, whereas people whose art stems from temporal lobe epilepsy would at first glance seem — given that seizures are like electrical storms — to have increased activity. Must we then say that both decreasing and increasing temporal lobe activity are associated with creativity? No, because the changes in epilepsy are more complicated than a simple increase in activity. There does seem to be an increase during seizures, but between seizures there is often a paradoxical decrease in activity near the epileptic focus or scar in the brain. The decrease may reflect brain tissue that is exhausted or damaged by the seizure. It is between seizures, not in them, that people with temporal lobe epilepsy are hypergraphic.

Therefore, both temporal dementia and temporal lobe epilepsy may decrease temporal lobe activity. If that is true, it might be more accurate, if less complimentary to the temporal lobe, to say that it acts not as the seat of creative drive, but as the seat of creative drive suppression. In fact, the situation is probably even more complicated; during creative activity there may well be local increases and decreases in temporal lobe activity simultaneously. That would explain why people who have had their temporal lobes surgically removed to control their epilepsy do not become wildly creative. It is perhaps best to be circumspect and say merely that creativity is associated with altered temporal lobe activity.

Does the temporal lobe control drive in the visual arts and music as well as in literature? The temporal lobe dementia patients are evidence that it does, because most of the sufferers who become creative do so in music or the visual arts. And although temporal lobe epileptics and manics seem more likely to resort to written rather than visual or musical expression, there are also some whose desire for artistic expression has been visual or musical.

Vincent van Gogh is a vivid example. He almost certainly had temporal lobe epilepsy, manic-depression, or both. However, scholars who have reconstructed van Gogh's medical history are an example of pathography run wild. They have put forward over one hundred other medical diagnoses. Nonetheless, many of the other diagnoses are indirect causes of epilepsy or mania.) To my mind, the diagnosis of epilepsy is relatively certain, with the artist's own documented seizures and a family history of seizures. He had many manic-depressive features too, but we know that violent mood swings can also be seen in temporal lobe epilepsy. Van Gogh was diagnosed with epilepsy just after slicing off his left ear. The doctor who diagnosed him was influenced by having recently seen another epileptic patient who had cut off his own ear. It was not entirely coincidental: both van Gogh and the other patient removed their ears because of epilepsy-related hallucinations of threatening voices coming through that ear.

The neural activity underlying hypergraphia and hallucinations of voices may share some of the same brain regions. Both processes require activity in the language comprehension area (Wernicke's area), which is in the temporal lobe. They may also be linked through the phenomenon of the inner voice, the voice that narrates our daily experiences and may dictate a writer's literary compositions but can, if it becomes pathological, be interpreted as hallucination.

Van Gogh painted in a fury that amazed others and even himself. He was one of the most prolific artists ever, painting more by himself than many Renaissance painters did with a stable of assistants. Even on the day he fatally shot himself, he brought his easel out to the fields to paint. At his peak, he painted a new canvas every thirty-six hours. He described his motive force as emotional as much as cognitive or aesthetic: "Sometimes I draw sketches almost against my will. Is it not emotion, the sincerity of one's feeling for nature, that draws us? . . . The emotions are sometimes so strong that one works without knowing one works, when sometimes the strokes come with a continuity and coherence like words in a speech or a letter."

Van Gogh's direct comparison of painting to writing reflects the fact that his drive to express himself was not restricted to painting. He was hypergraphic as well as a compulsive painter, writing his brother Theo as many as two or three six-page letters a day — excessive even for the profuse letter writing of the nineteenth century.

Besides hypergraphia, van Gogh had other signs of the temporal lobe Geschwind syndrome. He had violence and mood swings. He was hyperreligious — he worked for a time as a minister and was, impressively, fired for "excessive zeal." He had an unconventional sexuality — he lived with prostitutes and may have had an affair with Gauguin. He was overinclusive — Gauguin's memoirs document how difficult it was to end a conversation with him. The episode in which van Gogh sliced off his ear reveals many temporal lobe traits: auditory hallucination, aggressiveness, altered sexuality, and hyperreligiosity. The left-ear amputation was after a violent fight with Gauguin. Through that ear he thought he heard a voice telling him to kill Gauguin. He then cut off his ear, he reported, because of the biblical injunction, "If thine eye offend thee, pluck it out."

Besides van Gogh, a few patients reported in the medical literature have had temporal lobe epilepsy and were compulsive painters. One of them stopped painting when his temporal lobe was removed to control his seizures. A disproportionate number of famous musicians and composers have had epilepsy or manic-depression. (A notable example is the manic-depressive composer Robert Schumann, also a prodigious letter writer.) It is still true that we know of fewer nonliterary artists than literary artists with temporal lobe changes. In contrast to painters and musicians, writers tend to leave more documentation of their lives and their disorders — what with writers' own usually copious personal writing and descriptions by their writer friends.

A colleague introduced me to one of her patients — a healthy woman with no significant medical problems — who abruptly became a passionate sketcher. Previously, she had drawn a little; but a year before I met her she was "suddenly compelled by a pad and pencil" to start drawing. She draws faces of people on the subway and filled thirty-five notebooks in a year. "Drawing is like scratching an itch," she told me; "it is not really a pleasure." On the other hand, she said she likes her complete concentration when drawing — something few people say about their itches. When I asked whether she was equally passionate about writing, she said that she does not keep a journal, but has very elaborate handwriting and has always written poetry "at the drop of a hat." She is a middle-school principal who once gave a presentation on traffic safety entirely in verse. Not wanting to make her feel pathologized, I asked timidly about seizure symptoms (she had none) and mood problems. "Mood problems?" she said, laughing, "you bet!"

The temporal lobe contains brain regions that are crucial to visual object and musical perception. Indeed, to a large extent music is the right hemisphere equivalent of the left hemisphere function of language. It is no coincidence that the brain structures in the left hemisphere that are important for speech recognition are, in the right hemisphere, important for recognizing melodies. Singing and melody are closely tied to the right hemisphere's ability to produce and recognize prosody, the intonational and emotional component of speech. (Chanting is an ancient example in which the distinction between singing and prosody blurs.) Similarly, the brain structures in the left hemisphere that are critical for logical and mathematical calculations are, in the right hemisphere, significant for visuospatial thinking.

Most of the scientific evidence so far described has been from studies of people with brain damage. In the past few years, several new techniques have been developed that give information about brain activity in normal people. These include the PET scans mentioned earlier and functional magnetic resonance imaging (MRI). Functional MRI is different from the more familiar structural MRI used by doctors to identify strokes and brain tumors. Instead of presenting a static picture of the parts of the brain, functional MRI gives a dynamic image, showing the activity levels of various brain areas. Functional MRI can show how brain activity changes during tasks such as moving a limb, watching images on a screen, responding with emotion, or remembering. The changes allow researchers to determine the function of a particular area. By scanning people thinking creatively (with the usual caveat that judging creativity is difficult), researchers may soon be able to see which patterns of brain activity underlie creativity.

Another new tool that has already cast light on creativity is transcranial magnetic stimulation (TMS). Like functional MRI, TMS uses a magnet, but instead of requiring a giant machine circling the head the way functional MRI does, TMS needs only a handheld device. Also unlike functional MRI, which gives a picture of brain activity, TMS allows researchers to alter the activity. Low-frequency TMS inhibits the brain region under the device, whereas high-frequency TMS stimulates it. TMS can help to diagnose the function of brain areas, and sometimes even treat symptoms. Its two modes make it possible to determine whether TMS over the temporal lobe, but not other lobes, would selectively inhibit or stimulate the creativity of a person performing a creative task.

One very preliminary study has used TMS over the temporal lobe to induce the sensation of being visited by the muse — an experience presumably linked to drive more than talent. Another preliminary study has, within minutes, apparently, increased subjects' drawing and mathematical abilities by giving TMS over the frontal lobe. And TMS given daily to the left prefrontal cortex, an area whose activity changes dramatically in depression, significantly improves mood. This effect is a reminder that the temporal lobe is not the only cortical region controlling motivation and emotional response.

The concept of treating mood and creativity disorders by simply waving a wand over the head is delightful. But what are the risks of TMS? So far, few problems have been discovered — but the field is in its infancy.

Creativity is transcendent; it is also, paradoxically, immanent — something science can help. The enterprise, while fraught, is full of promise. Problems with creativity cause individual suffering and economic hardship. And on a global level, the number of threats facing the world over the next hundred years means that greatly increasing human creativity may be necessary for all our survival.

3

Writer's Block as State of Mind

Creative imagination and work go together with me; I take no delight in anything else. That would be a prescription for happiness were it not for the fact that one's productivity depends entirely on sensitive moods. What is one to do on a day when thoughts cease to flow and proper words won't come? One cannot help trembling at this possibility.

— Sigmund Freud

June 7. Bad. Wrote nothing today. Tomorrow no time.

— Franz Kafka

HYPERGRAPHIA IS NEITHER PAINFUL (except sometimes to the reader) nor common. Writer's block is both. All of us have had twinges of it, 10 percent of college students have significant writer's block, and half of all graduate students end up All But Dissertation. In professional writers the syndrome is an obsession, and many writers have transferred the obsession to their characters. In George Eliot's *Middlemarch,* for instance, the idealistic Dorothea, who has married Mr. Casaubon to devote her life to his scholarship, is filled with horror as she begins to realize that he will never put out: "'And all your notes,' said Dorothea . . . 'all those rows of volumes — will you not make up your mind what part of them you will use, and begin to write the book which will make your vast knowledge useful to the world?'" Or there is Joseph Grand in Albert Camus's *The Plague,*

Figure 5. *Rebus Charivariques* (c. 1840). A French drawing from one of the fanciful alphabets popular at the time. It is, perhaps accidentally, a wordless illustration of writer's block.

pathetically filling page after page with versions of his novel's first sentence. Or even Margret and H. A. Rey, authors of the children's book *Curious George,* who also wrote a book about a penguin who ran out of stories to tell his audience.

Dissecting writer's block is as difficult as carving meatloaf at the joints. We are not always even sure we are blocked. (Am I blocked or just talentless? Am I blocked or do I just hate my assignment?) But everyone agrees that block is a mental state. In this chapter I attempt to figure out what that means and then look at explanations of block in those terms. The next chapter looks at the beginnings of our understanding of block as a brain state.

What It Feels Like

Although writer's block can have many manifestations and many causes, all blocked writers share two traits: they do not write despite being intellectually capable of doing so, and they suffer because they are not writing. That definition, though simple, allows us to peel away several other states that have important differences from writer's block.

In some ways block is a phenomenon opposite to hypergraphia. Yet in some surprising ways the two brain states are complementary without actually being opposites, which is why a writer can alternate between hypergraphia and block. Writers can even be hypergraphic and blocked at the same time, as when Joseph Conrad frantically wrote letters to friends while putting off his novels:

I sit down religiously every morning, I sit down for eight hours every day — and the sitting down is all. In the course of that working day of eight hours I write three sentences which I erase before leaving the table in despair. Sometimes it takes all my resolution and power of self-control to refrain from butting my head against the wall. I want to howl and foam at the mouth but I daren't do it for fear of waking the baby and alarming my wife. After such crises of despair I doze for hours, still held conscious that there is that story that I am unable to write. Then I wake up, try again, and at last go to bed completely done up. So the days pass and nothing is done. At night I sleep. In the morning I get up with that horror of that powerlessness I must face through a day of vain efforts. . . .

I seem to have lost all sense of style and yet I am haunted by the necessity of style. And that story I can't write weaves itself into all I see, into all I speak, into all I think, into the lines of every book I try to read. . . . I feel my brain. I am distinctly conscious of the contents of my head. My story is there in a fluid — in an evading shape. I can't get hold of it. It is all there — to bursting, yet I can't get hold of it any more than you can grasp a handful of water. . . .

I never mean to be slow. The stuff comes out at its own rate. I am always ready to put it down . . . the trouble is that too often, alas, I've to wait for the sentence, for the word. . . . The worst is that while I'm thus powerless to produce, my imagination is extremely active; whole paragraphs, whole pages, whole chapters pass through my mind. Everything is there: descriptions, dialogue, reflection, everything, everything but the belief, the conviction, the only thing needed to make me put pen to paper. I've thought out a volume a day till I felt sick in mind and heart and gone to bed, completely done up, without having written a line. The effort I put out should give birth to Masterpieces as big as mountains, and it brings forth a ridiculous mouse now and then.

This long passage, even longer in the original, paints vividly the sick horror of feeling blocked. But its verbosity also shows how closely related hypergraphia and at least some writer's block can be in the overpowering desire to write.

Defining block as writing less (much less) than the writer wants to has the result that there can be writers with normal productivity who have an agonizing sensation of block because they are not as productive as they want to be. Conrad, for instance, despite the harrowing passage on the previous page, turned out books quite regularly. While those of us who are less productive may grumble that his was not true block, the sensation of block is so closely related to true block that the two should be considered together.

The sensation can arise from different roots. There is the writer's throbbing self-criticism, which may itself be the source of the block. There is also the strangled feeling of inarticulateness, of ideas coming faster than words, of not being able to express what is inside. And there may also be the dull gnawing of feeling empty, of having no ideas to express.

Why is suffering a major criterion for writer's block? Because someone who is not writing but not suffering does not have writer's block; he or she is merely not writing. Such times may instead be fallow periods for the development of new ideas, periods Keats famously described as "delicious diligent indolence." You might think it would be easy to tell not writing from writer's block, but that is not always so. As an example, the novelist Paul Kafka-Gibbons decided to take a relaxing summer off from writing his novel. He then spent those months wrestling with his psychoanalyst, who thought he should face the fact that he had writer's block.

Kafka-Gibbons's experience highlights the role that other people's attitudes can have in creating at least the appearance of writer's block. Students who seem blocked often turn out instead to have a secret dislike of their subject — or their teacher, or their parents. Conversely, a sort of external block can arise when the not-writer wants to write but is repressed by society. The oppression can be internalized until the not-writer believes the block is something within her, that she cannot write because she has nothing valuable to say. Such cases are common, and if the not-writer has internalized the authority figure's values well enough, they may shade smoothly into true writer's block.

Thus, some writers are left with self-criticism or perfectionism as a source of block — in Franz Kafka's words, having "to see the pages being covered endlessly with things one hates, that fill one with loathing, or at any rate with dull indifference." Kafka's self-assessment led to his famous deathbed plea to Max Brod to burn all his work. Instead, of course, Brod published it. Did he betray Kafka? Or was he the external force that Kafka invoked to help him fight his internal critic? (Kafka-Gibbons, a distant relative of Kafka, plans to avoid this sort of controversy by making sure his epitaph reads "Publish all I'd burn.")

Much popular psychology aimed at curing writer's block explicitly attempts to defang internal critics. Here, though, issues of skill arise — some internal critic is necessary for good writing. One poet has said that there is no such thing as writer's block if your standards are low enough. Should we want to bring every writer's judgment down to the level of his or her ability? Or is curing a mediocre writer of the inhibitions of perfectionism a disservice to writer and reader alike?

Writer's block is not agraphia, the selective loss of the skill to write (usually caused by strokes, and strikingly rare). Unlike agraphia, writer's block tends to be restricted to a genre or particular project, with all other forms of writing normal. Coleridge, for instance, was a fluent — sometimes even hypergraphic — journalist, correspondent, and metaphysical speculator. Yet when he tried to write poetry, Coleridge complained, he "beat up Game of far other kind — instead of a covey of poetic Partridges with whirring wings of music . . . up came a Metaphysical bustard, urging its slow, heavy, laborious, earth-skimming flight over dreary and level Wastes." Why was poetry different from metaphysics or journalism for Coleridge? Crucially, he thought of himself primarily as a poet, not a journalist; his poetry mattered most to him and he worked hardest on it. Thus, what mattered most to him was most difficult. I will discuss one of the brain mechanisms by which this may occur in the next chapter.

Further evidence that writer's block is not closely related to agraphia is a variant of writer's block in which the blocked writer actually writes more, even if badly. Oliver Sacks tells of an agonizing block while writing *Uncle Tungsten* that caused him to write and throw away about two million words for a book of one hundred thousand words. This sort of "high-output block" presumably needs a different sort of treatment from low-output block.

Nonetheless, there is something that writer's block shares with agraphia and also aphasia (loss of the basic ability to speak). That is the suffering inherent in being unable to communicate. It characterizes high-output as well as low-output block; the panicked writing is a desperate attempt to be understood. And being unable to communicate can cause depression, which in turn can cause an inability to communicate.

Some aspects of block may be culturally determined. The phrase "writer's block" was coined by an American, a psychiatrist named Edmund Bergler. Jay Parini has slyly suggested that not only the name "block" but even blocked writing itself may be a peculiarly American habit:

> Trollope's calmly professional attitude towards writing . . . remains a kind of unspoken ideal for contemporary British writers like Graham Greene, Anthony Burgess, Iris Murdoch, and A. N. Wilson — all of whom regard productivity as a virtue. . . . By contrast, contemporary American writers — Saul Bellow, Mary McCarthy, William Styron, Norman Mailer and Thomas Pynchon — often harbor long silences, publishing in gigantic, well-publicized spasms. A few of our best writers — J. D. Salinger, Ralph Ellison, Grace Paley and Harold Brodkey — have fashioned whole careers out of the sound of one hand clapping.

In other ages and cultures, writers were not thought to be blocked but straightforwardly dried up. One literary critic points out that the concept of writer's block is peculiarly American in its optimism that we all have creativity just waiting to be unlocked. By contrast, Milton when he could not write felt that he was empty, that there was no creativity left untapped.

If writer's block is more common in the United States, it would not be the first weakness that is peculiar to our culture. The modern American idea of the literary writer is so shaped by the towering images of Ernest Hemingway and F. Scott Fitzgerald struggling with every word, that there is a paradoxical sense in which suffering from writer's block is necessary to be an American writer. Without block once in a while, if a writer is too prolific, he or she is suspected by others of being a hack. Nonetheless, of the first six descriptions of block in this chapter — Freud, Kafka, Eliot, Camus, the Reys, and Conrad — none were American. Gustave Flaubert, for instance, had a drive to write that was nearly matched by his drive to rewrite, at one point leading him to exclaim, "What a waste of paper, what a number of crossed-out passages."

As a thought experiment, take away from writer's block the problems of motivation and skill. What is left, arguably, is the problem of inspiration — skilled writing that is highly motivated but without the quality that makes some writing transcendent. Fitzgerald was one of many writers who believed that inspiration is finite, something that can be used up:

> I have asked a lot of my emotions — one hundred and twenty stories. The price was high, right up with Kipling, because there was one little drop of something — not blood, not a tear, not my seed, but me more intimately than these, in every story. It was the extra I had. Now it has gone and I am just like you now.
>
> Once the phial was full — here is the bottle it came in.
>
> Hold on, there's a drop left there. . . . No, it was just the way the light fell. . . .

Although most psychologists and writing teachers distrust the Romantic notion of an inspiration that is separate from skill or hard work, and doubt the claim that one can write at one's best only when "in the mood," so many professional writers take these notions seriously that perhaps we should too. After all, psychologists, as opposed to professional writers, are not known for writing well. Perhaps it is in part because they follow their own advice to write while not inspired. As Norman Mailer put it, "Writing at such a time [against one's inclinations] is like making love at such a time. It is hopeless, it desecrates one's future, but one does it anyway because at least it is an act. Such writing is almost unsprung. . . . If you can purge it, if you get sleep and tear it up in the morning, it can do no more harm than any other bad debauch."

Perhaps the most practical implication is not to keep yourself from writing when not inspired, but to be ruthless about writing whenever inspiration hits. This approach requires always having paper or a palmtop computer with you, and above all to avoid answering the door or e-mail when you are in the middle of something good. Keep in mind the useful (if probably apocryphal) cautionary tale of Coleridge's person from Porlock — the businessman who, by detaining Coleridge for an hour, terminated the composition of "Kubla Khan."

Literary critics often use the notion of inspiration to explain the careers of writers who stopped being able to write. Thus they sometimes describe Wordsworth's career as falling into three stages. In the first he had both inspiration and judgment, and produced such radiant works as *Lyrical Ballads*. In the second, he still had judgment but wrote explicitly about his lack of inspiration, as in *The Prelude*. In the third stage he seemed to have lost his judgment as well and produced endlessly dull verse. (Even literary critics tend to adopt the medicalized language of disease when discussing late Wordsworth, as in Francis Jeffrey's 1814 review of *The Excursion* — which starts with the immortal line "This will never do!" and goes on to argue that "we can only watch the progress of [Wordsworth's] symptoms" and "wait in patience for the natural termination of the disorder.") To some extent Coleridge took an approach opposite to Wordsworth's in later life; when his inspiration stopped, he more or less stopped writing.

Nonetheless, writing regularly, inspiration or no, is not a bad way to eventually get into an inspired mood; the plane has to bump along the runway for a while before it finally takes off. In practice, most writers find some balance between bowing to their muse and doggedly writing, whether inspired or not. My own balance flipped after my postpartum break. Before, I felt I had my muse firmly by the throat and wrote, if in a pedestrian way, when it pleased me. Since my illness, I have given up any pretense of being in command. I strain my nerves for the faintest sense of the feeling that I should write, the feeling that my feet are starting to lift off the ground. Although I sit down to write every day at five in the morning, on the days when my muse has left me, I can no longer pretend that I sit down because I am in control of the situation. I am not writing but doing penance for all the days when the muse spoke and I failed to listen.

What is the relationship between writer's block and block in other fields — musician's block, sculptor's block? Is writer's block more common, or is it just that more is written about it because it interests writers more? Probably the latter. When we look carefully, there is ample evidence of other blocks. The Hungarian composer György Kurtág, for instance, described an intermittent "compositional paralysis," of which he said dryly, "The child decides when it wants to be born — not its mother." All forms of block cause frustration, feelings of inadequacy, and sometimes financial worry; but writer's block, tied to language more directly than other art forms, is perhaps most likely to bring with it the suffocating feeling of being unable to express oneself.

What tends to be called block, whether painter's or potter's or physicist's, is generally restricted to a field seen as creative or artistic, in which the problem is not well defined and requires more divergent than convergent thinking. At the other end of the spectrum are careers where the problem is well defined, where most of the thinking is convergent. One of the paradoxical joys of medicine and other applied sciences is their relative freedom from block. When you find a vascular surgery patient with blood spurting from her graft site, the response required — if you have medical training — is usually immediate and obvious. At least, it is obvious compared to a task such as writing the great American novel.

Block as "All in Your Head"

Explanations of writer's block in terms of mental states have varied wildly. Nearly all, however, follow a simple formula. The explainer takes his preferred school of psychology and finds examples of writer's block that fit his theory best. Very few theorists try to address all the different types of block. And, for obvious reasons, few writers on block are writers *with* block — blocked writers are not the ones who get the book deals. Some explanations can get fairly theoretical. All the same, there may be something to learn from theories that think about us a little differently from the way we think about ourselves. In Albert Einstein's words, a chemical analysis of a cup of soup shouldn't be expected to taste like the soup.

Of all the academic explanations of writer's block considered here, those of cognitive psychology have the most familiar tone. Cognitive psychology falls between behaviorism and the depth psychologies such as psychoanalysis. Unlike behaviorism, cognitive psychology talks freely of mental states and sees them as crucial in understanding behavior. Unlike depth psychology, it does not focus strongly on the effect that unconscious emotion can have on performance. It stresses the role of conscious skills like evidence collection, problem definition, and decision making.

The writing researcher Mike Rose argues that many cases of writer's block stem less from emotional problems than from deficits in cognitive skills; for instance, having overly rigid compositional strategies. Such as a rule against sentence fragments. Another skill problem is too-early editing: a writer begins criticizing and altering a text before there is enough of a rough draft to evaluate. Rose's cognitivist model explains why writers are more likely to get blocked on hard projects than on easy ones. The model would seem to best fit unskilled writers, but Rose grants that, surprisingly, professional writers are as likely to get blocked as inexperienced ones. It may be that when faced with compositional problems that are knotty enough, even gifted professionals can end up blocked.

The literary critic Zachary Leader raises the example of Mark Twain, who had a long period of apparent writer's block while writing *The Adventures of Huckleberry Finn*. Was the block caused by a cognitive problem with plot and structure? Twain began the book in 1876, and quickly reached a point at which he had Huck and Jim escaping north up the Ohio River to free Jim. Then he broke off, as if he did not know what to do next with the plot. Over the next few years, Twain added only a few chapters — although he was able to complete other books successfully. Eight years after starting the book, Twain finally abandoned the trip north and allowed Huck and Jim to continue to float down the Mississippi. In a sudden outpouring of some of his best writing, he finished the book in only three more months, often writing three thousand to four thousand words in a sitting. Thus, on a cognitivist description, a rough spot in the plot — the trip north — caused Twain's block.

Nonetheless, Leader argues that when Twain and most fluent professional writers are blocked, what appear to be cognitive problems actually have emotional causes — as when a poet begins to edit too early in his composition not because he doesn't know better, but because his disapproving father's recent visit has made him more self-critical. On Leader's retelling of Twain's block, Twain had trouble writing about going up the Ohio River because he had no strong emotional tie to that river. Floating down the Mississippi, on the other hand, resonated with his early experiences as a steamboat pilot. Changing the direction of Huck and Jim's journey was not a logical solution to a technical problem, but an emotional solution. In fact, it would have been more logical for them to escape north than to drift downstream farther away from Jim's freedom.

The divide between Rose's cognitivist and Leader's emotivist interpretations of Twain's block (I am oversimplifying their thoughtful positions) reflects a long-standing divide in Western psychological theory between affective and cognitive processes, between thought and feeling. Although the divide has been conceptually fruitful, in real life it is often hard to separate the two phenomena. Emotions influence the content of thought; beliefs shape emotions. The two intertwine tightly in the very process that leads someone to become a writer, or indeed to take up any true vocation. We learn to do well what we love, and we learn to love what we do well. Conversely, in writer's block, we often learn to hate what we don't have the skill to do well, and that makes us do it even more poorly.

What would a cognitivist approach to treatment of writer's block look like? It might, of course, look uncomfortably like the sort of freshman composition class that provides block diagrams with named stages — Brainstorming, Outlining, Writing, Editing, and so on — that to me were about as helpful as trying to learn how to dance by looking at those diagrams with the little footprints. Slightly more advanced approaches might include more sophisticated tips (Chekhov's "a rifle hanging on the wall in the first act must be fired by the third act") — although these guidelines sometimes act more as soothing emotional supports than as cognitive ones.

In some parts of the country, writer's workshops are as common as gun clubs are in others (one adult school near me gave five courses on writer's block in a single semester). Such workshops often take a cognitive approach at a third level of abstraction, roughly equivalent to cognitive-behavioral therapy. CBT is a widely used psychotherapeutic technique that can help problems such as depression that, although emotional, also have cognitive aspects. CBT attempts to change beliefs that lead to negative views of the self ("I am a bad writer"), of experience ("Unless everything is perfectly quiet, I can't try to work"), and of the future ("I will be blocked forever"). Such cognitive strategies couple to behavioral ones: breaking tasks into smaller chunks, diversion from tortured thoughts through exercise or socializing, desensitization of the writing tasks that cause the fear.

Psychodynamic explanations of writer's block emphasize the importance of unconscious desires and fears rather than conscious cognition. As a neurologist, I was trained to think of psychodynamic and especially psychoanalytic therapy as unscientific, if grudgingly necessary in cases where patients had issues with their parents, hated pills, or had Ph.D.s in comparative literature (a field still alive with post-Freudians). During my postpartum break I watched in amusement and horror as my beliefs shifted. Discussions of fantasies and unconscious motives fascinated me; pills, previously such clever little tools, became barely tolerable assaults on my thoughts. Although drugs could dull what was happening to me, psychodynamic explanations seemed more likely to give the events meaning. The very appeal of psychoanalytic theory was how literary it is, although Freud (himself a remarkable prose stylist) tried his best to remain a scientific neurologist. In Lionel Trilling's words, "Of all mental systems, the Freudian psychology is the one which makes poetry indigenous to the very constitution of the mind. Indeed the mind, as Freud sees it, . . . is in the greater part of its tendency exactly a poetry-making organ . . . It was left to Freud to discover how, in a scientific age, we still feel and think in figurative formations, and to create, what psychoanalysis is, a science of tropes, of metaphor."

Nearly all psychodynamic schools have been shaped by Freud's approach. This chapter started with an epigraph in which Freud movingly described his fears of block. What he thought causes block has less resonance for most of us.

> Analysis shows that when activities like playing the piano, writing or even walking are subjected to neurotic inhibitions it is because the physical organs brought into play — the fingers or the legs — have become too strongly eroticized. . . . As soon as writing, which entails making a liquid flow out of a tube onto a piece of white paper, assumes the significance of copulation, or as soon as walking becomes a symbolic substitute for treading upon the body of mother earth, both writing and walking are stopped because they represent the performance of a forbidden sexual act. The ego renounces these functions, which are within its sphere, in order not to have to undertake fresh measures of repression — in order to avoid a conflict with the id.

Yikes. In this era, when even the Freudians are a little post-Freudian, we can once again read such a statement with almost as much shock as early twentieth-century readers had. Yet sanitized versions of Freud's model still underlie much of the psychotherapy practiced in this country, Europe, and South America. For Freud, the blocking agent was the internalized, punishing father, and writing was symbolically associated with the writer's childhood sexual desire for his mother. In fact, he believed that all creative work was driven by such neurotic associations — a twentieth-century version of the Romantics' link between creativity and mental illness. Many modern psychotherapists would hurry past the infant sexuality part — at least when there are patients listening who might find it off-putting — but would still argue that blocked writers often keep themselves from writing because of either fear of punishment by or rebellion against parent-like authority.

Many psychoanalysts since Freud have developed their own theories of writer's block or creative block. Although Jung shared Freud's belief that fear and guilt cause block, he looked to earlier sources of childhood conflict, in the child's ambivalence about becoming an entity independent of the mother. Jung was less interested in the idea of art as neurotic escape, instead emphasizing the role of the unconscious — especially the collective unconscious — as the source of creative inspiration. A striking feature of Jung's theory is the extent to which the artist, at least the artist's ego, is a passive recipient of the message of his or her work. Such passive "visitations from the muse" will come up again in Chapter 7.

I have described Ernst Kris's theory that creative work requires both a strong ego and a strong id, to allow rapid alternation between primary- and secondary-process thought. If either conscious or unconscious processes gain ascendancy, the creative project fails. Block arises when the ego is too dominant: unusual ideas are repressed, and the work, if it continues, becomes arid. When the id is dominant, the work falls apart because it is undisciplined, because it expresses rather than communicates.

In describing how modern psychotherapy is often sanitized psychoanalysis, I have not been fair to the many therapists who have thoughtfully incorporated a number of different theoretical views. Such eclecticism, at its best, can allow awareness that there are many reasons to have writer's block. Charles Ducey, the director of the Bureau of Study Counsel at Harvard University, offers such a list:

> Some procrastinate because of their perfectionism; others experience being "blocked" as a result of their unbearable self-criticism and negative judgment. Some unconsciously associate writing with anxiety-

arousing sexual or aggressive assertiveness, and consequently experience writing inhibitions; still others rebel against perceived demands of the "authorities" (parents, teachers) and engage in a sit-down strike against their own writing. Yet other students seem as yet developmentally unable to define their sense of self in either their work or their lives. Writing for them becomes an act of self-definition. Added to these issues of intrapsychic conflict and/or developmental lag is the ever-powerful behavioral vicious circle and impact of cognitive set, the self-reinforcing positive-feedback loop of being ever more incapable of writing, the more one believes that one has a condition known as "writer's block."

One systematic and accessible psychodynamic exploration of creative block, Abigail Lipson and David Perkins's book *Block,* sees writer's block as a special case of all counterintentional behaviors. These are behaviors in which you do what "you" don't want to (such as sabotage an exercise program, or shout at a supervisor, or lack the nerve to ask a boy to the dance). Behaviors are interactions between forces or motivations. The will, or conscious intention, is only one of the many forces that drive us, and not one of the strong ones. Overcoming block requires not only insight to identify the relevant forces but then changing those forces — usually by changing the environment rather than by relying on an act of will alone.

Thus a writer who procrastinates by answering e-mail the instant it arrives generally finds willpower of little help in handling his e-mail addiction. But he may well be helped by an environmental change: disabling his e-mail so that he can check it only once a day at the local cybercafé (where he has to pay high rates for on-line time).

It is not uncommon, of course, for someone to overcome one obstacle to his work only to quickly replace it with a new one. The reformed e-mail addict may now find that chatting at the cybercafé is more and more eating into his writing time. If the force driving him first to e-mail and then to the café is the loneliness of writing, a simple change such as working at the café, among the comfortable buzz of the other customers, might be enough. If the force driving him is something more complicated, such as the desire to constantly com-municate with others in order to impress them, he might find therapy helpful to temper that desire. Or he may admit to himself that it was the need to reach others that drove him to writing in the first place. Perhaps if he abandons the well-paid writing for specialty journals that he has ended up doing, and goes back to trying to write for a general audience, he will be able to give up his cybercafé cronies, whom he doesn't much like anyway.

The Lipson and Perkins model, rather than assigning major im-portance to any one psychological theory or psychic force — such as libidinal urges, or conditioning experiences, or self-esteem — pre-sumes that some or all of these may cause block in any given situa-tion. Such psychodynamic approaches have both the advantage and the disadvantage of becoming very complicated very quickly.

That is rarely the case with the self-help literature on writer's block, a genre that includes hundreds of books. It tends to provide theoreti-cally meager instructions to be confident, brainstorm, and prioritize, and to order the set of audiotapes advertised at the back of the book. At their best, self-help books combine a systematized version of com-mon sense with a more digestible version of psychodynamic ther-apy's complex theories — again usually including a dollop of well-disguised Freud.

Much of the self-help literature on writer's block falls into the broader category of creativity enhancement. One popular approach tries to decrease the writer's perfectionism, or to silence his or her in-ner critics. This theme implicitly draws on the psychoanalytic con-cept of the superego, that internalized, harshly judgmental represen-tation of parental and societal values. Yet lofty values alone are not sufficient to cause block. Writer's block requires not just the inability to write as well as you want, but the inability to write anything less than you want. What drives that inability is the belief — usually un-conscious — that it is better to write nothing than to write poorly. Whereas in fact, as G. K. Chesterton put it, "If a thing is worth doing, it is worth doing badly." (This quotation is usually misattributed to Oscar Wilde, as are most witty British-sounding epigrams.)

Perfectionism certainly causes some block. But it is invoked as a cause a little too often; it is such a comfortable explanation of your block. It is easier to tell people that you haven't published much because you have such high standards, than that you are disorganized or inhibited or love to play tennis.

Self-help techniques for quieting the perfectionist's inner critics include brainstorming, nurturing self-esteem, and visualization. In brainstorming, the inner critics are consciously suppressed and the goal is to write down as many ideas as possible without regard to quality. Only afterward is the editor allowed to throw out the trash. A related technique, called freewriting, does not even ask that the ideas be related to the topic — the writing is simply a way of loosening up the writer and decreasing his or her fear of paper. Anecdotal evidence tells us that brainstorming is effective in other fields as well as writing, for instance a ceramics teacher who divided his class into two groups. One group was graded solely on the quality of its best work; the other, solely on the quantity of work (fifty pounds of pots rated an A, forty a B, and so on). Students in the quality group needed only produce one perfect pot to get an A. Ironically, the best pots were produced in the quantity group.

Such anecdotes are appealing, and it is true that finding a good idea usually requires considering many bad ones with an open mind. But few scientific studies have been able to show in controlled situations that brainstorming significantly increases the quality of the best idea, although the volume of ideas grows. Most likely, this occurs because the quality of the average idea declines.

Several trials have shown that brainstorming done in groups (the preferred corporate method) is actually harmful, perhaps because no one is going to relax his or her editing superego in the presence of the boss. The modest effect of brainstorming even when done in private may reflect the fact that typical brainstorming is a "storm" only in the tamest sense. Brainstorming does not bear much relation to vivid primary-process thought or divergent thinking: it may produce more ideas, but not more unusual ones.

That brainstorming is a watered-down descendant of the Freudian technique of free association is clear. In an amusing example of back-and-forth borrowing, Freud himself got the idea for free association from an 1823 essay called "The Art of Becoming an Original Writer in Three Days." But the way in which brainstorming differs from free association is important. Brainstorming is usually presented as easy ("all you have to do is relax"), whereas psychoanalysts eventually realized that true free association is quite difficult. The difficulty of escaping rigid thought patterns set up over a lifetime is encapsulated in Sandor Ferenczi's famous statement that the patient is not cured through free association; he is cured when he can free associate.

The self-help approach to nurturing self-esteem often involves the writer's giving himself unconditional praise. On Al Franken's *Saturday Night Live* parody show "Daily Affirmation," he would look into the mirror and say, "I'm good enough, I'm smart enough, and, doggone it, people like me." Techniques proposed seriously by writer's block coaches often don't differ much from Franken's parody, and include making up rave reviews from famous critics, penciling yourself onto best-seller lists, and springing for a massage ("because I'm worth it"). Strong evidence exists that creative, productive people do have high self-esteem — often to the point of arrogance. There is much less evidence that insecure people can be made more secure, and more productive, by techniques such as these. Inaccurately high self-esteem can even cause poor performance, as well as sociopathy. This area is full of controversy.

Some writers have tried to defang their superego by visualizing a scene in which its personifications are silenced, as in Anne Lamott's description:

First there's the vinegar-lipped Reader Lady, who says primly, "Well, *that's* not very interesting, is it?" And there's the emaciated German male who writes these Orwellian memos detailing your thought crimes. And there are your parents, agonizing over your lack of loyalty and discretion; and there's William Burroughs, dozing off or shooting up because he finds you as bold and articulate as a house plant; and so on. . . .

Close your eyes and get quiet for a minute, until the chatter starts up. Then isolate one of the voices and imagine the person speaking as a mouse. Pick it up by the tail and drop it into a mason jar. Then isolate another voice, pick it up by the tail, drop it in the jar. And so on. . . . Then put the lid on, and watch all these mouse people clawing at the glass, jabbering away, trying to make you feel like shit because you won't do what they want — won't give them more money, won't be more successful, won't see them more often. Then imagine that there is a volume-control button on the bottle. Turn it all the way up for a minute, and listen to the stream of angry, neglected, guiltmongering voices. Then turn it all the way down and watch the frantic mice lunge at the glass, trying to get to you. Leave it down, and get back to your shitty first draft.

A writer friend of mine suggests opening the jar and shooting them all in the head. But I think he's a little angry, and I'm sure nothing like this would ever occur to you!

Although I should point out that there's not much more scientific evidence for visualization than there is for brainstorming, Lamott writes so well that I can't resist promoting her technique.

Along with combating perfectionism, a second self-help approach to fighting writer's block often puts the writer in touch with his or her inner child. The inner child is roughly the self-help name for what psychoanalysts would call the id, minus the lust and aggression that make the id not fit for family viewing. The inner child is an ideal child, playful and curious, and has little relation to actual children, who may insist on having the identical book read to them at bedtime each night and who would rather starve than try a new vegetable.

Getting in touch with the inner child shares with silencing internal critics the belief that the id-like force and the superego-like force are antagonistic and in a struggle to control you, the ego-like force. Techniques for getting in touch with the inner child tend to involve relaxation and visualization; they may encourage the writer to be more playful, sometimes through formalized writing games. One writing coach suggests that you "move around the room in a joyful way — skip, spin, sway — and say, 'I'm a writer,' about ten times." If such an approach increases the writer's intrinsic enjoyment of the project, it might foster creativity. To the extent that it merely embarrasses the writer and disturbs the neighbors, it is probably less helpful.

We now come to the explanations that writers give about themselves. Of course, some literary critics would argue that we shouldn't ask writers about their writing — as the linguist Roman Jakobson remarked when the novelist Vladimir Nabokov was proposed for a chair in the English department at Harvard, "Are we next to invite an elephant to be professor of zoology?" (The result of Harvard's hiring policy was that Nabokov was recruited by Cornell and became a wildly successful lecturer on literature there.)

Questions from audiences at writer's workshops soon push authors into having opinions about writer's block. Often, authors' advice is practical: edit something you wrote the day before, always stop at an easy spot, start with an outline that gets more and more elaborate until it becomes your text, start with stream of consciousness writing, don't edit too early, drink lots of coffee, take a break. Some recommended treatments for writer's block are much more esoteric:

> Another method which may be helpful for others (it helps me) is the use of binaural signals through a binaural signal generator or music which incorporates this technology. The signals basically help one change brain wave states from Alpha to Beta to Theta and down to Delta. The optimum brain wave state for learning and creating is the state between Theta and Delta. This can be reached by various means including the use of sound-light machines, binaural signal generators, music with the signals incorporated within it or tapping on key points along the meridians of the body.

The question would-be authors ask authors over and over is about their writing habits: whether they write in the morning or evening, lying down like Capote or standing up like Hemingway, in Proust's cork-lined room or Woolf's room of one's own. Answers are often elaborate:

W. Somerset Maugham's day began at 8 A.M. with breakfast on a tray and the morning papers. He shaved in his bath, consulted with his Italian cook about the day's menus and then repaired to his den, where he wrote with a special fountain pen until precisely 12:45 P.M. "My brain is dead after 1 o'clock," Maugham decreed. The rest of the day unfolded with a one-martini lunch, a nap, golf or tennis, the cocktail hour and then a formal black-tie dinner, always with champagne. This rarely varied routine produced 74 novels, plays, collections of essays and short stories in 65 years at his writing desk.

These habits are amusing, but usually not helpful to anyone but their inhabitors. Writers write every which way; the only ingredient their habits have in common is that having habits helps, and that, as a rule it's better not to be interrupted much. (Even this isn't universal. I like to work in a room where my family is milling about. It keeps me from missing them, and the mindset required to filter out the crashes — my children are throwing spoons at the moment — somehow helps me to focus.)

It is evident that the existence, if not the detail, of the habits is important. As a scientist would put it, habits have a highly stabilizing effect on behavior; in the vernacular, without habits we would be a mess. The loss of habits accounts for much of the fatigue we feel when in a new country or on a new job. If it weren't for habits, who could bear the misery of rising before dawn to run shivering to the car and then repeatedly risk death on the highway to go to work every day? Similarly, writers depend on writing habits to get them going each time they lift a pen or strike a key.

Habit is a phenomenon that can be understood neuroscientifically. Eric Kandel, a Nobel laureate in 2000 for his work on the neurobiology of habit, was the first to show the electrochemical changes that occur at nerve synapses when primitive habits are being formed. He originally performed his experiments in sea slugs; similar although more complicated mechanisms exist in higher animals. In mammals, habit learning proceeds through a different mechanism than declarative learning (the learning of memorized facts) and requires subcortical brain regions more than it does the cerebral cortex.

Declarative memory, however, depends crucially on the temporal lobe, in the hippocampus. The extensively studied amnestic patient H.M., for instance, has lost his declarative memory after sustaining damage to both temporal lobes. After hearing of his father's death for the hundredth time, he is as piteously distressed as he was the first time. But he can still learn habits and nondeclarative motor skills, such as riding a bicycle.

Writers describing their blocks are more likely than the self-help literature is to attribute their problems to lack of ideas or to the difficulty of finding words to express what is floating inarticulately in their heads. (It is no surprise that the relentlessly optimistic self-help literature does not stress these difficult-to-fix factors.) Many writers have explicitly Romantic notions of inspiration, seeing themselves as its passive recipients (while not denying the hard work it takes to wrench the inspiration into some publishable form). Such notions present writer's block not as an obstruction but as a lack. To fill such a void writers may try to assimilate the ideas of others — or hope for divine grace.

Writers such as Stanley Kunitz describe not writing as a way of retaining one's ideas and options, of not losing them to the harsh realities of written language. "The poem ['On the Edge']," Kunitz said, "also came out of not writing. I was going through one of my extensive three month dry spells or maybe I was simply dissatisfied with what I was writing. . . . The poem is really, I guess, about not writing, about the power one gains by not committing oneself; one becomes almost God-like."

Writers are more vocal than the upbeat self-help literature about the external forces that frustrate their work: poverty, the need to work a day job, the callousness of publishers, racial or gender discrimination. Some writers faced with such external blocks may be well aware that the problem starts outside themselves; others may have internalized society's messages ("As a Mexican, I have no words worth saying") or blame themselves ("I don't write because I'm lazy," as opposed to "I don't write because I have a sixty-hour-a-week day job"). In an ideal world, many of these factors would be absent. But not all of them — most writers would stop short of wishing their family away. The tension is expressed in Yeats's poem "The Choice," which begins

> The intellect of man is forced to choose
> Perfection of the life, or of the work,
> And if it take the second must refuse
> A heavenly mansion, raging in the dark.

Parents, at least those who have a substantial role in taking care of their children, are often told that they must choose between having children and being creative. "Balzac, you remember, described creation in terms of motherhood," said the poet Tillie Olsen. "Yes, in intelligent passionate motherhood there are similarities, and in more than the toil and patience. The calling upon total capacities; the reliving and new using of the past; the comprehensions; the fascination, absorption, intensity. *All almost certain death to creation — (so far).* Not because the capacities to create no longer exist, or the need . . . but because the circumstances for sustained creation have been almost impossible." (italics added)

Is it true that parenthood and creativity are so similar that they are in direct conflict? Sometimes the energy and discipline of parenthood spills over into one's writing. For instance, a friend, parent of four children, finished her novel only after firing her full-time nanny. This is the opposite of the sabbatical effect that has crippled several other friends. They finally get a year off to write, and their output plummets. As the old adage says, "If you want to get something done, give it to a busy person."

Writing and parenthood are tangled in my own mind since it was after the death of my twin sons and again after the birth of my twin daughters that writing pushed everything else from my head. Because my daughters were premature, they were conveniently small enough to both fit on my desk in a bureau drawer, where they slept while I wrote. Once in a while a little arm would come out and pat the screen. When they woke up, I could nurse one on my lap while I typed across her, simultaneously rocking her sister in an infant bouncy chair with one foot.

The baby in the bouncy chair always went to sleep first. Once they were both asleep, I would put them in the crib, lie down in my own bed next to them, and continue writing in the small circle of a book light and my children's soft breathing in the dark. When one woke up, I would write on the floor as I rocked her again in the bouncy chair. For some reason I wrote in tiny tiny writing on tiny tiny Post-its, which I would stick to the wall and collect in the morning. My husband, who was remarkably tolerant throughout the periods of my intensest writing and who was much more help than any medicine, said that my trying to write an entire book on the smallest size of Post-its was the act that most convinced him I was deeply disturbed.

I think Olsen was wrong about parenthood's hurting writing, at least in my case. I believe I wrote, and write, better when I can smell my daughters' hair and hear the little grunts they make in their sleep. Even now that they are in preschool, I love it when one sits on each knee as I write — although there admittedly is a problem seeing the computer screen over their heads. Their voices ("Let's play I'm a mice." "No, let's play tickle ourchother.") keep me from floating too far into my own world.

There remains the more critical question of the degree to which obsessive writing hurts parenthood. How abnormal is it that I am so absorbed in my writing that I am scarcely distracted by the conversation of my daughters six inches from my head? I would like to think that writing is the least of my many faults as a parent, that writing while my children play under the table is not much more harmful to them than was my ancestor's hoeing the potatoes while her children played among the rows. Of course, my abilities as either a mother or a writer will be for my daughters and my readers to say. But to have a parent who takes joy in something, especially if she can share that joy with her children, is better than to have a parent who resents her children for keeping her from her vocation.

My admittedly airbrushed picture of writing and motherhood

may anger people whose babies cry more than mine did, and who make trying to write like wading through tar. Yet we had our share of month-long colic, hospital stays for asthma, and even a complicated bacterial meningitis that had all four of us living in a tiny quarantine room for several weeks. Maybe it is irrational to believe that if you love your family and your vocation enough, if your concentration on each is pure enough, then you will find time for both of them. It is true, anyway. Who said all true things are rational?

This is not to deny the block caused by distractions such as raising children, getting a plumber for the leaky shower, deciding what car to buy, answering absolutely vital e-mails from colleagues. Typically, the advice given to people grappling with such blocks emphasizes a cognitive solution: listing tasks in order of importance and postponing or jettisoning the unimportant ones. The companies that sell day-planners announce heroically that their little planners "unleash the power of employees to focus on and execute priorities." The women's magazine version of the same advice is "Don't try to be Supermom — relax your standards for cleaning house." What both approaches neglect is that it is painful to jettison those other tasks — they are important to us although we don't want them to be. For many people it is very unpleasant to live in a dirty house, or to buy a car without researching it intensively.

The manic goal-directedness of my postpartum hypergraphia leads me to suspect that many of the people who "get things done," who seem able to resist the pull of alternative tasks, are not having to make the effortful cognitive choices or acts of will that the above approach requires. Instead, they are in a mood state that is so focused on one goal that the distractions hardly register. In other words, the solution is not to choose to stop cleaning and live in squalor — that would be misery. The solution is never even to see the squalor because you are so wrapped up in your project. Although that sounds even harder, it is not always the case. (Chapter 6 outlines what is known of the biochemistry of inducing such goal-oriented motivational states.)

One characteristic of people in such states is that they often make quick decisions, saving a great deal of fussing time that can then be used to work. Quick decisions are not always the best decisions, however. Thus, people who are so involved in their work that they ignore their bills and make snap decisions about car purchases are best suited by having a spouse, collaborators, or employees with temperaments opposite to theirs, who can keep their affairs in order.

Finally, after considering the opinions of writers about their block, I want to look too at the opinions of literary critics, the zoologists of the authorial bestiary. Much of the literary theory on block has focused on the Romanticists' view, both because Romantic ideas about block are still enormously influential, and because so many Romantic writers were so terribly blocked. The Romantics' belief that creative inspiration arises from an irrational, uncontrollable inner source did not originate with them. What was new for the Romantics was their emphasis on the sublime, the experience of transcendence in the presence of a phenomenon — frequently a natural object — with grandeur too great to be expressed.

If the sublime is that which cannot be expressed, a painful inarticulateness and writer's block seem inevitable. So much Romantic work was incomplete because of block that the unfinished literary fragment became its own genre, as in Coleridge's famously interrupted "Kubla Khan: A Fragment." Writing fragments let the Romantics symbolize, by their act of falling mute, how much the object of their poem transcended their description of it. Most modern genres, however, do not allow this treatment of block.

The Romantics also managed to deal with writer's block by the common strategy of writing about it. Coleridge, for instance, described the mute dejection associated with the failure of his "genial spirits" (his faculty of creativity):

> A grief without a pang, void, dark, and drear,
> A stifled, drowsy, unimpassioned grief,
> Which finds no natural outlet, no relief,
> In word, or sigh, or tear. . . .

My genial spirits fail;
And what can these avail
To lift the smothering weight from off my breast?

Modern critics have pointed out that the towering presences that struck the Romantics speechless were as often the great writers of the past as they were majestic crags. Walter Jackson Bate has argued that as printing became less expensive and more of the great writing of the past was available to intimidate younger writers, poets began to see poetry as in a decline, unable to meet the standard of Shakespeare or Milton. Of course, even Shakespeare had his own worries, as in Sonnet 26. It begins by describing the "beautiful old rhyme" that flowed from the "antique pen" of the superior, ancient poets, and ends with the starkly moving couplet, "For we, which now behold these present days, / Have eyes to wonder, but lack tongues to praise." Or, in Mark Twain's rather different voice, "What a good thing Adam had. When he said a good thing he knew nobody had said it before."

This emphasis on the burden of the past shares much with the psychoanalytic approach. For literary critics, the most significant past is the literary past, the vast weight of talented writers. For psychoanalysts, the blocking agent is not the literary forefathers but the actual father. Harold Bloom made more explicit the Oedipal overtones of a writer's being blocked by towering predecessors and argued that writers respond to their literary forefathers the way children respond to their parents. Because of the requirement that great works be original, the artist must try not to be what he admires — a recipe for suffering similar to that of a small boy who wants to be his father and have all his father's privileges. In Bloom's account, only a few of the most notable poets manage to escape the blocking influence of their literary parents, and they do so by misreading the predecessor's work in a way that clears imaginative space for their own work. In a crude sense, the successful poet invents a fault in the predecessor in the same way an adolescent invents reasons to criticize her parents as she is trying to become less dependent on them.

Bloom proposed six ways in which such creative misreading allows escape from writer's block. I will not attempt to define them, but list them because their names are so euphonious, if shamelessly opaque — clinamen, kenosis, tessera, daemonization, askesis, and apophrades. (Is it ill-bred to point out that terms like these make medical words such as hypergraphia sound colloquial?)

Although Bloom and Bate focus on some of the most talented writers in English, even a child writing a class paper can feel the anxiety of influence when faced with the superior prose and knowledge of his junior encyclopedia. Much plagiarism starts from such situations. Would teaching writers about clinamen, kenosis, and the like provide them with an alternative to writer's block or plagiarism? I admit to being dubious.

The theories of Bloom and Bate, that great precursors are barriers to a writer's aspiration to originality, predict an inevitable decline in literature as the sheer mass of predecessors increases over time. This puts the two critics squarely in the "things were better in the old days" school, a position that has been historically more popular with people over forty than under. In fact, writer's block is not an inevitable response to masterpieces. They can inspire, as in Keats's exhilarated response to reading the Chapman translation of Homer:

> Then felt I like some watcher of the skies
> When a new planet swims into his ken;
> Or like stout Cortez when with eagle eyes
> He star'd at the Pacific — and all his men
> Looked at each other with a wild surmise —
> Silent, upon a peak in Darien.

Silent — briefly. Why was Keats inspired and Coleridge blocked by past writers? The answer brings us back from literary history to personal history: the individual experiences and temperaments of each writer.

The notion that writer's block is an inevitable, even fitting, response to the sublime natural and literary world neither began nor ended with the Romantics. It arose much earlier, from a deep distrust of language's tendency to distort the real world. That distrust, perhaps first put into writing by Plato, has persisted in modern and postmodern writers in many forms. For Roland Barthes, the conflict between writing and truth arises by definition: a creative writer is someone for whom writing is a problem.

Writers and theorists sometimes take the argument for writer's block one step further, proposing that it is a necessary stage in the composition process, a period of preparation. As the writer Victoria Nelson remarked: "Writing/not writing represents a natural alternation of states, an instinctive rhythm that lies at the heart of the creative experience. To steal a metaphor from Coleridge (who stole it from the Germans), they are the inseparable systole and diastole, the contraction and expansion, of the creative experience." Or as James Thurber more graphically put it: "There's a time to go to the typewriter. It's like a dog — the way a dog before it craps wanders around in circles — a piece of earth, an area of grass, circles it for a long time before it squats. It's like that — figuratively circling the typewriter."

It is difficult to imagine that the term "writer's block" should apply both to such pregnant silences and to the smothering state described by Coleridge. Yet an inexperienced writer might mistake the former for the latter, become depressed or anxious, and then have the depression or anxiety truly create a block in the latter sense of the word. Once we start using these clinical terms, however, the landscape suddenly changes. Depression and anxiety are disorders that we are increasingly comfortable describing as brain disorders, and if writer's block is caused by them, it is a very different phenomenon indeed. Or is it?

4

Writer's Block as Brain State

You don't know what it is to stay a whole day with your head in your hands trying to squeeze your unfortunate brain so as to find a word.

— Gustave Flaubert (1866)

They have cut off my head, and picked out all the letters of the alphabet — all the vowels and consonants — and brought them out through my ears; and they want me to write poetry! I can't do it.

— John Clare (1860)

FROM LITERARY THEORY to neuroscientific explanations of writer's block is a dangerous leap. What would it mean to talk about writer's block as a neural response to stress, or a psychopharmacologic imbalance, or even as a disease? In practice, if perhaps not in theory, psychiatrists and internists already do — when they give out the antidepressants, antianxiety drugs, and other psychoactive pills currently prescribed to people who say they are blocked or without motivation. Some types of writer's block fit such a biological model better than others. By considering them here, I do not mean to give the impression that there are types of block that are "biochemical" and types that are somehow less real or, as some of my patients paradoxically put it, merely all in your head. Everything in your mind, including your present happiness and your memory of yesterday's phone call to your mother, is all in your head in as concrete a way as your heartbeat is in your heart. It is a way that includes your head's anatomy, biochemistry, and genetics, but is also exquisitely shaped by experience.

I assert this with confidence — yet, of course, most people who are not scientists or doctors believe there is a dividing line between biological and mental phenomena that lies somewhere south of personality changes caused by stroke and north of taste in music. Over the last fifty years, schizophrenia, manic-depression, autism, and many other diseases have migrated into this metaphoric northern hemisphere. Notably, nothing has migrated south. Aggression, intelligence, creativity have for most nonscientists remained on the "mental" side of the line; indeed, the idea that they might be biologically determined is threatening to many people. One reason is their false confusion between "biological" and "genetic," the belief that if our thoughts are shaped by brain states, they must be subject to strict genetic constraints; aggression, intelligence, and creativity then are relatively uninfluenced by experience. However, the fact that a mental state can be influenced by drugs does not preclude its being influenced by experience as well: education, the sight of a sunrise, or noticing a dress sale at Agnès B.

A second reason why people fear thinking of problems with creativity as neurobiological problems is that they disapprove of what they see as medical attempts to enhance or pathologize normal traits. This argument, which groups medical treatment of writer's block with Ritalin for rowdy boys and nose jobs for girls depends crucially on the definition of "normal." In this context, normal certainly has nothing to do with actual population averages. For instance, many upper-middle-class parents panic if their child performs at the school's average level; they demand every educational resource available to them. That they are eager to enhance their child's normal performance through education, even though they might fear doing so with a pill, shows that fear of enhancement is to a large extent not a fear of manipulating normal traits, but primarily a fear of medical

technology. People who have no objection to using education, meditation, exercise, megavitamins, even "herbal" drugs to enhance normal characteristics are often horrified to take a pill approved by the
Food and Drug Administration.

People fear drugs, rightly, because they fear the very real side effects. But behavioral techniques have significant side effects, too, and
not effects we can necessarily predict. A student who goes to college to get a liberal arts education may inadvertently pick up values
that turn her into a stockbroker. In Muriel Spark's *The Prime of Miss
Jean Brodie*, Mary MacGregor has an educational experience that, by
changing her political beliefs, causes her futile death in the Spanish
Civil War. Although we worry more about the side effects of medication than of behavioral interventions because they are easier to see,
that is actually an advantage. For instance, the 1960s saw both the introduction of lithium for manic-depression and the beginning of the
phonics method of teaching reading. Since then, it has become clear
both that lithium allows previously disabled people to return to productive lives and that lithium has many well-defined side effects. The
debate between the phonics and whole-language methods, on the
other hand, remains contentious and politicized — not because of
lack of money, effort, or intelligence, but because of the difficulties of
social science research.

Sometimes what people fear about drugs is that drugs are the easy
way out, that the pills will do for them what they should do for themselves. Yet if a person has enough willpower to overcome a problem
such as creative block, depression, or obesity, then he or she doesn't
truly have a problem. There is scientific evidence that willpower and
the process of making a decision are brain states. Many of us have
been inspired by a famous story about William James. After being
tortured by indecision for six months, he one day had the sudden revelation, "My first act of free will shall be to believe in free will," and
immediately resumed his forceful and productive intellectual life.
Even that stirring event, though, is also an example of an abrupt
change in neurochemical state in a man who had many such changes,
not always so invigorating:

> I went one evening into a dressing-room in the twilight . . . when suddenly there fell upon me without any warning, just as if it came out of the darkness, a horrible fear of my own existence. Simultaneously there arose in my mind the image of an epileptic patient whom I had seen in the asylum, a black-haired youth with greenish skin, entirely idiotic, who used to sit all day on one of the benches . . . with his knees drawn up against his chin, and the coarse gray undershirt, which was his only garment, drawn over them inclosing his entire figure. He sat there like a sort of sculptured Egyptian cat or Peruvian mummy, moving nothing but his black eyes and looking absolutely non-human. This image and my fear entered into a species of combination with one another. That shape am I, I felt potentially. Nothing that I possess can defend me against that fate, if the hour for it should strike for me as it struck for him.

In this mood James's belief in his free will vanished. Perhaps rather than hoping that we can invoke free will to solve our procrastination or bad temper, we should realize that when we are healthy enough to have a vigorous sense of free will, our problem has to a large extent already been solved. There are many ways of sidestepping a feeble or recalcitrant will that do not involve medical treatment. Nonetheless, James himself was not hesitant to compare his mental condition to the biological problem of epilepsy. He combined exceptional literary and introspective ability with an openness to the neuroscientific advancements of his day in a way paralleled by few other writers.

If pills could replace free will — and it is not at all clear that they could, at least for long — then some worry that the pills could be forces for mind control by others. Teenagers taking medicine for attention deficit hyperactivity disorder (ADHD) sometimes describe feeling as if their new ability to focus on their schoolwork feels alien to their true nature and feels forced on them (crucially, by their parents). Of course, diabetic teens often resist taking their insulin with similar indignation.

It is hard to imagine either the U.S. government or civilian employers acquiring the power to require that workers take creativity or productivity treatments. It is easy to imagine unofficial pressure from employers to do so — the same sort of pressure that athletes feel to use blood doping or steroids, or that employees currently feel to comply with equally unhealthful behavioral demands for hundred-hour workweeks. Monitoring such pressures from employers will be necessary. In fact, there will need to be careful monitoring of voluntary overuse by employees as well. If treatments actually make the work more bearable, employers will probably find employees eager to use them. Even now, many teenagers would prefer to take ADHD medication (whether or not they have ADHD) than be subjected to a behavioral substitute such as expensive, time-consuming, dull tutoring courses.

Whenever possible, the person receiving the treatment should be the one who decides whether to take it. Treatment for writer's block may seem frivolous to some, but the blocked writer may see the affliction as a work disability. Conversely, except for the incompetent (which would include the severely mentally ill), no one should be pressured into taking any medicine, even though families and doctors know it is "best" for them. Most of us feel we have a basic civil right to do self-injurious things, whether overeating, bungee jumping, repeatedly marrying badly, or writing inflammatory editorials. If a pill exists that will remove someone's taste for extreme skiing and cause her to finish her papers on time, does she have an obligation to take it? Doctors, whose goal is often to minimize suffering, might argue that she should. If her goal is to maximize joy, perhaps she should not.

Brain-State Analogies of Block

All this concern about mind control is, although important, slightly premature. We don't yet have enough understanding of higher cognitive or motivational brain function to develop, say, a writer's block pill, or an electrical treatment for logorrhea, or a way to change a lyric poet into a writer of scientific journal articles (note that education can rarely do that either). But there are states that often accompany block, or have useful similarities to it, whose brain basis is better understood.

WRITER'S CRAMP

The analogy between writer's block and writer's cramp may help show how the brain malfunctions in block as well as in cramp. Writers cramp, as neurologists use the phrase, is a brain disorder of the movements that form words. (It is not the pain the average person experiences when she writes too fast for too long.) Writer's cramp is neither a basic muscle problem nor the high-level disorder of the composition process seen in writer's block, but somewhere in between. Henry James had writer's cramp, which required him to dictate his later works — and the switch may have contributed to the more natural although more rambling diction of his later writing. (Some friends claimed they could tell the exact chapter in *What Maisie Knew* when he switched from writing to dictating.)

Often patients with writer's cramp can still perform other skilled hand movements, such as playing the violin, even though they cannot write — recall the genre specificity of writer's block. Stress and repeated attempts potentiate writer's cramp, just as they can worsen writer's block. The harder the sufferer tries, the worse the performance. Writer's cramp involves, among other regions, the primary and supplementary motor cortex in the frontal lobe. Could writer's block affect, in an analogous way, the regions farther forward in the frontal lobe that are thought to be involved in composition and planning? No one yet knows, but the thought is intriguing.

The parallel between cramp and block has significant practical implications. In cramp, there is growing evidence that repetitive stereotyped practice causes the injury. An epidemic of writer's cramp occurred among nineteenth-century clerks, who worked essentially as human photocopiers. Periods of enforced arm rest, or learning an unrelated skill such as braille, may help the brain unlearn the abnormal movements of writer's cramp. Block, too, may be more common in situations in which writers are under stress and force themselves to sit down day after day, hammering at the same problem. Rests or distractions from the task may give relief.

Repeatedly getting stuck may from a neurologist's point of view

be related to perseveration. In patients with severe frontal lobe damage, perseveration can be remarkable. Like perseverating patients,
writers with block can sometimes snap themselves out of an aber-
rant mindset with a sudden change: a shower, a walk, a vacation.
Attending to personal hygiene has always been especially popular.
Laurence Sterne wrote that when

> the thoughts rise heavily and pass gummous through my pen . . . I never
> stand conferring with pen and ink one moment; for if a pinch of snuff
> or a stride or two across the room will not do the business for me — . . .
> I take a razor at once; and have tried the edge of it upon the palm of my
> hand, without further ceremony, except that of first lathering my beard,
> I shave it off, taking care that if I do leave hair, that it not be a grey one:
> this done, I change my shirt — put on a better coat — send for my last
> wig — put my topaz ring upon my finger; and in a word, dress myself
> from one end to the other of me, after my best fashion.

Sterne's cleaning-up strategy recalls the incubation and eureka
stages of creativity discussed in Chapter 2. Perhaps it was no coincidence that Archimedes' original cry of "eureka" was made in the bath.
One practical implication of these anecdotes: Put a wax pencil in the
shower stall for wall writing, so that you don't forget your insights.

PROCRASTINATION

Another phenomenon that has many similarities to writer's block
and that fits a biological model surprisingly well is procrastination —
a topic that fills most of us with sick fascination. In theory, procrastination and block are separate problems. A blocked writer has the discipline to stay at the desk but cannot write. A procrastinator, on the
other hand, cannot bring himself to sit down at the desk; yet if something forces him to sit down he may write quite fluently. Samuel
Johnson's essay on procrastination for *The Rambler* in 1751 dissects
such a pattern — an essay made more amusing, or more poignant, by
the fact that it was written at the last minute as a boy from *The Rambler* waited to carry it to the press.

In practice, though, writer's block can cause behavior that looks very like procrastination. Few people have the fortitude of Gene Fowler, who said: "Writing is easy. All you do is stare at a blank sheet of paper until drops of blood form on your forehead." Most of us, instead of a painful confrontation with the empty sheet, put it off by doing something else that suddenly seems terribly, terribly urgent. Charles Dickens described this dynamic when he found himself, during the composition of *Little Dorrit* "prowling about the room, sitting down, getting up, stirring the fire, looking out of the window, tearing my hair, sitting down to write, writing nothing, writing something and tearing it up, going out, coming in, a Monster to my family, a dread Phaenomenon to myself."

Procrastination is a very complicated phenomenon, but behaviorism, surprisingly, gives one a handle on it. Behaviorism as an academic discipline is, of course, so fifteen minutes ago. Nonetheless, behaviorist models still underlie much study of animal behavior, as well as the successful school of cognitive-behavioral therapy. Behaviorism describes simple rules guiding the way that reward increases or decreases the likelihood of a behavior. Many of these rules were first observed with the famous Skinner box, in which an animal presses a lever to get food pellets. Positive rewards such as food or money increase the frequency of the behavior; negative rewards such as physical pain or bad book reviews decrease the behavior.

Behaviorists developed an animal model of procrastination with implications for human work habits. When they trained a pigeon to press a lever for food and required it to press a high, fixed number of times before getting the food, it pecked slowly at the beginning of each series as if it were putting off the hard work it had to do. The scientists found that they could get rid of this slowdown by making the rewards more frequent, or by spacing them randomly.

According to behaviorists, people learn to avoid their writing task when they are negatively rewarded for writing, whether by rejection slips or by the sheer boredom and hard work that writing entails. One behaviorist treatment might be simply to change the environment so that the writer received more frequent — and less predictably delivered — rewards for sticking to his or her task. Behaviorism predicts the benefit of having a comfortable chair to make staying at the desk more attractive. And if, for instance, computers had a slot below the disk drive which, after a random number of words written, slowly extruded a crisp five-dollar bill, writers would miss far fewer deadlines.

Do frequent deadlines increase writing speed in the same way as frequent rewards? Certainly, journalists working under deadline are less likely to have writer's block than novelists whose publication date is vague. Of course, there is a selection bias: few journalists with writer's block keep their jobs. Book writers, on the other hand, deal with editors who are famously soft on deadlines. (I once received a letter from a book editor that said: "We *must* have your manuscript by August 15. If you do *not* submit it by this date, could you please give us an estimate of when you might submit it?")

The neural circuits underlying the responses to reward and punishment have been elaborately worked out, at least in simple animals. Although the circuits are more complicated in humans, they obey the same neuropharmacological laws. Already many drugs block pleasure (for example, naloxone, which can treat opiate overdose) or enhance pleasure (name the street drug of your choice). Even complicated psychological pleasures and pains are starting to have an understood pharmacology. Antidepressants such as the serotonin reuptake inhibitors can help painful shyness. Would such medications be useful for a writer whose fear of negative reviews kept him from publishing? Could we get the long-awaited sequel to *The Catcher in the Rye* if J. D. Salinger were on Paxil? If we did, would it be worth reading, or would it be made bland by the dampening of the neuroses that seem to have driven his writing?

Another neural factor in procrastination, partly independent of reward and punishment networks, may be attention and distractibility. Goal-directed behavior on the one hand, and a tendency to get sidetracked on the other, seem, oddly, to be increased in idiosyncratic ways both by drugs such as stimulants and by the endogenous excitatory systems involved in mania. It may be that mild levels of stimulation produce the focus seen in hypomania or in successful treatment of ADHD by Ritalin, whereas higher levels lead to scattered flight of ideas and the sort of procrastination that stems from starting one task only to start a second only to start a third.

Procrastination has a long evolutionary history — even pigeons do it. Why should that be? Part of the reason is that procrastination is sometimes advantageous. Ancient Egyptians had two hieroglyphs that have been translated as "procrastinate." One meant harmful laziness in completing an important task, such as tilling the fields at the appropriate time in the Nile flood cycle. The other hieroglyph denoted the useful habit of avoiding unnecessary work and impulsive effort.

Looking at procrastination as an energy-conserving mechanism that has spun out of control explains why many techniques aimed at helping procrastinators don't work. Attempts to improve "time management" fail because the procrastinator generally knows exactly when he should be doing what, but simply cannot bring himself to do it. An energy-conservation model has some trouble explaining procrastinators who frantically do a minor task to repress the anxiety resulting from not doing the major task. In such cases, though, the minor task is always easier or less painful than the major one. Perhaps the most successful antiprocrastination device known to man, the tight deadline, works by introducing the threat of an imminent greater pain (that of missing the deadline) to counteract the pain of working. Unfortunately, there are other factors to consider beyond getting the job done. Recent evidence suggests that although people may feel they work better with deadlines, in fact deadlines hinder creativity.

DEPRESSION

When diagnosing a mental illness as the cause of a patient's writer's block, most clinicians think first of depression as the cause. Whether unipolar or bipolar, depression afflicts writers at a rate eight to ten times higher than the general population. Many of the classic symptoms of depression are also classic symptoms of writer's block: increased self-criticism; decrease in enjoyment of the project; loss of energy, imagination, and the ability to concentrate. And most depression directly disrupts a writer's motivation to write. Because depression is not only a mental state but also a brain state that is at least partially understood, what we know about depression can serve as a window on the neurological basis of some types of writer's block.

Every medical student learns a legalistic definition of clinical depression as a state lasting longer than fourteen days in which the sufferer (1) either has a "blue" mood or loses interest in most activities, and (2) also has at least four symptoms of the following seven: change in sleep, change in appetite, lack of concentration, decrease in energy, exaggerated feelings of guilt, slowed or disorganized thinking or action, and thoughts of death or suicide. Depression can be agitated, with increased activity, or what is sometimes called melancholic depression, with apathy and lethargy. This "one from column A, two from column B" approach to diagnosis, although reductionist, is fairly useful: it is better to have your internist inquire about your mood with nine rote yes-no questions than to ignore it altogether.

The many writers with intimate knowledge of depression have provided far more vivid, if less systematic, definitions of the state. Although culture influences the way depression is expressed, similarities across cultures and time are even more striking, as King Saul's episode in the Old Testament and Ajax's suicide in the *Iliad* make clear. Shakespeare fills *Hamlet* with descriptions of one of depression's most characteristic features, its anhedonia, or inability to take pleasure in life. This couplet's progressively shortening vowels musically evoke the decay of Hamlet's enthusiasms:

> How weary, stale, flat, and unprofitable
> Seem to me all the uses of this world!

He continues later, with greater agitation:

> I have of late — but wherefore I know not — lost all my mirth, forgone all custom of exercise; and indeed it goes so heavily with my disposition,

that this goodly frame, the earth, seems to me a sterile promontory; this most excellent canopy, the air, look you, this brave o'erhanging firmament, this majestical roof fretted with golden fire, why, it appeareth nothing to me but a foul and pestilent congregation of vapors. What a piece of work is man, how noble in reason, how infinite in faculties, in form and moving, how express and admirable in action, how like an angel in apprehension, how like a god! the beauty of the world; the paragon of animals; and yet to me what is this quintessence of dust? Man delights not me.

Depression can cause block in any field of creativity. But some psychiatrists think that depression is especially intertwined with and harmful to language because of the way depression drains away meaning. The French psychoanalyst Julia Kristeva described this process:

> For those who are racked by melancholia, writing about it would have meaning only if it sprang out of that very melancholia. I am trying to address an abyss of sorrow, a noncommunicable grief that at times, and often on a long-term basis, lays claim upon us to the extent of having us lose all interest in words . . . , actions, and even life itself. Such despair is not a revulsion that would imply my being capable of desire and creativity, negative indeed but present. Within depression, if my existence is on the verge of collapsing, its lack of meaning is not tragic — it appears obvious to me, glaring and inescapable.
>
> Where does this black sun come from? Out of what eerie galaxy do its invisible, lethargic rays reach me, pinning me down to the ground, to my bed, compelling me to silence?

Leon Wieseltier agrees that complete depression makes writing impossible: "Whenever I read Kafka, I wonder: what sort of dejection is this, that leaves one the strength to write, and write, and write? If you can write about the wreckage the wreckage is not complete. You are intact. Here is a rule: the despairing writer is never the most despairing person in the world."

Of course, that is one reason why we write, to prove to ourselves that the wreckage is not yet complete.

The evidence for — and continued public resistance to — the

idea of depression as a brain disease is by now an old story. Different brain chemicals have different roles in controlling mood. Many of them are neurotransmitters, substances released by neurons to communicate with other neurons. Scientists first noticed their role in mood by accident, when they observed that drugs affecting neurotransmitters given for other reasons, such as for high blood pressure, also had effects on mood.

The transmitter that has recently received the most attention is serotonin, in part because of the success of the antidepressants known as SSRIs — the selective serotonin reuptake inhibitors. Other neurotransmitters, especially norepinephrine, are important as well. Depression seems to involve a complicated underactivation of serotonin and overactivation of norepinephrine. Drugs that raise serotonin levels (like the SSRIs) or lower norepinephrine levels generally help depression. Because no two people get depressed in exactly the same way, there is variation both in the symptoms of their depression and in how they respond to medication.

Other neurotransmitters, perhaps especially the opiate neuropeptides, may be crucial to depression but are less understood. Sudden crashes in brain opiates occur during grief and separation anxiety, states that often trigger depression. Some psychologists have proposed that the apathy of severe depression is a protective mechanism run wild, that it was originally intended for cases of grief that would otherwise cause overwhelming agitation. After extreme loss, depression can be less an illness than a relief.

While the view of depression as a distorted protective mechanism may not fit with the experiences of many who have suffered hideously during depression, it may be that their suffering stems from being not depressed enough. They are in mixed states, partly manic or anxious. This may help to explain why depressed people are more likely to attempt suicide when emerging from a depression than when deeply within it. Similarly, it seems that writer's block during mixed states or agitated depressions is more painful than writer's block during the deepest, most melancholic depression. As the passage from Kristeva shows, those who are the most depressed are often the least likely to care about their depression — or their inability to write.

Depression is beginning to have a neuroanatomy as well as a neurochemistry, by which I mean that we are starting to define the brain regions as well as the brain chemicals that are most important in depression. Although serotonin and norepinephrine are widely distributed in the cerebral cortex, each originates in tiny discrete nuclei in the brainstem (the dorsal raphe and locus ceruleus, respectively). The limbic system plays a crucial role in mood. And studies using functional brain imaging techniques have begun to show patterns of cortical activity during depression. Frontal lobe activity, in particular, decreases — roughly the opposite of the frontal lobe increase seen in creative thought. When the patient's depression is treated — whether by drugs or by psychotherapy — frontal lobe and other activity changes too. Limbic regions such as the anterior cingulate cortex and the amygdala are also relevant.

Preliminary evidence suggests that writer's block may also have a special link to the frontal lobe. Part of the evidence is similarities between writer's block and Broca's aphasia, which results from damage to Broca's area in the frontal lobe (see Figure 2a in Chapter 1). Like Wernicke's aphasia, Broca's aphasia causes difficulty with normal use of language, either spoken or written. In Broca's aphasia, patients can comprehend language better than they can produce it. Most are frustrated, struggling with each word, and very often become depressed.

No doubt some of this depression stems from being speechless, from being able to communicate only the simplest needs. But frontal lobe lesions can cause depression even in patients without aphasia. As they become depressed, they become apathetic and tend to speak less. When their depression is treated with antidepressants, they become more communicative again. The depression and wordlessness of Broca's aphasia strikingly resembles the plight of people with writer's block. Thus language inhibition and depression appear to be cousins, different manifestations of frontal lobe malfunction. By contrast, Wernicke's patients can produce language better than they can comprehend it, the brain damage is in the temporal lobe, and they tend to be garrulous and manic. In this they are similar to hypergraphics.

The advent of powerful antidepressant drugs has made the chemical underpinnings of depression easier for people to accept. Yet many nonmedical people still distinguish "chemical depression," by which they usually mean a depression that begins spontaneously, and "depression for a good reason," one that follows a painful life event. Psychiatrists increasingly find that this distinction (also known as endogenous versus exogenous depression) is, at least as far as brain mechanisms go, merely one of degree. Life events trigger depression, not through an ethereal mental mechanism but through brain changes. Conversely, repeated depressions triggered by life events predispose people's brains to spontaneous, "endogenous" depressions.

An antidepressant will ease depression that follows a bereavement, just as it helps an endogenous depression. Nonetheless, many people would choose not to take an antidepressant after someone they love dies, in part because their grief is one of the few things they have left of their beloved. Some people who can turn their depression into a tool or an aid to contemplation may reasonably choose not to treat it. But for the vast majority, whose depression brings only suffering, preserving a depression because it is "appropriate" may be not only agonizing but life threatening.

On this model of writer's block as an aspect of depression, treatment options range from many types of psychotherapy through the ever-expanding array of antidepressants. These therapies are not mutually exclusive; many depressions that are well treated by drugs can also be treated by psychotherapy, and vice versa. In fact, most people do best when treated with both simultaneously. It is, of course, vital that the treatment be tailored to the patient.

Antidepressants do not act only in the brain regions most intimately involved in depression; that is why the drugs often have side effects. Startling new methods are being developed that may allow more precise targeting of particular brain regions. In one such technique, deep brain stimulation, a neurosurgeon permanently places an electrode in the brain of a depressed patient. The treatment is still experimental for depression, but is governmentally approved for some movement disorders. Many of my clinic patients have deep brain stimulators. Their electrodes allow me to increase or decrease the activity of the brain tissue around the electrode, and thus dial up or down particular symptoms.

Parkinson's disease has some interesting links with depression — not only do many of my Parkinson's patients have depression, but nearly all of them *look* depressed, because of their mask-like faces and slow movements. The reverse phenomenon occurs too: a depressed teenager can start to look Parkinsonian. In some cases my electrode settings will have not only the effects on movement that are intended, but effects on mood as well. Have I cured anyone's creative block? Proving an effect will require rigorous clinical trials. But one patient, not originally a writer, did compose an inspirational memoir afterward, and rather rapidly. But that could have been the hypergraphic response to any illness or stress. Another patient shoots off quite impressive research proposals while hypomanic on some stimulator settings, but stops generating them on settings that make her depressed. Still another patient with what was probably stimulator-induced hypomania turned his energy toward baking loaves of bread all night, so the effect is not clearly selective for writing.

In initial trials, deep brain stimulation has helped the depression of people whose illness was so severe that they did not respond to any other treatment. It also had a surprising side effect. Because some electrode settings have different effects on patients' moods than others, certain patients found they preferred to vary the setting depending on what they were doing. One patient said: "When I am home sitting around the house, I like setting 2 because it helps me feel calm. But if I am going out to a party, I like setting 4 because it gives me more energy."

The thought of controlling our brains this flexibly is intoxicating and frightening. It calls up images of a world in which we have special settings for job interviews, or for writing lyric passages as opposed to philosophical ones. More ominously, it raises the question of who would control our settings and why.

We can reassure ourselves that techniques like deep brain stimulation will never be common, for few people will want a procedure that removes a piece of their skull and pokes a (thin) piece of metal into their brain. (As Woody Allen said, "The brain is my second-favorite organ.") But transcranial magnetic stimulation (TMS) may achieve some of the same results without the need for electrodes in the brain. If so, it may soon be possible to ward off depression and at least some types of writer's block by holding a magnetic wand over a precise location on our skulls while we are watching television.

Although most writers who have been successfully treated for depression find that their writing begins to flow again as their mood improves, paradoxically, a few writers have linked their desire to write to their depression. Producer Joseph Papp told his staff to avoid all therapy, "because then my writers can't write any more."

One justification for such a position is that an artist must suffer to create, and what more effective way to suffer than through mental illness? "The intensest light of reason and revelation combined," wrote Herman Melville, "can not shed such blazonings upon the deeper truths in man, as will sometimes proceed from his own profoundest gloom. Utter darkness is then his light, and cat-like he distinctly sees all objects through a medium which is mere blindness to common vision. Wherefore have Gloom and Grief been celebrated of old as the selectest chamberlains to knowledge? Wherefore is it, that not to know Gloom and Grief is not to know aught that an heroic man should learn?"

Other writers argue that depression is not necessary for creativity directly, but is an inevitable side effect of the mechanism that produces elated, creative states. As Rilke said, when it was suggested that he be psychoanalyzed, "If I lose my demons, I will lose my angels as well." Several more recent writers have described how their desire to write disappeared as their depressions lifted, but blame the antidepressant — not the loss of their depression — for their decreased creativity. Lauren Slater depicts such a state a year after starting Prozac:

> It's been almost a year now since I've composed a short story or a poem, I who always thought of myself as a writer, all tortured and intense. I can just manage this journal. So maybe I'm not a writer anymore. Maybe Prozac has made me into a nun, or a nurse, or worse, a Calgon Lady. Why can't I manage a simple story? Why is my voice — all my voices — so lost to me?
>
> Every morning, before work, I come to the blank page and look at it. It looks like winter. It is February in my mind. I think of the things people have said about the blank page, all the images. Sheet of snow. Anesthetized skin. To those images I add my own: the white of Prozac powder, spread thin.

The biochemistry of this side effect, if it is real, is unknown. One possibility is that it occurs through mood flattening. Some antidepressants, at least in some people, seem to not only decrease their low moods but diminish their excited or high moods. Without their highs, patients may find they have less drive to write. This occurrence can be misinterpreted as more depression breaking through the antidepressant — sometimes causing the physician to increase the dose, which only worsens the symptom.

CYCLES OF PRODUCTIVITY

Performance often waxes and wanes systematically. Artists or athletes may enter the Zone one day, only to be expelled like Adam and Eve the next. Three ingrained cycles are important for both mood and creativity: sleep, the seasons, and hormonal cycles. Sleep rhythms deserve the closest look, because they are the easiest to change and because it can be hard to tell block (usually treated as a work issue) from depression (usually treated as psychiatric) from fatigue (usually treated as medical) from sloth (usually treated as one of the Seven Deadly Sins).

Sleep rhythms are controlled by the suprachiasmatic nucleus in the brain. Even without day and night cues, most people continue on a fairly normal sleep-wake schedule — with one strange exception: it will be roughly twenty-five hours long, rather than twenty-four. This explains why most people sleep and rise an hour later each weekend day, when not forced to wake on time for work — and then wake on Monday with something unpleasantly like jet lag. Not surprisingly, few individuals get their best writing done on Mondays. The treatment, studies have shown, is to keep the time one rises as constant as possible. The time one goes to sleep is less important.

Most writers — most everyone — has tried to determine how little sleep they can get away with. The U.S. Army has poured money into the problem of sleepiness, but so far has not developed a non-circadian man. It did demonstrate that sleep can be kept to a minimum by means of a twenty-minute nap every four hours. The same conclusion was reached five hundred years earlier by Leonardo da Vinci, with a much smaller research budget.

What about the role of snooze buttons in all of this? They are notoriously addictive. I have a theory, based on the exquisite morphine-like rush that follows hitting the button and going back to sleep, that the act of returning to sleep releases endogenous opiates in the brain. Admittedly, the only research supporting my opiate theory is my own introspection: looking through the literature turned up only a couple of papers on how to make snooze buttons easier to hit in the dark and a publication called "Don't Hit the Snooze Button on God." One way to cure a snooze button addiction is to find a loud alarm clock, disable its snooze button, put the clock on the other side of the room, and set it for the true time the snooze addict actually gets up. Within a week or so addicts will usually be able to rise even without the alarm, and will find themselves less groggy than if they had been dozing for half an hour before getting up.

Rising in an alert state increases early-morning productivity. Dawn simulators, which shine a gradually stronger light in the face just before rising, may also help. Those who find themselves still groggy after all these changes are, most likely, severely sleep-deprived, and must simply get more sleep each night.

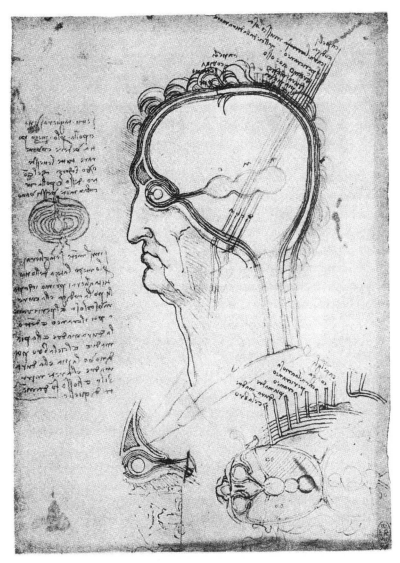

Figure 6. A page from Leonardo da Vinci's notebooks (c. 1490). He thought the three fluid-filled cerebral ventricles (drawn incorrectly as stemming from the eye at the level of the temporal lobe) controlled inspiration and creative dry spells. His own inventiveness alternated with severe block — he left many of his major works unfinished. His famous mirror writing, shown here, is a trait often linked to hypergraphia.

Treatments with stimulants ranging from caffeine to amphetamines can help decrease sleep for short periods. Unfortunately, the
body soon becomes tolerant to the drug and needs to take more and
more to get the desired effect. And heavy use triggers rebound sleepiness and disrupts sleep at night. So for most people, stimulants help
only if they have the willpower to use one or two cups a week. There
are some exceptions, though, such as the power user and prolific
mathematician Paul Erdös, who said that a mathematician is a machine for turning caffeine into theorems.

One new medicine, modafinil (Provigil), holds promise because it
has few side effects and seems to promote a state of quiet alertness
rather than the jittery high of caffeine and other stimulants. The exact way it works is unclear, but it seems to affect a discrete part of the
limbic system, a sleep-wake center in the hypothalamus, rather than
the widespread cortical arousal network. Although modafinil was
originally developed for people with narcolepsy, its use is quickly
spreading to people with fatigue from many causes. Its crossover into
the writing community was recently documented in the *New Yorker*
by Jerome Groopman's paean to its virtues.

Occasionally, what may seem like writer's block is merely a matter
of writing at the wrong time of day. The distinction between morning people and evening people is not entirely understood, but it can
influence creative productivity. Many writers write very early, perhaps because the early-morning increase in stress hormones such as
cortisol provides a natural rush. The artist Ted Orland, on the other
hand, tells of watching his output inexplicably shrivel up until he realized that the problem began when he switched from working in the
evening to working in the morning.

Because sleep rhythms change with age, it helps to experiment pe-
riodically with new regimens. Adolescents, who annoy their parents
by insisting that they need to stay up until all hours and then sleep
late, recently received support from scientists who have shown that
their sleep melatonin rhythms really are different from normal human beings, and that adolescents do best going to sleep between midnight and two in the morning. Some school systems have changed

their hours in an effort to decrease classroom sleepiness and perhaps even increase SAT scores. As people get older, their total need for sleep decreases and they often wake earlier and earlier. Some seek treatment for insomnia or depression; others interpret the same symptom as an opportunity to do several hours of work before their official workday starts.

Although fatigue is not really the same as block, it certainly feels like block when you try to write and your mind refuses to move. A short (less than fifteen-minute) nap during such a lag may be much more effective than coffee. The length of your nap, however, is important. Naps longer than fifteen minutes usually allow you to transition into dream sleep (rapid eye movement or REM-stage sleep), and you will wake up much groggier than if you had remained in nondream sleep.

Dream sleep, whatever we speculate about the relation between dreams and creativity, actually seems to have a negative effect on mood. If you keep a depressed patient awake all night, his or her mood will improve significantly. (Unfortunately, the benefit only lasts until the first nap that contains dream sleep.) Most (but not all) antidepressants suppress dream sleep, and some researchers have speculated that this property might be essential to their effectiveness. I hope not. I have experienced this drug-induced dream suppression and disliked it. A dream, even when somber, gives flavor and depth to a day. There are worse things in life than being unhappy.

Writers who are feeling too manic and hypergraphic, with too many scattered ideas, may benefit from a sleep regimen opposite to that for depressed or blocked writers. Sleep deprivation doesn't calm down overenergetic writers, it often only disinhibits them further. They may find that their writing becomes more organized if they are forced to go to bed two hours early. Some have speculated that an all-nighter may help writer's block by using sleep deprivation to disinhibit the writer. Perhaps it is the approaching deadline that finally spurs the writing to begin, but sleep deprivation itself seems to decrease creativity, rather than increasing it.

The first rule a medical resident learns is "Sleep when you can, eat when you can; you may never get a second chance." But the resident's life, while tiring, is also pleasantly loaded with call-room beds. What about writers whose work situation is not so well equipped? In my first job after my residency, I had no office and took naps under a very deep desk. I stopped when I woke up one day to find a colleague borrowing my computer, her shoes close enough to my face that I could have tied her laces together. She stayed for what seemed like forever, as I tried not to sneeze. Afterward I found a convenient closet to sleep in, an arrangement that lasted until one of the departmental administrators came to look for paper plates. He screamed, and later told me that he had been sure I was dead. So naps are problematic productivity strategies for people who have to write in public places. One such problem even had a technical name when I was in college: the "snarf mark," the imprint of a spiral notebook wire on the face of someone who had fallen asleep facedown in the library.

Humans are driven by seasonal cycles as well as sleep cycles. In earlier times, food supplies and activity levels varied a great deal from summer to winter. These days, although the most seasonal activity is often preparing taxes for April 15, seasonal brain changes remain. Circadian and seasonal rhythms are related, for increased night length is what tells the body that winter is coming. In some animals the increase triggers hibernation; in humans, the effect is often weight gain and a desire to watch reruns. On average, people are less productive and less creative during the winter. Kay Jamison has collected evidence that artistic and other creative works peak in the early fall, with a smaller peak in the spring.

Some people, especially sensitive to day length and seasonal cycles, show an exaggeration of the productivity dip that most of us experience in the winter. A fraction have seasonal affective disorder, in which the short days of autumn trigger depressions every year. They can be helped by light therapy, a simple but effective technique in which the sufferer looks at a bright full-spectrum light for thirty minutes early each morning, tricking the suprachiasmatic nucleus into thinking it is summer again. There is some evidence that winter light therapy can help the mood and energy even of people without depression.

Behavioral strategies too can aid writers whose output drops in the winter. Some are able to edit in the winter even though they lack the energy for new writing. If they shift their writing to the summer and their editing to the winter, they may greatly increase their productivity. Finally, choice of habitation is crucial. The expatriate writers who have long flocked to Paris should particularly beware short days, since Paris is on the latitude of Vancouver. (On the other hand, Parisian health insurance, unlike that in this country, covers light therapy — providing more justification for its description as the city of (full-spectrum) lights.) Writers in the United States often self-medicate with a winter trip to Key West (Ernest Hemingway, Elizabeth Bishop, Walker Percy . . .).

Finally, rhythms in reproductive hormones can have effects on productivity that dramatically imitate block. The best understood of these is premenstrual syndrome (PMS), or, more accurately, the psychiatrically more intense form of PMS known as premenstrual dysphoric disorder. I will blur the two. Most women — up to 75 percent — have moods that worsen just before their periods, although only about 5 percent have symptoms strong enough to interfere significantly with their work or home life. These symptoms are generally mood swings and depression, but can include decreased concentration and short-term memory. Doctors have long suspected a role for the sex hormones estrogen and progesterone. The situation is complicated, however: PMS seems not to be directly a function of a patient's hormone levels, since most women with premenstrual mood changes have normal hormone levels. And treating premenstrual syndrome with serotonin reuptake inhibitors turns out to be more effective than manipulating hormone levels.

Sylvia Plath's poetry is a fascinating example of how a body's rhythms can affect a body of work. Scholars have for some time believed that Plath had bipolar disorder, but the publication of her unexpurgated journals has confirmed that her poetry's content and style also fluctuated dramatically with her menstrual periods. (In fact, bi-polar women often have severe PMS.) The influence of her menstrual cycle is perhaps most notable in her famous "Ariel" poems. The recurrent rise and fall in the tone of the poems, with their themes of barrenness, fertility, misery, bleeding, and relief, are overseen by the image of an inspiring but indifferent moon goddess. "If I could bleed, or sleep!" Plath wrote in "Poppies in July." Eventually, she did both: her suicide, like the writing of her bleakest poems, was during a premenstrual period.

Presenting a work of literature as influenced by PMS will no doubt offend some readers as reductionist. Others will see it as perpetuating the gender stereotype of the irrational, labile woman. Actually, I held both positions until I had a bout of severe PMS for a few months after I stopped nursing my daughters. (PMS often starts or is worst during the first few menstrual cycles postpartum; indeed, it was during one of these that Plath killed herself.) It was disorienting to feel my mood worsen rapidly each day, to feel my ink dry up before it reached the page, to watch the lines between infertility and literary sterility blur. And then suddenly have it all disappear, and feel normal again. Now it makes more sense to me that someone would bother to write an entire poem cycle about PMS.

Of course, women are not alone in having writing shaped by hormones. Testosterone, though, does not cycle as women's sex hormones do; or rather, it is one long cycle accelerating in adolescence and tapering off in old age. Late in life is when the risk of depression and suicide rises dramatically in men; some have argued that depression can be helped by testosterone. The writer Andrew Sullivan is perhaps the most articulate fan of testosterone as a mood elevator, based on his own experiences with testosterone replacement. Some doctors are now attributing many of the ills of middle-aged men, including depression and decreased productivity, to "andropause," the midlife decline in testosterone, and treating it with supplements — even in men whose testosterone is not low. So far, however, the data supporting these treatments are highly controversial.

While the relation between low testosterone levels and depression is still not completely understood, the relation between high levels and aggression is clear. In both animals and humans (male and female alike), after a fight, testosterone increases in the victor and decreases in the loser. The hormone has a complicated relationship with social rank: it turns out that a high testosterone level benefits upper-class men, but in lower-class men it is associated with unemployment and being unmarried, perhaps because a poor man's aggression is more likely to get him into trouble than a CEO's is. In some primate species, the alpha male actually has less testosterone than the males in middle management, perhaps because the alpha male does not have to fight as much.

Is high testosterone useful to creative people? Or is it merely a distraction in the relatively peaceful creative life? Did Hemingway's presumably high testosterone help him, or merely cause his violent death? Science may eventually have answers to these questions.

A friend, on reading these passages about testosterone, argued that I was an essentialist, one who believes there are inalterable biological differences between men and women. That took me aback. I had always been in the unthinking "I can do anything you can do" post-feminist school, perhaps because I had never suffered much from men (other than occasional bits of patronizing if well-meant advice from oldish ones, and the ubiquitous annoyance of abrasive beard stubble). Then I started to think more about my writing. Why was I writing a female-style book full of unsolicited personal confessions about how emotions and childbirth and PMS and choosing daycare centers (see the next chapter) had changed my writing? Why couldn't I have written a purely objective scientific treatise, or chosen a less female topic — fly fishing, perhaps? Of course, it's possible for women to write like men; my own first book was clipped and distant. Yet I have the disturbing feeling that something has been turning me from a writer into a woman writer. Is it the hormones in the pregnancies? The activity of raising young children? Part of me wishes that whatever is doing it would stop. But part wonders why scientists are supposed to hide the reasons why they care about their research. And why fly fishing is considered of general interest, anyway.

ANXIETY AND EXCESS MOTIVATION

After depression, anxiety is probably the second-clearest link between writer's block and a psychiatric illness. Anxiety and depression share many features, but may cause writer's block through different mechanisms. One of the chief ways in which depression causes block is by sapping the energy and motivation to write. Paradoxically, the increased energy and motivation of anxiety can also interfere with writing. This is an example of the venerable Yerkes-Dodson law. Yerkes and Dodson first described the connection between a subject's arousal and task performance in 1908, in a study of the beguilingly named dancing mice. (These mice have a brain mutation that causes them to run in circles and toss their heads — enough to make them popular pets at the turn of the century.) Yerkes and Dodson proposed that performance has an inverted U-shaped dependence on arousal, so that both very low and very high levels of arousal interfere with performance. Low arousal produces immobility because of torpor; high arousal does so through the frozen deer-in-the-headlights phenomenon. Yerkes and Dodson also noted that the optimal level of arousal varies with different tasks; cognitively difficult tasks have lower optimal levels of arousal than tasks requiring endurance or physical strength.

The excessive motivation that can paradoxically cause writer's block can derive from a number of sources, whether external, such as parental pressure, or internal, such as a consuming desire for fame. Frequently the arousal comes from negative emotions such as anxiety; but the emotion need not be negative. Even states of increasing elation, as seen in manic episodes (or the beginnings of love affairs), can progressively disorganize and distract the writer. Note the surprising fact that this form of writer's block is not the motivational opposite of hypergraphia. Rather, both share the quality of being excessive states of motivation to write. What would make one person with extreme motivation hypergraphic while another was blocked? Some evidence indicates that strong internal motivations are less disorganizing than strong external ones. High-arousal block may alternate with hypergraphia in the same person, as in graduate students who ricochet between feverish nonwork on their dissertations and reams of e-mail and blogging.

Writer's block that is linked to anxiety is often also tied to procrastination — the process that leads you to suddenly clean out your basement the week before a writing deadline. Procrastination of a different sort can accompany depression. For at the most fundamental (or simplistic) level, there are perhaps only two types of writer's block, high energy and low energy. Unlike low-energy block, high-energy block may worsen as your deadline approaches; it makes you sweat, makes you sit down only to jump up again. When your work is part of who you are, and you fear that it is bad, you become more and more frantic. Perhaps you have ideas, but you quickly reject them as worthless. Perhaps you do not even let them into your consciousness, but feel them swelling, purulent — an abscess where your brain used to be. In low-energy block, the desire that makes you sit down to write is a dull sense of guilt. Instead of ideas, you have only sterile ruminations on how things used to be when you could write, when the world had color.

The Yerkes-Dodson law explains why the bigger the project, the bigger the block. It explains why a writer like Coleridge could be blocked in writing poetry, the genre most important to him, but could freely write essays. It explains part of the second-book phenomenon, in which writers freeze trying to live up to their first success, and it gives one reason why the harder a writer tries to fight his block, the more he mires himself in it. The Yerkes-Dodson law also gives strong and specific recommendations for combating this form of writer's block; namely, by lowering the blocked writer's arousal, even if that includes lowering his or her motivation.

At first glance, decreasing arousal is a counterintuitive way to combat writer's block — typically, a blocked writer will do the opposite, drinking black coffee or mentally whipping himself in the hope that increased motivation will drive increased productivity. Moreover, little in the standard literature addresses this aspect of block. Instead, we have to look at stage fright as a model.

Psychotherapeutic approaches to stage fright or performance anxiety usually divide into psychodynamic psychology and symptomatic treatment. In the former, the sufferer uncovers past events contributing to the anxiety. In the latter, relaxation techniques, meditation, or biofeedback teach the sufferer to control the physical symptoms of anxiety (tremor, quavery voice, sweaty palms) without necessarily understanding them. Only a few centers have approached writer's block with symptomatic treatment, perhaps because getting rid of your racing heart doesn't usually help you to write better.

Pharmacologic approaches to performance anxiety are used too. Unfortunately, antianxiety drugs such as diazepam and alprazolam (Valium and Xanax) have sedative effects that tend to take the edge off the sufferer's performance. Alcohol has similar effects. Is alcohol's temporary effect on anxiety one reason why so many writers and other artists have become alcoholics? (Of the seven U.S. Nobel laureates in literature, five have been diagnosed as alcoholics.) The writer Stephen King, a recovering alcoholic, argues that although writers may say they drink because alcohol helps their writing, they really drink simply because they are alcoholic. They use their status as writers, though, to invoke what King calls the Hemingway defense: "As a writer, I am a very sensitive fellow, but I am also a man, and real men don't give in to their sensitivities. Only *sissy*-men do that. Therefore I drink. How else can I face the existential horror of it all and continue to work? Besides, come on, I can handle it. A real man always can." Ultimately it is likely that so many writers drink because they have mood disorders and mood disorders correlate independently with alcohol and drug abuse.

Whether or not alcohol helps any artist in the short term, it appears to hurt creativity in the long run. Tom Dardis has argued persuasively that the reason Faulkner, Hemingway, Fitzgerald, and others did their best work in their twenties and thirties was the progressive brain damage that alcohol caused later in their lives.

Besides sedatives, a second class of drugs used for performance anxiety is the beta-blockers, such as propranolol (Inderal). Beta-blockers have little central nervous system effect on the brain and do not dull thinking. Instead, they treat the adrenaline-induced peripheral nervous system effects of anxiety, most notably tremor. Beta-blockers have been useful for musicians and public speakers, for whom a shaky hand or voice can be disabling. They do not help writer's block, which doesn't depend on physical dexterity — unless you count the typing.

A third class of antianxiety drugs is the antidepressants, especially SSRIs such as fluoxetine (Prozac) and newer agents such as venlafaxine (Effexor). More and more, these drugs are being used, instead of tranquilizers like Valium, as first-line antianxiety agents, and most of them are not sedating. We would therefore expect them to be effective in writer's block and, with the caveats mentioned earlier, they seem to be. Whether this is because of the antianxiety effect or the antidepressant effect, or both, is not clear.

Thinking of this type of writer's block as a less physical form of stage fright raises the question of how self-consciousness relates to both problems. Self-consciousness depends on our awareness of how others see us, of our audience. Philosophers sometimes talk of self-consciousness as the trait that makes us fully human. Yet, as anyone can attest who has ever appeared in an elementary school play, self-consciousness can subjectively feel as if it only interferes with our ability to act and live fluidly.

In a relevant parable, a centipede walked past a spider who said: "I can't tell you how much I admire your walking. I can hardly manage my eight legs; how can you possibly manage a hundred?" With that, the centipede, who had never before given his legs a thought, collapsed in a tangle. If self-consciousness disrupts skills primarily by making them slower and less automatic, it may be less of a problem for writers and visual artists than for athletes, musicians, and centipedes. Indeed, a heightened self-consciousness may be necessary for at least a certain kind of introspective artist. As Franz Kafka wrote in his journal, "This inescapable duty to observe oneself: if someone else is observing me, naturally I have to observe myself too; if none observe me, I have to observe myself all the closer."

The novelist Claire LaZebnik has pointed out the danger of being conscious of the possibility of writer's block. When she once brought up the subject at a party, she got angry phone calls afterward from several of her writer friends, who said that just hearing the words had made them unable to write for days. On hearing this story, a writing counselor I know said in exasperation: "People are so suggestible! This is why it's so hard to prove block even exists."

I would draw a different conclusion. Beliefs about block can influence block, because beliefs are important things. Important biochemical things, too. The suggestibility of block points to a practical question: the trade-off between offering well-publicized help groups that deal with block, and downplaying the existence of block to avoid suggesting anxious writers into it. The trade-off is similar between publicizing the problem of campus suicides and avoiding the problem of "copycat" suicides. Despite the derogatory term, copycat suicides are real, tragic suicides. Similarly, thinking oneself into a block is a real block, one caused by the failure of helpful repressive mechanisms.

Although I have never had the experience LaZebnik described, of being knocked off balance by hearing the word "block," perhaps that is because I am never able to forget the possibility of block. Paradoxically, it drives my writing — compelling me to put aside everything else because of the possibility that today may be the last day I will ever be able to write. It's another way writer's block is sometimes not the opposite of hypergraphia but the cause. Perhaps writers could reclaim the concept of block as Saint Jerome in his study used a memento mori (a skull, or an hourglass with the sands of time slipping away) to drive his work, in those lovely Renaissance paintings where he sat at his manuscript with a conveniently cat-sized lion purring at his feet and a casement window opening from the room onto a jewel-like Flemish landscape. The perfect writer's life.

OTHER BIOLOGICAL FACTORS

The left brain–right brain theories of creativity may have implications for the treatment of block. As I described in Chapter 2, creativity seems to require a high level of interaction between the two hemispheres. Self-help writers often go far beyond the neuroscientific evidence, stereotyping the left brain as the exclusive seat of logic and the right brain as the seat of holistic thinking and creativity. On such a view, block arises when the left brain dominates the right brain.

The proposed treatments, which are claimed to increase right brain activity, use many of the same techniques — relaxation, brainstorming, visualization — as do other self-help approaches to writer's block. One physiological technique unique to left brain–right brain enthusiasts is the memorable advice that plugging the left nostril can decrease the amount of oxygen going to the left hemisphere and thereby cause an artist to perform more creatively. Although this theory apparently is based on a medieval notion of oxygen traveling directly from nostril to brain without mixing in the lungs or heart, there has been one laboratory group — a single one — that has tested the proposition empirically and found some support.

Another technique proposed to alter hemispheric activity and creativity is called broadly the Mozart effect, in which listening to music (usually classical) produces an increase in creativity, SAT scores, and other cognitive tests. A small industry of audio recordings has sprung up, claiming to manipulate brain state by altering EEG rhythms by selectively increasing blood flow in certain areas of the brain. However, a review of sixteen studies of the Mozart effect shows that its average effect is minimal (roughly two to nine IQ points for only thirty minutes after hearing the music) and depends on "enjoyment arousal." You have to enjoy Mozart's music for the phenomenon to work — and in fact, one study showed that for Stephen King fans, reading one of his short stories work just as well. Thus, if music while you write helps you stay awake, so much the better — but it's probably not because of music's right hemisphere effect.

Finally, a few other classes of drugs have been anecdotally reported to help writer's block, at least in some people. One is the neuroleptics, sometimes called the antipsychotics. These drugs act mostly on dopamine, a neurotransmitter important for motivation, initiation of movement, and many other functions. The neuroleptics would not appear on anyone else's list of drugs to combat writer's block (if anyone besides myself were rash enough to make such a list). Yet as the newer ones are becoming safer, they turn out to be useful for milder mood disorders and anxiety. Also, unlike traditional anxiety drugs such as diazepam, neuroleptics help suppress the critical internal voices that, as Anne Lamott described, can distract from a writer's true voice.

One final class of drugs that might be helpful in writer's block is the anticonvulsants. A few people with abnormal temporal lobe activity do not have the classic hypergraphia of Geschwind's syndrome; rather, their desire to write is combined with block or word-finding trouble. The epileptic Flaubert, who crossed out nearly as many words as he wrote, was probably an example.

In a recent case report, an excellent public speaker who wanted to write a book visited a neuropsychiatrist because he felt he could get words out of his head when he spoke, but not when he wrote. Functional imaging of his brain showed abnormal temporal lobe activity on both sides. Once started on a low dose of anticonvulsant, he was reportedly able to write for hours at a time. It is not certain that the anticonvulsant worked by preventing low-grade seizure activity, however, because anticonvulsants usually have mood-stabilizing effects as well.

The Risks and Benefits of Self-Experimentation

In this chapter and the previous one, I have touched on many different techniques for getting around creative block, all with different theoretical justifications, few with extensive testing. Even treatments that clearly work well on average may not work well for a given person. The multiple aspects of block show how specifically tailored an effective treatment — behavioral or medical — should be. Determining the best treatment for a creative problem depends on subtle, subjective descriptions of the writer's mental state before and during treatment. A description in mental language is at present better than any brain scan or neurochemical measurement to reveal what is going on inside a writer's head. Determining the best treatment nonetheless requires objective knowledge of the treatments under consideration, and objective record keeping of how the writer responds. Without a clinician with an infinite amount of time and sympathy, no one is better suited to do this than the writer (perhaps with help from his or her family).

Therefore, overcoming a creative problem, whether it is low-energy block, perfectionism, or having too many too disorganized ideas, often requires what in the Introduction I gave the inflammatory name of self-experimentation. Although I could have called it something blander, the fact is that self-experimentation, although it is essential, can occasionally be dangerous. You should proceed cautiously, and of course with supervision when medication is involved. It is critical — and sometimes difficult — to define your primary goal. To write a successful book at all costs? To make yourself feel creative, independent of success? To more comfortably balance the demands of work and family? These goals might indicate quite different treatment regimens.

Start with techniques recommended by reliable sources. Anecdotal evidence ("Someone in my writer's group knows someone who wrote a book in thirty days") is probably the least reliable. Inspirational publications and seminars usually contain advice that has been endorsed by more than one person, although it is often in the frustrating category of advice that could be followed only if you had already solved your problem (such as "Write for half an hour each day"). As you might expect, someone with my training prefers dull peer-reviewed scientific articles. But since there are very few on creative block, people with problems now, who can't wait for science to catch up with their needs, have to make compromises.

As much as possible, control for other variables besides the treatment you are introducing. For instance, try not to compare the effects of a light box at 7 A.M. in the fall with sleeping until 10 A.M. in the summer. Will you be able to control for everything? No. Often you will need to run the same experiment repeatedly as conditions change, which is another way of saying that a technique that didn't work in the past may help later on.

Never underestimate the effects of suggestion or placebo; these are two phenomena that make many people have at least an initial response to a persuasively advertised but inert nutritional supplement, or a twelve-step writing technique. You may believe you are above that sort of manipulation, but you also probably feel more alert immediately after your first few sips of coffee, when your brain has registered the taste and not yet received the caffeine. This is a classic placebo effect, and it reflects not stupidity but a neurochemically conditioned brain change, despite being independent of the actual caffeine.

Try to put the placebo effect and suggestion to use; for instance, by going to seminars by inspiring teachers rather than dull ones (the former will have more impact even if the content of the messages is the same). Cults often can strongly affect behavior through suggestion, but they do tend to have disadvantages.

A common mistake is to hear of a new treatment, start it with exaggerated enthusiasm, then give up on it after the first bad day. Trying the new technique long enough is very important. I have patients who have tried as many as forty therapies for a severe neurological problem, but quickly give up because of side effects that they find frightening — say, dry mouth from a medicine. Yet if they step back from the new problem, they may realize that it is trivial compared to the original one. Allowing yourself time to get used to a new symptom will let you put it in perspective, especially since such side effects are usually temporary.

Some people give up a treatment too early because they underestimate the improvement they have made. This is a significant problem in depression. I am always torn when a patient comes in saying that nothing has changed, and his wife and children vehemently disagree — pointing out how much more active he is, how he is taking walks and writing again. Even his behavior in my office is different; he smiles and jokes with me. I want to give his perceptions priority — it is his body, his life — but I also know that his perceptions are skewed by his illness.

An essential technique to help escape perceptions colored by mood is to create an objective rating scale by which you can judge your performance. It could be as simple as using your computer's word-count tool at the end of each day or week. (Seeing the number creep up can even be mildly rewarding.) You may also want to keep track of other factors you suspect influence your writing: hours of sleep, exercise, amount of alcohol or other drugs used, visits from children, lunch with worst enemy. Especially if you are a perfectionist, subjective judgments of your writing's quality tend to be less helpful than cruder but more objective quantitative ratings. Blocked writers are often so full of self-loathing that they may rate the quality of their writing every day as -2 on a scale of 0 to $+10$. Choosing a scale that always bottoms out in this way is useful only as proof of your gloominess. As a measure of your response to treatment, it is like putting a meat thermometer in your mouth to try to detect a fever. Select a new scale — for example change -2 to $+5$, to allow you to see changes around your average performance.

Daily quantitative evaluations (or even more frequent ones, if you want to know how diurnal rhythms affect your writing) can help you think objectively about your writing; they can also swamp you with data. The ability to summarize changes by means of anecdotes can be useful. My patient with Parkinson's disease who brought me hundred-page color printouts of his symptoms might also document his progress by noting whether he can flip pancakes and have them land on the griddle again. Someone who procrastinates might say, "This term I handed in four of five papers on time; last year it was only one."

Let me conclude by giving the usual doctor speech about the importance, in the case of prescription drugs, of taking them under the supervision of a physician trained in that field. Your own personality will influence with whom you work best. If you don't like the first or second doctor, see another. (If you don't like the fifth, though, it just might be you that is the trouble.) Remember that finding a doctor exactly like you may not be useful — if you are a risk taker, get someone more cautious. If your physician emphasizes the value of trying a medicine for a month or two before deciding whether it works, it usually pays to listen. But if after a reasonable interval, you still believe the side effects outweigh the benefits, you have the right to be firm about stopping even if your doctor tells you the sedation you're experiencing is "minor," and your family says, "But dear, you're so much easier to get along with these days." It is easier for others to downplay the side effects of a treatment if they have not tried it themselves. When your block is accompanied by significant psychiatric illness, though, you may have to resign yourself to taking your doctor's and family's advice very seriously.

This book is partly, among the other genres it has jumbled, one of those doctor-turned-patient narratives in which the physician (played by William Hurt, of course) should become a better, more sensitive doctor because of his experiences. In my case, so far I am merely confused by divided loyalties. It still sometimes frustrates me when a patient irrationally turns down the wonderful treatment I offer because it has a trivial (to me) side effect. Yet the period when I tried so many treatments for excesses and dearths of words and moods did teach me something: I am more aware of how double-edged powerful treatments can be. I was lucky that, despite having at one time or another about nine different side effects, none was severe except the antidepressant-induced agitation that hospitalized me. But even my mild tremor was physically tiring; it made it harder to get a key into a lock, and when I stroked my daughters' hair, it caused my hand to stutter or slap across their foreheads.

Of course I still recommend pills to my patients. It is nonetheless clear that exercise or psychotherapy or education or moving out of one's parents' house may be a more specific and effective treatment — if sometimes requiring greater effort. Accepting a medical model of mental functions doesn't restrict treatment to pills. Educational and behavioral techniques are still available. They affect the brain too, sometimes in much more focused ways. Greater knowledge of the biomedicine of learning and psychotherapy and meditation may evolve to make these treatments become more effective than standard medical treatment.

Relating the Causes of Block

There is little reason to believe that the "mental" varieties of writer's block I described are fundamentally different from the more obviously brain-based varieties. How far have we come in this chapter and the previous one in discussing writer's block in both mind language (thoughts, experiences) and brain language (neurochemicals, brain regions)? Both are complicated propositions.

I will consider mind language first, but in a backward way, by using a physiological metaphor to relate the mental phenomena of perfectionism, suffering, lack of skill, procrastination, inspiration, oppression, and the many other states related to writer's block (sloth, fear of rejection, and simple confusion). Imagine the writing process as a heart pumping blood. How well it pumps depends on a number of factors. The first is the heart's ability to pump strongly, which requires both muscle energy and rhythmic coordination. Second, the heart pumps against a pressure, the afterload, which must be low enough that blood can move out of the heart. The afterload depends both on the mass of blood in the outflow vessels and on the stiffness of the heart's exit valve. Third, the pumping also requires an adequate supply of blood delivered to the heart, in what is called the preload.

On my heart model, the writer's intrinsic ability to pump out work depends on his or her energetic state (normal motivation with absence of depression or fatigue) and ability to coordinate the rhythmic contractions (skill, good work habits, avoidance of procrastination). The writer's afterload is inhibiting disapproval, whether internal to the writer (the tight valve of perfectionism, oedipal fears, generalized anxiety) or external (the burden of the past, critical colleagues, sociopolitical pressure). Finally, the writer's preload is the inspiration or set of ideas needed to prime the pump. Just as the blood that the heart pumps out eventually returns to feed it and prime the next contraction, so a writer's output is the basis for further ideas. When that output falters, there is less inspiration and energy for further work, a vicious cycle that has given many writers the literary equivalent of a heart attack.

Why is it better to describe lack of inspiration as lack of blood than, say, as an unwell inner child? Partly, a heart model takes into account many phenomena that are not explained by inner-child psychology. Partly, too, a taste for the more scientific- and manly-sounding heart metaphor is to some degree just a doctor thing. Because the heart's physiology is better understood than that of most organs, physicians tend to use it to explain metaphorically everything from biochemical cycles to bowel function. (The heart metaphor for the gut function leads to the useful warning that when treating constipation, dire things happen when you increase preload — the pressure in the intestines — without first decreasing afterload, the sphincter pressure).

As metaphors go, the heart pumping blood is a more romantic image for creative work than, for instance, a salivary gland squirting out its product. But the heart metaphor is romantic in another way, since it implies the Romantic belief that a writer's inspiration is delivered passively, the way the heart's preload blood flows into the right atrium. Antiromantics would argue that this is inaccurate, that a writer actively sucks new ideas and observations into his or her work. And once inside, they might argue, the ideas are altered and . . . digested. A bowel metaphor of creativity. If we shift to this rather less romantic organ, the preload becomes food, the contractility and coordination of the bowel takes the place of the heart muscle, the anal sphincter becomes our pinched or expansive self-judgments, and our finished work is a glistening stool.

Freud, of course, famously argued that the bowel metaphor of creativity is not just a metaphor; that our attitude toward our later work is shaped historically by how we were rewarded or punished for our first "jobs." Although as adults we need a great deal of imagination to take such a position seriously, there was a time when eating was a strange and sometimes alarming process of taking alien material from the outer world into an equally mysterious body. Bringing products forth from that body, and casting them into the outer world of limitless space, was no less frightening. The process of creating a book is not so different.

Finally, how to summarize mental descriptions of writer's block in terms of brain states? I began this book with the suspicion that writer's block might be the opposite of hypergraphia from a neurological point of view as well as from the viewpoint of productivity and pleasure. Hypergraphia — and metaphor, and inspiration — are associated with altered activity in the temporal lobes. Might writer's block be the opposite temporal process?

The more research I did, however, the more likely it appeared that writer's block is a frontal lobe process rather than a temporal lobe process. (Granted, the two lobes influence each other strongly.) Block shares the strangled muteness of Broca's aphasia, the inflexibility of perseveration, and the task specificity and stress dependence of writer's cramp — all frontal lobe neurological disorders. And the two psychiatric disorders most closely tied to writer's block are depression and anxiety, both with evident neurobiological underpinnings and both showing decreases in brain activity that are especially severe in the frontal lobes. The parallels between depression and anxiety on the one hand and what I have been calling low-energy and high-energy block on the other suggest pharmacological treatment for block. They also support the effects on block of behavioral treatments (exercise, psychotherapy, meditation) that can help anxiety and depression.

Of the many drugs discussed in this chapter, none are approved by the Food and Drug Administration for writer's block — and of course, writer's block is not even something that the FDA would consider a medical condition. Moreover, these drugs have other, primary, effects — on depression, anxiety, and other mental states. This is not a surprise: current drugs work on neurochemical systems that are widespread through the brain. But it is not clear whether writer's block ever appears as an isolated problem. Even if it did, wouldn't the unhappiness and sterility that come with being blocked soon infect other aspects of the writer's life? Thus it is to some extent not a disadvantage that these drugs affect mood as well as writing.

Often, people self-treat their block in ways that merely exacerbate it neurochemically. A depressed person may stop exercising, while an anxious person may drink more and more coffee in an attempt to stay vigilant. When a drug affecting a particular neurotransmitter system has an effect on writing, it is evidence for the role of that system in driving the writing. Just as no two depressions are biochemically identical, so no two blocks are. In the many people who have low-energy blocks with a depressed character, the success of antidepressant drugs, which work on serotonin, and also norepinephrine and dopamine, implicates these three systems. People with high-energy block may benefit from these same drugs, but in addition may be helped to some extent by sedatives, which decrease cortical excitation. Whether blocks are high-energy blocks or low-energy blocks, their association with intense mood states demonstrates the importance of the limbic system in the desire to write.

5

How We Write: The Cortex

Language can be regarded as a psychic parasite which has genetically earmarked a section of the cortex for its own accommo-
dation.

— Christopher Dewdney, *The Immaculate Perception*

A few years ago I did my first reading. . . . Eventually my turn
came, and the words that I had written in silence . . . unfolded
themselves like lawn chairs in my mouth and emerged one by one
wearing large Siberian hats of consonants and long erminous
vowels and landed softly, without visible damage, here and there
in the audience, and I thought, Gosh, I'm reading aloud, from
Chapter Seven!

— Nicholson Baker, *The Size of Thoughts*

FOR THE MANY who no longer believe that it is souls that separate
men from beasts, it is language, an almost equally magical substance,
that does the job. The most vicious and highly publicized fights in
linguistics have been over whether other primates can be taught true
language. Animals may communicate, whether through noises, visual
displays, or scents, but their interactions lack key aspects of true language such as syntax and the ability to generate novel sentences.

The lack of talking animals has made research into the brain basis
of language more difficult than studies of more basic phenomena
such as movement, sensation, and even drug addiction. While you
can quickly turn a rat into a cocaine addict, a chimpanzee like Nim

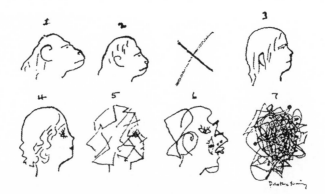

Figure 7. Max Ernst's interpretation of the ascent of man ("Le Musée de l'Homme," 1965) seems also to be a commentary on the evolution of language, from primate grunt to modernist scribble. There is some Creator's block after stage 2, and woman appears more highly evolved than man.

Chimpsky (named for the linguist Noam Chomsky) never learned crucial aspects of language despite living with a human teacher for several years. Thus the research described in this chapter on how our brains speak and write is based almost entirely on humans. That is not the case for the next chapter, on *why* we write, because the limbic system's control of the drive to communicate in animals seems to have important similarities to its control of human language. In previous chapters I have argued that it is difficult to completely separate skills and drives. In this chapter and the next though, I partially separate them anyway. At least at a neurobiological level, it can sometimes help to discuss skill and drive independently.

Although the neuroscience of writing is in some ways parasitic on the neuroscience of speech, the two skills are significantly different. Most fundamentally, speech is nearly an instinct for humans, partially wired into our brains by many thousands of years of evolutionary selection, whereas writing is a recent cultural acquisition, useful but no more necessary to a fully human life than mowing the lawn or bowling. As a consequence, writing is a more fragile skill than speech is, and more likely to be affected by brain injury.

*　　　*　　　*

A tendency of neuroscientists to think of the brain as modular has governed a large part of the push to separate skills and drive. The doctrine of modularity proposes that brain functions such as face recognition or language comprehension are generally found in discrete locations, rather than being spread throughout the brain. Modularity is a popular working hypothesis among neuroscientists, in part because it simplifies things — it is easier to think about the brain as little chunks than as diffuse networks.

Critics of modularity call it neophrenology, after Francis Galton's discredited practice in the nineteenth century of trying to predict aspects of human character — such as Patriotism, Criminality, and Godliness — by the location of bumps on the skull. But to a first approximation, the brain has graciously complied with our desire for modularity, allowing many of the discoveries that are the subject of this book. Now computers are becoming able to store and manipulate network-based, nonmodular aspects of brain models that are too complicated for our human brains to handle.

At the simplest level of modular explanation, most brain regions divide into sensory (brain input), motor (brain output), and association areas. Association areas often integrate sensory and motor information, but in some parts of the cortex their activity may be far removed from basic sensory and motor processing, mediating such high-level functions as abstraction and judgment (not "Will I move my arm?" but "Would it be better for my husband and children if I moved my arm?"). Most language processing occurs in association areas, although of course language depends crucially on sensory regions (those controlling hearing for speech, sight for reading or sign language) and motor regions (those controlling larynx and mouth, or the hand). The brain is sensibly organized so that speech comprehension areas are near auditory areas, and speech generation areas are near those that govern motor control of the face. (See Figure 2a in Chapter 1.)

A different type of modularity is based on neurochemistry. Neurons concerned with specific functions often use specific neurotransmitters. For instance, many of the neurons that regulate pain perception release endogenous opiates, chemicals that closely resemble man-made opiates such as morphine and heroin. Although endogenous opiates have effects besides pain suppression — which is why people get constipated when they take opiates — their role in pain is selective enough that the opiate system can be seen as a pain module. Because the cerebral cortex has a relatively homogeneous distribution of neurotransmitters, physical modularity and connections are more relevant to the cortex's language ability than neurochemical modularity. But neurochemical modularity — and therefore medicinal interventions — play a critical role in the limbic system's control of the drive to communicate.

One of the original reasons for hypothesizing a modular organization of the brain was that it helped to explain the results of brain injuries restricted to only part of the brain. Most localized brain injuries, rather than making the victim a little worse in every ability, affect only some functions and leave others relatively spared. Studying the effects of localized injuries showed neurologists that language is controlled by the left hemisphere. A similar approach has even allowed the cortical areas most important for using nouns to be roughly distinguished from cortical areas controlling verbs. Understanding health and understanding illness intertwine.

Interpretation of the effects of brain injuries is not always straightforward, however. Just because a lesion to an area damages a particular function does not mean that the area specifically controls that function. The famous, if somewhat grisly, frog parable taught to beginning neuroscience students illustrates this well. In it, a researcher trained a frog to jump when it heard the word "jump." He removed the frog's legs, found it would no longer respond to the word "jump," and concluded that frogs hear with their legs. Wrong, of course. Yet if he had been studying crickets, he would have been accidentally correct, as crickets do hear with their front legs.

Understanding the effect of brain injuries is made easier if the modular approach is tempered by a more connectionist way of thinking of the brain. Skills are not really isolated modules, but exist in a network of other skills that can be divided up as finely as patience will tolerate. The task of writing a sentence, for instance, beyond the desire to write the sentence, requires the ability to generate an appropriate idea, to translate it from "mentalese" into English, to generate the words in their written form, to find a pen, to hold it correctly on the paper, to respond to the fact that at first nothing comes out of the pen by shaking it a few times, to do so without getting ink on your clothes, to form the letters correctly, and to simultaneously read the sentence for errors. As all this is going on, the next sentence probably is already being generated.

Thus to understand how the brain controls writing, we don't merely need a lesion that blocks writing — anything from comas to amputations can do that. We need the lesion to be in a location that blocks only writing. For many years, scientists sought such a center. All the candidate regions, however, turned out to be merely areas involved in hand control or vision, not the compositional aspects of writing. Reading and writing are visual skills: instead of auditory cortex and the music of speech, they involve occipital cortex and the visual beauty of alphabets. Outputs of writing do not go through the mouth region of motor cortex, but through the hand region. Any deficit that truly affects written composition also affects spoken language. This interdependence supports the idea that the new skill of writing seems to have adapted areas of cortex that were previously specialized for speech.

Lesion studies are not the only tool that neuroscientists use to study language function. I've already mentioned the ability of electrical stimulation to reversibly activate or inactivate brain areas. Surgeons often use it to locate language areas in surgeries where they want to remove unhealthy brain tissue without impairing speech. Functional imaging and transcranial magnetic stimulations are less invasive ways of obtaining similar information.

Speech

I want to return to what was perhaps the first discovery about the relation of language to the brain: the fact that in most people, language control resides in the left hemisphere. This asymmetry is in sharp contrast to a brain organization that is mostly symmetric and crossed, in which the left side of the brain controls the right side of the body and vice versa.

That crossed organization in itself is fairly strange. One theory postulates that sometime during the evolution of vertebrates, our heads rotated 180 degrees with respect to our bodies. Thus, at least from the point of view of our ancestors who preceded the rotation, we literally have our heads on backward. This sort of transposition is not impossible genetically — it can even be caused by a single gene — and would explain, among other things, the massive crossing of nerve fiber bundles in our necks.

How would a brain go from a symmetrical, paired organization to one in which a function such as language is lateralized, that is, controlled by a single hemisphere? One clue may be the types of functions that get lateralized. Most are higher cognitive functions, and lateralization is well seen only in humans. Language is by far the most obvious example, but other functions are lateralized to a lesser degree: visuospatial reasoning (as in solving the Rubik's cube), the ability to recognize melodies and speech intonations, some higher emotional processing, and so on. One reason why such higher functions have evolved on only a single side of the brain may be that spreading the function over two hemispheres would have required much longer nerve fiber connections between related brain areas, and would have slowed processing speed. It may have been more efficient for all the language regions to be clustered as close together as possible.

Cognitive functions are not the only ones that are lateralized. One prominent example is handedness. Why do most of us prefer our right hand? The neurologist Marsel Mesulam has somewhat ironically pointed out that we should, at least in principle, be able to figure this out, since the brain has given us a perfect experiment of nature to study. Both hands have identical genetic composition and the same socioeconomic background. The left hand gets to sit next to the right hand and watch all the nimble things the right hand can do. But even after decades of this cultural enrichment program, the left hand never learns. Why? Mesulam speculates that in order to maintain lateralization, the left hemisphere actively suppresses the right hemisphere and thus the left hand.

The strange syndrome of left-sided neglect supports his theory. When the right hemisphere is damaged, the left hemisphere's unopposed activity can make the patient completely ignore his left side. (Damage to the left hemisphere does not produce an equivalent right-sided neglect.) I once had a patient who suffered a right hemisphere stroke and fell to the ground, unable to walk because of a paralyzed left leg. She lay on the floor for two days, not because no one came to her aid, but because she kept blithely reassuring her husband that she was fine, that there was nothing wrong with her leg. Only on the third day did he bring her in for treatment. When I asked her why she could not move her left leg, and held it up for her to see, she said indifferently that it was someone else's leg. I don't know what her husband's neurological problem was in responding so slowly, although in his defense, some people ignore horrific symptoms if they are not painful. A major function of pain is to motivate you to seek aid, to call for help.

The neurology of language made great progress during the nineteenth century, in part because during the Franco-Prussian War musket balls were replaced by smaller and more penetrating rifle bullets. The latter were more likely to cause specific syndromes such as aphasia, rather than to leave their victims diffusely "cracked in their intellectuals," to use Patrick O'Brian's phrase.

The first speech region to be discovered, Broca's area, was named after the nineteenth-century neurologist who found that patients with damage there had much more trouble speaking than understanding speech. The fact that Broca's area is more important for speech production than for speech reception fits with its location in the left frontal lobe, just in front of the part of the motor cortex that controls mouth and tongue movements. Thus Broca's aphasia, the defective use of language that arises after Broca's area is damaged, is also known as motor aphasia.

People with Broca's aphasia have much more trouble with syntax than with semantics, with grammar than with meaning. Their speech is halting and telegraphic, usually including only the major words and leaving out small parts of speech. Here a patient with Broca's aphasia is asked to tell the story of Cinderella:

> PATIENT: Cinderella . . . poor . . . um 'dopted her . . . scrubbed floor, um, tidy . . . poor, um . . . 'dopted . . . Si-sisters and mother . . . ball. Ball, prince um, shoe . . .
>
> EXAMINER: Keep going.
>
> PATIENT: Scrubbed and uh washed and un . . . tidy, uh, sisters and mother, prince, no, prince, yes. Cinderella hooked prince. (Laughs.) Um, um, shoes, um, twelve o'clock ball, finished.
>
> EXAMINER: So what happened in the end?
>
> PATIENT: Married.

The words are often in the wrong order. In severe cases they are no more than a word heap. Broca's aphasics lose language in a way that mirrors how children gain it. Complicated structures and uncommon words are lost in mild cases, whereas in the most severe aphasias even the simplest words are lost. The last word to go is often the word "no," just as it is often one of the first words that children use fluently — over and over, to reject those loathsome string beans or sometimes just for the relish of saying the word. In Broca's patients, "no" is more often used with an anguish that reflects the depression they commonly have.

The role of Wernicke's area in speech comprehension reflects its location in the temporal lobe, close to the cortical regions that control hearing. Because aphasia caused by damage to Wernicke's area is closely linked to the inability to take in speech sounds, it is often called sensory aphasia. Wernicke's aphasia must, of course, be distinguished from a simple inability to distinguish speech sounds. One of the telling differences is that patients with Wernicke's aphasia are relatively unaware that they are having trouble understanding speech. Their happy oblivion contrasts sharply with the strangled frustration of patients with Broca's aphasia.

Also unlike Broca's aphasics, patients with Wernicke's aphasia have much more trouble with semantics than syntax, suggesting that syntax is primarily a frontal lobe function and semantics a temporal lobe function. Wernicke's aphasics frequently substitute one word for another and produce grammatically correct forms with all the meaning leached out, the "politician-speak" mentioned in Chapter 1.

In the following example, a patient with Wernicke's aphasia describes the "cookie theft" picture from the standard Boston Naming Test. The patient is shown a picture in which two children steal cookies from a jar while their mother's back is turned. She is also oblivious to the fact that her sink is overflowing and that her son is about to topple from a high stool.

> Well its a its a its a place and its a girl and a boy . . . and they've got obviously something which is is made some made made made well its just beginning to go and be rather unpleasant (ha! ha!) um and this is in the this is the the woman and she's put putting some stuff and the its its that's being really too big to do and nobody seems to have got anything there at all at all and er its . . . I'm rather surprised that but there you are this this er this stuff this is coming they were both being one and another er put here and er um um I suppose the idea is that the er two people should be fairly good but I think its going to go somewhere and as I say its down again . . . let's see what else has gone er the the this is just I don't know how she di' how they did this but it must have been fairly hard when they did it and er I think there isn't very much there I think.

Although this passage is about as incoherent as the example of Broca's aphasia, it is dramatically more fluent, and longer. Wernicke's aphasics don't just talk nonsense, they talk a great deal of nonsense. Perhaps because they don't care that they are not making sense, they are notably voluble and often hard to interrupt. Their pressured speech is a characteristic they share with manic-depressives and temporal lobe epileptics, and the fact that it is of temporal lobe origin lends support to the hypothesis that the pressured writing of hypergraphia is a temporal lobe phenomenon as well.

The rough analogies between the two principal types of language deficits, Broca's and Wernicke's aphasia, and some aspects of writer's block and hypergraphia, extend also to the two major flavors of agraphia (the inability to write). There is a motor agraphia from frontal lobe damage, like Broca's aphasia, in which the patient's writing is labored and he or she has trouble sequencing letters and words. And there is a sensory agraphia from temporal lobe damage, like Wernicke's aphasia, which is fluent, nonsensical, and in which the letters may be mirror-written or have exuberant extra loops.

It is not at all intuitive that speech production and reception could be separated the way they are in Broca's and Wernicke's aphasias. Intuitively, you might expect poor comprehension always to be accompanied by poor production. Once you realize that the two speech functions are neurologically distinct, you may notice the distinction even in normal speakers. Such a medicalized look at normal language may be useful. For instance, analogies of the two aphasias can show up when college students try to write essays: their problem may be productive or Broca-like when their writing is halting but thoughtful, or their problem may be receptive or Wernicke-like when the writing is relatively fluent but empty.

Parsing their problems this way may help to tailor educational strategies or, in the future, medical ones. The advent of transcranial magnetic stimulation raises the question of what would happen if the brain of such a student were stimulated over the appropriate region. Would the student's writing improve? If so, would a visit to a TMS salon make the current practice of buying term papers from the Internet unnecessary? This may be frivolous speculation — but my guess is that it is not.

The linguist Roman Jakobson has made the surprising argument that the nature of aphasia is bound up with the nature of figurative language and that it selectively affects speech patterns we normally associate with poetry, not neurological conditions. On his scheme, Wernicke's aphasia is in part an error of metaphor, of comparison between unlike things, because of the way that Wernicke's patients incorrectly substitute one noun for another. They have great difficulty in defining things, in naming words that are similar. They may not define "boat" as "ship" but will talk around the subject by naming things physically contiguous, or associated with it by cause and effect. In this way, they may call a boat a sail, or a knife a fork. As metaphor fails them, they resort to another figure of speech, metonymy — the substitution of one concept for a related, often physically nearby, concept, as in "the crown" for "the king." The importance of the temporal lobe in metaphor will come up again in Chapter 7, where I discuss some of the ways in which brain regions involved in metaphor also play a role in delusions.

In contrast to Wernicke's aphasics, Jakobson argues that Broca's aphasics display a failure of metonymy rather than of metaphor. Their trouble is with word relationships and order, with causing subject and verb to agree, and even with letter order (as in "forg" for "frog"). In attempting to define words, they use not metonymy but quasi-metaphoric expressions such as "spyglass" for "microscope." Thus metonymy seems to require an intact frontal lobe. The troubled sequencing seen in Broca's aphasics is also seen in other patients with frontal lobe damage. The problems that Broca's and Wernicke's patients have with figurative language probably affect their written language even more than their spoken language, simply because writing is more difficult than speech. Many aphasics lose the power to write at all.

For Jakobson the distinctions between metonymical and metaphorical modes of thought, between frontal and temporal lobe function, have more than neurological implications. He suggests that they can categorize various literary genres. On this scheme the metaphorical (temporal lobe) mode of thought predominates in poetry, especially of the romantic and symbolic schools. Metonymical (frontal lobe) thought is dominant in realism, with its emphasis on cause and effect and on actions contiguous in time and space. Jakobson also believes the distinction can extend outside literature, arguing that cubist painting transforms an object into a set of metonyms, whereas surrealist painting has a metaphorical attitude.

Is the parallel between frontal and temporal, metonymical and metaphorical, function useful or merely ornamental? It is at least scientifically testable. Functional brain imaging shows that the temporal lobe's function in metaphor may be relative rather than absolute, and that there may be input from the right hemisphere as well. Even if only partly true, though, Jakobson's theory deserves attention as one of the rare places where poetry and neuroscience directly intersect. (It could be said that poems such as the sciency bits of James Merrill's *The Changing Light at Sandover,* or the brain imagery in Emily Dickinson, approach the same intersection from the other direction.)

Besides Broca's and Wernicke's aphasia, there are many other types of aphasia — and presumably of agraphia, although this has been less well studied. Some patients can comprehend and speak, but not repeat others' speech. Some cannot initiate sentences on their own, but can repeat the speech of others. Some have "pure word deafness": they can understand written sentences but not spoken ones (although their hearing is otherwise normal). Some patients have the ability to use nouns but not verbs, or verbs but not nouns (this is called anomia); some are unable to name colors, to name animals, to name fruits. Edward Zurif has pointed out how tempting it is to call this last problem banananomia.

The existence of many small brain areas devoted to such semantic categories is possible, although definitely not proven. They may, of course, be devoted to more than one category at the same time. But the typical brain lesion is too large, or incorrectly shaped, to accurately wipe out a discrete semantic category. Functional imaging likewise does not have the resolution to see these putative category areas, while electrophysiology, because it is dangerous, is rarely performed. Thus there is so far very little evidence about the nature of language processing on a scale finer than a centimeter or so of brain.

*   *   *

If language function is so strongly lateralized in the brain that Broca's and Wernicke's areas are found only in the left hemisphere, what are the equivalent areas in the right hemisphere doing? They are not irrelevant to speech processing, but their role appears to center around interpreting and producing vocal inflections and the emotional tone of speech. For instance, a lesion in the right hemisphere counterpart of Wernicke's area produces an insensitivity to tone that can block the ability to appreciate humor, irony, passion. A lesion in the right hemisphere counterpart of Broca's area produces speech with unusual inflections and tone that neurologists have called, for lack of a more confusing Latin name, robotic speech or sudden foreign accent syndrome. Neurologists, whose dreams are different from those of other folks, dream of finding a patient with this syndrome. When I was a resident, we thought we had found one, but it turned out that he was just from Montreal.

The neurologist Oliver Sacks tells of a ward of aphasic patients listening to President Reagan give a speech on television. Although unable to fully understand his words, the patients compensated by being particularly sensitive to his tone and inflections, which they found farcical. A patient with a right hemisphere lesion who could not judge tone was also present. She concentrated on Reagan's exact words — which she too found ridiculous. Sacks concluded from this that it takes a fully working brain to be deluded by politicians. Nancy Etcoff and her colleagues confirmed Sacks's anecdote experimentally by showing that in a controlled setting aphasics had better lie-detecting ability than undergraduates at the Massachusetts Institute of Technology. Lest anyone object that MIT students do not count as completely normal controls, she also had a smaller group of more typical control subjects.

Right hemisphere counterparts of Wernicke's and Broca's area are also important for the interpretation and generation of melody. This fact fits with the hypothesis that the first music was song and that it arose directly from highly inflected, emotional speech. Electrical stimulation of the right hemisphere equivalent of Wernicke's area can cause musical hallucinations. In fact, the composer Dmitry

Shostakovich, who reportedly had a metallic shell fragment resting against his temporal lobe, said, "Since the fragment has been there, each time [I lean] my head to one side, I can hear music — different each time!" Reportedly he would use this method while composing, producing melodic ideas for his symphonies.

Reading and Writing

How does writing differ from speech? Writing is harder, and more culturally dependent. Nearly everyone learns to speak but in many countries almost no one learns to write. Even in the United States, with its universal public education, 10 percent of adults are functionally illiterate and write at less than a sixth-grade level. Why? Writing is not obviously a more complex task than speech. If anything, the much greater speed at which speech is produced and deciphered, the smaller territory allotted to auditory than visual processing in the brain, and the contortions of the tiny larynx should create even more of a challenge than writing. One argument has it that writing is more difficult for humans because it is evolutionarily recent, not hardwired the way speech seems to be.

Oral language probably evolved more than one hundred thousand years ago, most likely from nonlinguistic grunts and hoots and gestures. (The comedian Lily Tomlin has proposed that the first human sentence was "What a hairy back!") There has been a great deal of controversy about the extent to which oral language is genetically controlled. Proponents of this position, notably the followers of Noam Chomsky, argue that all languages share a universal "deep grammar"; they also point to evidence that if children do not learn language before a certain critical period, thought to be sometime around puberty, they never successfully learn it. (Woody Allen has responded that while sentence structure is innate, whining is acquired.) The existence of regions in the brain that are specialized for language, such as Broca's and Wernicke's areas, are probably also evidence for the innateness of language.

By contrast with oral language, writing probably evolved only about five thousand years ago, in part from primitive art and pictograms, but perhaps primarily, at least in Sumeria, from tally marks used in commerce. This latter theory, which the work of Denise Schmandt-Besserat has securely established, is appealingly clever but saddens me. How could poetry and literature have arisen from something as plebian as the cuneiform equivalent of grocery-store bar codes? I prefer the version in which Prometheus brought writing to man from the gods. But then I remind myself that one of the themes of this book is supposed to be that we should not be too fastidious about where great ideas come from. Ultimately, they all come from a wrinkled organ that at its healthiest has the color and consistency of toothpaste, and in the end only withers and dies.

Whereas speech may have only evolved once, writing developed several times spontaneously, with the major examples being Chinese, Sumerian, and Mayan culture. All speech shares the same structure, being made up of words and sentences, while writing has a more variable structure. In hieroglyphs and Chinese characters, symbols represent morphemes or units of meaning. In Japanese *kana*, Cherokee, and Ancient Cypriot, symbols represent syllables, whereas in Middle Eastern and European alphabets, symbols represent phonemes or units of sound.

In considering the difference in difficulty between oral and written language, we need to remember that we have very different standards for writing and speech. Take, for instance, Steven Pinker's excerpt of this Watergate transcript between President Richard Nixon (P) and his counsel, John W. Dean (D):

P: The grand jury thing has its, uh, uh, uh — view of this they might, uh. Suppose we have a grand jury proceeding. Would that, would that, what would that do to the Ervin thing? Would it go right ahead anyway?

D: Probably.

P: But then on that score, though, we have — let me just, uh, run by that, that — You do that on a grand jury, we could then have a much better cause in terms of saying. "Look, this is a grand jury, in which, uh, the prosecutor —" How about a special prosecutor? We could use Petersen, or use another one. You see he is probably suspect. Would you call in another prosecutor?

D: I'd like to have Petersen on our side, advising us [laughs] frankly.

P: Frankly. Well, Petersen is honest. Is anybody about to be question him, are they?

Pinker points out that when the Watergate transcripts were published, people were shocked, for a variety of reasons: "Some people — a very small number — were surprised that Nixon had taken part in a conspiracy to obstruct justice. A few were surprised that the leader of the free world cussed like a stevedore. But one thing that surprised everyone was what ordinary conversation looks like when it is written down verbatim."

One of the most striking features of this and other oral transcripts is how disorganized and ungrammatical speech is compared to writing. Why can't we get away with writing as sloppily as we speak? Perhaps we hold writing to a higher standard because we think that since it is more permanent, it is therefore more meaningful. And more powerful. For academics, writing can even save lives ("publish or perish").

There have been times when writing was viewed with mistrust. The ancient Greek alphabet apparently was the first to be user-friendly enough to allow general literacy, a phenomenon described suspiciously and mockingly by Aristophanes in *The Frogs* around 400 B.C.E. Factions in Afghanistan — and in the nineteenth-century United States — have considered literacy dangerous for women. Although most of us dismiss such attacks on writing out of hand, we may find Plato's defense of oral over written language unsettling. In the *Phaedrus* he described Socrates' fears that writing lets memory atrophy and that writing is deceitful; a writer can pretend to greater knowledge than he has by rereading what he cannot remember.

We can rephrase Socrates' fears more neurologically, if less elegantly, by saying that reading a passage aloud puts fewer demands on memory systems in the hippocampus than does reciting the passage. (Does this redescription add anything? Yes, practical implications. For instance, a theater actor who has suffered hippocampal damage might find a new job reading books on tape more manageable.) Socrates, of course, didn't write down his dialogues; Plato did. There is something both poignant and transgressive in the way that Plato lovingly preserved his mentor's advice by failing to follow it.

Socrates also pointed out that speakers can immediately respond to their audience's reactions, whereas writers and readers are alienated from one another. Accordingly, it is harder to make writing as emotionally charged as oration or shouting — and thus it does not activate the brain's limbic system as much as speech does. Part of writing's power, though, may come from the fact that although the audience is more distant, it can also be much larger. Writing can create a sense of community when there is no community to talk to. Thus the acts of writing and reading can still be relatively charged.

To some extent, computerized word processing blurs the distinction between writing and speech. The computer screen serves as a sort of audience, albeit one with a limited range of responses that, painfully, includes not only the screen saver that the computer uses to signal its boredom, but crashing. However, the prompting that the computer adds, and the ease of revision that it provides, give word-processed prose almost the fluidity of speech, especially as we increasingly need not spell, punctuate, or even organize our ideas. The poet Ted Hughes described the effect of word processing on the writing of children he judged in poetry contests:

> Usually the entries are a page, two pages, three pages. . . . But in the early 1980s we suddenly began to get seventy and eighty page works. These were usually space fiction, always very inventive and always extraordinarily fluent — a definite impression of a command of words and prose, but without exception strangely boring. . . . It turned out that these were pieces that children had composed on word processors. What's happening is that as the actual tools for getting words onto the

page become more flexible and externalized, the writer can get down almost every thought or every extension of thought. That ought to be an advantage. But in fact, in all these cases, it just extends everything slightly too much. Every sentence is too long. Everything is taken a bit too far, too attenuated.

By analogy, the relative ease of speech compared to writing may bring some disadvantages. Writing, because it slows you down, makes you think.

It is a melancholy fact about writing that it has had much of the vocal tone and inflections, the music of speech, drained out of it. An actor or orator moves us more viscerally than our own silent reading, although it is true that writing can describe emotion semantically ("I wandered lonely as a cloud") and has come up with conventions such as punctuation to take the place of the wordless pauses and emotional inflections of speech. These written conventions vary dramatically in different genres. The literature professor Alison Hickey tells of a student who sent her an e-mail ending in the cyber-convention :) indicating that he was intending to be humorous. When she asked him what the sideways smiley face added, he explained earnestly that written language was inadequate to convey emotions. She wondered if she should expect a paper from him saying that he didn't like *King Lear* because it was so :(

The fact that writing and reading do not permit direct interpretation of vocal inflections means that there may be less right hemisphere activity during writing than during speech. But when people read, they add imaginary inflections to the text. Sometimes they even subvocalize — read under their breath. During both these activities their right hemisphere activity increases. Actually, reading silently is a relatively recent invention. Saint Augustine, in his *Confessions,* marveled at the way Ambrose, bishop of Milan, read his manuscripts: "When he was reading, his eye glided over the pages, and his heart searched out the sense, but his voice and tongue were at rest." The carrels in medieval libraries, necessary to sonically isolate murmuring monks, gave way to the echoing nineteenth-century grandeur of reading rooms like that of the British Museum, where only sniffling and covert unwrapping of candies mar the silence. In Joseph Gold's words, language could finally, "like good Victorian children, be seen but not heard."

Most of us retain at least a faint inner voice and ear when we write and read. Their strength probably varies depending on the material. For full enjoyment, most poetry demands a fully functioning inner ear with natural inflections; that is one of the reasons why it should be read slowly. By contrast, the average formulaic biomedical journal abstract can be read by a skilled researcher without having to translate the visual input into an auditory stage before converting it into meaning.

Much stranger than the imaginary vocal inflections that we sometimes add to written text is the phenomenon of synesthesia, in which sensation of one modality, such as vision, produces a perception in another modality as well, such as hearing. Although synesthesia is possible in all the senses, it is most commonly triggered by speech sounds or letters. As one man with synesthesia described it, "'Ah' is something white and long; 'ee' moves off somewhere ahead so that you just can't sketch it, whereas 'yih' is pointed in form. 'U' is also pointed and sharper than 'yee', whereas 'yah' is big, so big that you can actually roll right over it."

A more exuberant description of synesthesia comes from Benjamin Blood who, despite his piratical name, was nearly everything but a pirate: farmer, inventor, pugilist, journalist, poet, and philosopher. He influenced William James and corresponded extensively with luminaries such as Emerson, Tennyson, and Grover Cleveland.

It was on a June morning in 1854 that I entered the publishing house of James Munroe and Company of Boston (and Cambridge) with a manuscript which soon evoked a discussion as to why the word *icicle* was not a fit name for a tub. . . .

Something in the natural sound of the spoken words was the first relevant suggestion: when you set down a tub it responds to that name. The shapes of the two things are also responsive: the tub is short and stubby, while the icicle is spindling and slim.

To illustrate this, . . . consider the use of the words *entrails, reins, bowels* — all good in scientific and social discourse, but for some un-mentionable reason classic culture draws the line at *guts!*

"Well, what is the trouble with guts?"

I expounded here that they were vulgarized by the absurd genius of u flat.

U, guttural, or flat, is a humorous savage, best described in his own words: a huge, lubberly, blundering dunderhead, a blubbering numskull and a dunce, ugly, sullen, dull, clumsy, rugged, gullible, glum, dumpish, lugubrious . . . a musty, fussy, crusty, disgusting brute, whose head is his mug, his nose is a snub, or a pug, his ears are lugs, his breasts dugs, his bowels guts, his victuals grub, his garments duds, his hat a plug, his child a cub, his dearest diminutive is chub or bub or runt . . . his doublet is of sturdy buff and though not sword, is 'cudgel proof'; budge he will not, but will drub you with a club, or a slug, nub, stub, butt, or rub you with mud.

I will stop his cadenza here; there's so much more where that came from that it's hard not to call it pressured speech.

One piece of evidence that synesthesia is a discrete brain state or neurochemical condition is the frequency with which it arises after use of psychedelic drugs such as LSD. Even drug-free normal people can have mild synesthesia, though usually as a strong mental associa-tion between the two senses rather than as an actual illusion or hallu-cination. As many as 0.2 percent of the population consistently asso-ciates certain colors with sounds. It runs in families and is more common in women than men.

People in the general population who lack strongly colored hear-ing have the synesthetic trait mildly. The most common example is to hear high auditory pitches as visually bright, and low pitches as dark. Similarly, certain speech sounds are heard as sharp and others as rounded or smooth. The Gestalt psychologist Wolfgang Köhler dem-onstrated this experimentally by showing his subjects two shapes, a sharply pointed one and a smooth one, and asking which shape was called "Takete" and which was called "Maluma." Normal subjects consistently paired the jagged visual image with the otherwise mean-ingless sound Takete, and the smooth image with Maluma. This was consistent across languages. Apart from these broad associations of high-pitched sounds with brightness, *t*s and *k*s with sharpness, and so on, synesthetic associations are idiosyncratic: one synesthete's mauve *a* is another's shiny green one. They are also remarkably consistent over time — a true synesthete will have the same color-sound associations if retested ten years later.

Because synesthesia is a little-known syndrome, few people are interested in it unless they have it — and I am no exception. Letters have always called up colors to me, except during my postpartum depression, when my synesthesia winked out like a string of colored lights after a bulb has blown. Until college I had assumed that my colored-letter imagery was merely an association to those plastic letter-shaped refrigerator magnets we all had as children. Only after I learned about the existence of synesthesia did I dig out those magnets and see that the letters had colors quite different from the ones that have always been in my head.

Scientists propose that synesthesia arises from brains with mildly crossed wiring, in which some nerve fibers that should go to one sensory center go to more than one. These exuberant fibers have been demonstrated in animals. When functional brain imaging is performed on people with synesthesia who are listening to letters, they show patterns of brain activity that are different from those of people who are not synesthetic. Primary auditory cortex is active, as expected, and primary visual cortex is not. But several higher-level visual areas in temporal and parietal cortex show increased activation, even though there is no visual stimulus. Some increased frontal cortex activation occurs, which may reflect multimodal sensory processing.

At first glance, it is tempting to dismiss descriptions of synesthesia as merely metaphors, figures of speech along the lines of Kipling's phrase "the dawn came up like thunder," rather than direct experiences or brain states. A second look suggests it might be more accurate to say that many metaphors are actually watered-down and culturally influenced forms of synesthesia. Vivid synesthesia may be more common in artists than in the general population. The novelist Vladimir Nabokov, the painter Wassily Kandinsky, and the composer

Alexander Scriabin were all well-known synesthetes. Another was the poet Arthur Rimbaud, whose poem "Vowels" shows how directly synesthesia leads to metaphor:

A black, E white, I red, U green, O blue: vowels,
I shall tell, one day, of your mysterious origins:
A, black velvety jacket of brilliant flies
Which buzz around cruel smells,

Gulfs of shadow; E, whiteness of vapours and of tents,
Lances of proud glaciers, white kings, shivers of cow-parsley;
I, purples, spat blood, smile of beautiful lips
in anger or in the raptures of penitence.

This close association between synesthesia and metaphor suggests that at least one aspect of being a poet may depend on overexuberant wiring. And the evidence that synesthesia activates temporal lobe structures fits nicely with Jakobson's thinking that the temporal lobe is important for metaphor. We should keep in mind, however, that a phenomenon as complicated as metaphor will likely require a network of different brain sites. Indeed, functional imaging of synesthesia shows frontal lobe as well as temporal lobe activity.

Reading and writing are tightly interconnected skills. As anyone who has tried to write in the dark can attest, it is hard to write more than a sentence or so without being able to read what you have written. Reading and writing do appear to be at least partly separable in the brain, however, just as speech comprehension and speech production are. The chief evidence is a rare syndrome called alexia without agraphia, the ability to write without being able to read. Alexia without agraphia can be considered a case of pure word blindness, in which words cannot be taken in visually even though vision is otherwise spared. Alexia without agraphia occurs when a brain lesion in the occipital lobe both destroys the left (language-dominant) hemisphere's visual cortex and thus its ability to see, and at the same time destroys part of the corpus callosum, the fiber bundle that connects the two hemispheres. Thus, the right hemisphere cannot transfer visual information to the left hemisphere to be read. A person with this syndrome can sometimes "read" words if they are spelled aloud, or if allowed to trace raised letters with a finger — thus bypassing the damaged visual reading system.

A second reading syndrome is alexia with agraphia, the inability to either read or write. It usually occurs when there is damage to a region called the angular gyrus, at the confluence of the left temporal, occipital, and parietal lobes. This region integrates auditory, visual, and tactile information. Damage to it causes problems connecting visual or tactile symbols (letters) with the sounds they represent. Generally the patient has trouble with spoken language as well, but it is less dramatic than the problems with visual language. As in lesions causing aphasia, when the lesion causing alexia with agraphia is small, it sometimes produces a startlingly specific deficit. One patient, for instance, had agraphia primarily of uppercase letters.

In a rare side effect of split-brain surgery, the epilepsy surgery that severs the connections between the two cerebral hemispheres, one patient, V.J., not only has a separation of reading and writing but turns out to have the two skills in different hemispheres. She has epilepsy, and in her forties she had split-brain surgery to help control her intractable seizures. After the surgery, she suddenly could not write, although she can still read and speak. Experiments that identified the performance of each hemisphere showed that the left side of her brain can read and speak but cannot write. The right side of her brain can write but cannot read. Thus, when words are shown in a way such that they reach only her left hemisphere, she can read them aloud but not write them. When words are shown to her right hemisphere, she will say she does not know what the word is. But her right hand will write down the word without her conscious awareness. Before the surgery this unusual pattern was hidden by the fact that her hemispheres could easily communicate with each other. Her problem is

further evidence that reading and writing can be separable neuro-
logic functions, and can in rare cases be as far away from each other
as the opposite hemisphere.

Learning to Read and Write

The process of learning to read and write has until recently been the
province of psychology, not neuroscience. But initial neuroscientific
findings have implications for the way written language should be
taught and how dyslexic children should be treated. One question
currently under debate is whether learning to read and write uses the
same brain networks as speech does, or whether the locations of
reading and writing control are less constrained, perhaps even grab-
bing whatever parts of the brain are relatively underused. The case of
V.J., where control of writing appears as far away as the right hemisphere, is evidence for the latter theory. But V.J. is probably not typical: she is left-handed and has severe epilepsy, both of which can
switch brain functions to unusual locations. It is likely that, in most
people, the networks for spoken and written language overlap.

If reading and writing depend heavily on speech areas in the brain,
we may be able to make inferences about the development of written language from what we already know about the development of
speech. What about the hypothesis that there is a critical period
around puberty after which fluent language is never mastered? This
theory originally stemmed from observation of children such as the
Wild Boy of Aveyron (the subject of François Truffaut's movie *The
Wild Child*) who grew up apparently without exposure to language
and who, despite intensive teaching, were then never able to grasp it.
The evidence has been complicated by the fact that some of these
children may have had cognitive deficits too. Still, the hypothesis of a
critical period fits with what we know about the development of
other sensorimotor skills in the brain — for instance, kittens who
grow up in the dark never develop normal vision.

Are second languages limited by the same critical period as first
languages? Popular American culture certainly says yes, driving up-

per-middle-class parents to send their children to preschools offering a choice between Spanish, French, and Mandarin (as a preschool we just looked at does). Functional imaging experiments of bilingual speakers seem to support this claim, showing slightly different patterns of left hemisphere activity depending on whether the subject is an "early adopter" who has acquired the second language before the putative critical period, or a "late adopter" who learned the second language after it.

There is a confounding factor in these experiments. Increasing task difficulty activates more cortex than simple tasks, even activating cortex in the opposite hemisphere. Thus the differences seen in late adopters partly reflect the fact that they had less adequate instruction in the language and were working harder when they spoke. This observation fits with the European view of second-language learning — they know their schools, which have better language programs than American schools, can turn out fluent speakers even when the students begin in middle school. Linguistic studies of how fluency declines with the age at which the second language is learned do not show an abrupt fall at puberty, only a linear decline throughout life (a pattern similar, sadly, to most other forms of learning). So we sent our daughters to the place that did not offer Mandarin but had a big place to make mud pies.

The next question to ask is whether we can usefully think of written language as a second language. A number of education theorists have argued that we can, and that toddlers can learn to read as soon as they learn to speak. They pepper their lectures with videotapes of charming two-year-olds — often their own — reading fluently, and they argue that teaching written language can be especially helpful to children who have trouble learning to speak because of hearing impairment. The key to teaching very young children to read appears to be making the reading a happy and meaningful communication with the parent, rather than a flash-card drill.

Nonetheless, as with second-language learning, there is no solid evidence for a critical period in learning to read and write. The fact that children can be taught to read when very young does not mean that parents need to pursue this goal. Many other skills are of equal value for very young children to learn. That being said, given my own interests I could not resist teaching my children their letters early, using the same refrigerator magnets that had not inspired my synesthesia. They were quickly able to spell through the "Styles" section of the Sunday *New York Times,* which has the advantage that most fashion ads are in full capitals: P-R-A-D-A, H-E-R-M-E-S. Will early designer-name spelling ability help anything other than their fashion sense in later life? Probably not.

One bizarre twist of early childhood reading is the phenomenon called hyperlexia. The term is used by neurologists to describe unusually advanced reading skills in children with autism or other brain damage. They generally learn to read without instruction, often at the same time they learn to talk. Although they are able to read many years above their developmental level, and may read dictionaries, technical manuals, or even sets of encyclopedias, they tend to have very limited comprehension of what they have read. Many hyperlexics have trouble *not* reading, and will recite every word they see. This compulsion can cause problems for the parents, as when a three-year-old taken on a subway ride loudly reads every obscenity scrawled on the car walls.

Not everyone with very early reading has autism, of course. Thomas Babington Macaulay supposedly learned to read at the age of two by listening to his father read the Bible aloud for an hour each night. (Because of the angle at which his father held the book, he learned to read upside down.) Samuel Johnson reportedly read the *Book of Common Prayer* by age three, Lord Byron read the classics in the original languages by age five, and all of these writers read insatiably throughout their lives. When the concept of hyperlexia is applied to people without autism, it becomes less clearly a "neurological syndrome" (although it is still, of course, a product of specific brain wirings and chemistries). Many who read voraciously would balk at being labeled hyperlexic. All the same, there may be a subset of avid readers whose reading has an especially compulsive quality. We make sure never to be without a book directly in front of us, partly because without one we can't help reading, over and over, cereal box labels or the newspaper used to wrap the fish.

Whether compulsive reading in normals is related to hyperlexia in autism is not clear. Most likely it is a combination of innate predisposition and learning and, occasionally, the desire to escape into a different world. One writer tells of seeing a four-year-old boy who tried to climb inside a large picture book. He opened it to his favorite page, spread it open on the floor, and stepped in. When nothing happened, he cried in bewilderment. Some of us spend our lives trying to climb inside books, often rather successfully. It is a passion that can extend from nearly the cradle to the grave. The poet Leigh Hunt said he "wanted to be caught dead while holding a book." He was.

Even in the average person who is not particularly compulsive about it, reading is an almost irrepressible skill. Consider the well-known Stroop test used by many research psychologists. A list of color names is printed with each word in a different color — but the color of the ink is not the same as the color of the word's meaning. (Thus the word "blue" might be printed in red ink.) When asked to list the colors the words are printed in, subjects find it difficult; instead, they often read the words. Ignoring the written color name turns out to be much harder than ignoring the actual color, even though reading is a learned skill and color perception a basic perception.

Is there a link between hyperlexia and hypergraphia? Some literary critics argue that reading and writing are the same activity, that when we read we bring our own experiences and images to the text and are essentially creating a new text. Like most scientists when they confront the humanities, I will now attempt to demolish a nuanced literary position with a few dismissive phrases. What we do in our heads when we are daydreaming or reading, however many of our own thoughts we are bringing in, has key neurological differences from writing. The cortical step that takes our mental images and translates them into words on paper is the one that makes all the difference. Thus many temporal lobe epileptics write all the time but rarely read, while many autistics with hyperlexia rarely write. Few voracious normal readers are also writers. And while it is true that most professional writers started out as fervent readers, the explanations may be practical rather than neuroanatomical. You write the book you want to read, or, as one novelist admitted, you become an author so that publishers will send you free reviewer's copies of other authors' books. In fact, writers in the throes of composition tend to read less, in part for the same reason that they mow their lawns less and don't return phone calls, and in part because, as one of my colleagues said after being needled for not keeping up with the relevant journals in his field, "At some point you have to decide whether you are going to be a producer or consumer of text."

An economist, on reading my manuscript, commented: "You go on about supply, why people want to write books. But what about demand?" Books and writing have been such extraordinarily successful inventions primarily because of what they can do for the reader, and readers may read something for reasons quite different from those of the author who wrote it. Above all, readers want useful information, whether from a road sign or an investment guide. This motive is not completely absent even in readers of fiction, although few people read *Madame Bovary* for straightforward advice on how not to run a marriage. At a more abstract level, readers want a narrative that makes the world seem to make sense, and they sometimes choose stories that fit with their worldview rather than stories that fit the facts. They want racy gossip, as all of us know who have surreptitiously chosen *People* magazine over *The Economist* in the dentist's waiting room.

Sometimes readers want a protagonist similar to themselves with whom they can identify; at other times they want a protagonist different enough from themselves that they can escape the rigid vault of their skull for a short while. Some readers' goal is aesthetic pleasure, or literature's ability to temporarily replace the chaos or desert in one's head with something ordered and beautiful. In that ability, reading is not so different from writing, or listening to or performing music, or devotion to one's children, or obsessively practicing a particular sport, or even workaholism — though we often assume workaholism is joyless. When others' obsessions are not ours, we are sad for them, and we talk of how empty their lives will be if they don't achieve their empty goal: the gymnastics prize, the firm partnership. But there is a monomania in which it is the focus, the sense of transport, that is the real pleasure. The kind of compulsive reading in which you lose yourself, which brings no medals or talk-show appearances, is one example of that.

Reading and writing are generally taught together, at least in the early grades. Later, students are expected to acquire writing ability incidentally in the process of acquiring knowledge in specific fields. Is that adequate training for a professional writer? The question worries me. Coming from Boston, a city with more universities per capita than anywhere else in the world, a city where virtually every writer has an MFA, I naturally believe that an advanced degree is the way to learn something. But until recently I have had almost no feedback about any nontechnical writing; what I wrote, I kept to myself. The first two "books" I wrote, at age five, were very short. Perhaps foreshadowing my later work, one was scientific and one more personal. The science one, written after an exciting demonstration of batteries by my kindergarten teacher, was called "Electersity." The other, illustrated with a weeping stick figure, was called "Loneliss." Don't feel too sorry for me; I wrote it when sent to my room after doing something aggressive with oatmeal.

Later writing was similar: little essays to relieve the pressure of an idea or an emotion. To the extent that I learned to write, it was through ruminating on an essay, setting it aside, and working on it again later, sometimes years later. Most often ideas came to me when my attention wandered in school lectures. This tendency sometimes caused trouble — not with the instructor, but with other students, who saw me writing furiously and wanted to borrow my lecture notes. When I tried to convince them that I hadn't been paying attention and was doing the written equivalent of daydreaming, they decided I was a competitive premed who didn't want to share.

How, then, did I and everyone like me who tries to write without workshops and writers' groups develop standards by which to edit my writing? Can you learn to write by reading? Can you learn to drive a car as a passenger? I hope so, because reading the *New York Times Book Review* every week was a major part of my literary education by the way it exposed me to the reviewers' often catty analyses of one another's styles. A second part of my education was what I learned about the rhythm of language by listening to poetry tapes while I was a neuroscience graduate student. The lab was fairly introverted; some of us went for weeks without saying anything more than "Pass the formalin," so I absorbed a great deal of poetry in the scientific silence.

Most dyslexics are denied many of the pleasures and advantages of reading and writing. Dyslexia, estimated as afflicting 5–10 percent of the population, makes school a misery, cripples future job prospects, and underlies much of the 10 percent incidence of functional illiteracy. Although by definition children with dyslexia have normal nonverbal intelligence, they often have deficits in skills besides reading: oral language, writing (poor handwriting and misspelling), mathematics, motor coordination, visuospatial abilities, and attention (attention deficit and hyperactivity disorder). Dyslexia sometimes decreases with intensive training, but may persist as a profound spelling deficit in adulthood. Occasional dyslexics nonetheless grow up to be gifted writers. Hans Christian Andersen is thought to be one example, and Winston Churchill, a Nobel laureate in literature, another. Of course, Churchill's terrible school performance may have stemmed from manic-depression, another diagnosis that has with significant evidence been pinned on him, but the general thought at the time was that he was a dunce as well as boisterous. His father wrote of him, "I have an idiot of a son."

Dyslexia tends to run in families, especially those with familial left-handedness, and this association made researchers suspect that dyslexia might have a neurological and genetic component. There have been preliminary associations of dyslexia with genes on several chromosomes. Postmortem studies demonstrate that neurons in the cerebral cortex of dyslexics are disorganized. And the left hemisphere language areas, especially a region called the planum temporale, are not as big in people with dyslexia as in people who read normally. Thus dyslexia has given us a revolutionary example of a phenomenon that what seemed until recently to be laziness or a failure of education could actually be a neurological disorder.

Currently three different theories try to explain dyslexia in terms of underlying perceptual problems. All agree that higher-level language processing of grammar and meaning is intact.

The first theory proposes that dyslexia is a problem with recognizing visual forms of words. This theory would explain why dyslexics can understand speech better than writing it, why they describe words as jumping around, and why they have such trouble on tasks requiring discrimination of letters and words that are visual mirrors of each other (*p* and *q, was* and *saw*) but do not sound alike. When tested, dyslexics tend to have basic visual perception difficulties that are not limited to words. Sensitivity to bright-dark contrast, for instance, is decreased in about 75 percent of dyslexics.

As attractive as the visual deficit theory of dyslexia is, more evidence has built up for a second theory, which explains dyslexia as a defect in auditory processing of language. Identifying the sounds (phonemes) that make up words is strikingly hard for dyslexics. Thus many have trouble distinguishing between related sounds such as *ba* and *ga*. Most children can break a word into syllables well before they can read, but dyslexic children have trouble doing so even after much exposure to reading and writing. Dyslexics can learn pictograms for words much more easily than they can phonetic spelling. Training in auditory skills improves dyslexics' reading and writing, and oral language exercises are widely used in treatment.

A third theory, the temporal processing theory, attempts to explain both the visual and auditory deficits in dyslexics as part of the same mechanism. On this view, dyslexics have trouble with rapid processing of sequences of all sorts. This difficulty would produce errors not only in language, which requires discrimination between word parts as quickly as hundredths of a second, but also between errors in other sensory and motor tasks.

Supporting the temporal processing theory is evidence that many dyslexics have general rate and timing problems; they may even have trouble tapping out rhythms with their hands. Moreover, when syllables are artificially slowed, dyslexics can learn to discriminate between them more accurately. The slowing technique has been used to develop a computer game that, although it teaches auditory discrimination, can increase dyslexics' reading level by up to two years after four to eight weeks of practice.

Finally, the temporal processing theory clarifies some of the mystery underlying the left hemisphere dominance for language in most people. It turns out that the left hemisphere is specialized for rapid sequence recognition, which it does better than the right hemisphere. This would explain not only why languages end up in the left hemisphere, but also other features of hemispheric specialization, such as the fact that in music perception the left hemisphere is better than the right at recognizing rhythm, whereas the right is better at recognizing melody.

If dyslexia emerges from a global defect in temporal processing, it nonetheless produces focal changes in brain activity. Reading in normal readers increases activity in several left hemisphere areas, especially the angular gyrus. When dyslexics are reading, they have much less activation of the angular gyrus. This is exactly the region damaged in adult patients who have acquired alexia with agraphia after brain injuries.

For a long time researchers did not recognize dyslexia as a neurological condition because its incidence varied widely from language to language. The line between nature and nurture is rarely sharp, and dyslexia is both a physiological and a cultural problem. Spoken languages are all of roughly the same difficulty for children to learn; in all cultures it takes the same time — three to four years — for a child to become fluent. Written languages, however, have widely different degrees of user-friendliness. A key factor, at least in Western languages, is spelling, or orthography.

There are two types of orthography, shallow and deep. In shallow orthographies, such as Italian and German, a straightforward correspondence exists between spelling and word sound. In deep orthographies, such as English and French, the mapping between print and sound is ambiguous. Children learning to write in languages with shallow orthographies learn much more quickly than children learning deep orthographies. This is especially true for dyslexics: German dyslexics, for instance, read significantly better than English dyslexics do. At the same time, the underlying neurological problem, as examined by tests of basic perception such as phoneme discrimination, seems to be the same across cultures.

Do these results provide neurological evidence that we should all learn Esperanto, with its perfectly phonetic spelling? Or — recalling that dyslexic American children find it easier to learn pictograms than phonetic spelling — perhaps we should all learn Chinese writing? Actually, other factors make ideographic languages like Chinese much harder to learn, despite the absence of messy phonetic orthography. It takes several years longer for a Chinese child to learn basic reading and writing skills than for children learning phonetic alphabets.

A chance to compare directly the difference for our brains between phonetic and ideographic writing comes in Japanese, which has two different writing systems. The first, *kanji,* is based on Chinese characters. It is ideographic and cannot be sounded out. The second, *kata kana,* is phonetic and can be understood syllable by syllable. Because the two systems rely on auditory processing to different degrees, one might predict that some brain lesions would affect one and not the other. This is in fact the case. Lesions of the angular gyrus, an area important for converting visual images of letters to sounds, disrupt reading of *kana* (syllabic) writing but leave reading of *kanji* intact. The latter seems to require activity in the left posterior inferior temporal gyrus, an area involved with visual recognition. The two writing systems thus give Japanese people some cultural protection against the neurological disorder of alexia, since they can sometimes resort to the second system after a stroke or other injury has damaged the first.

To conclude, writing is not hard-wired to the degree that speech is. There do not appear to be truly distinct brain regions processing written language but not spoken language, although the angular gyrus may help to integrate the visual and auditory aspects peculiar to written language. Perhaps we should even think of writing as a particular, unusually visual, language like sign language.

If writing is less innate, is it therefore less powerful? What is more effective, your supervisor's bellowing at you or her leaving an angry letter on your desk? Of course, it depends on context. The bellowing may initially penetrate your work haze more effectively, but it is fleeting. If the letter is notarized, it may be a more powerful and permanent incentive to change. It would be a mistake to underestimate writing on the basis of its being unnatural. Rather, it deserves to be said of writing what Queen Anne said admiringly of Saint Paul's Cathedral, "How awful, artificial, and amusing" (meaning awe-full, artful, and inspired by the muse). Our most powerful tools, and also — by definition — our arts, are artificial. At the start of this book I argued that science can help us write. One of the reasons is that writing is itself a technology. And writing, by spawning information technologies from the Gutenberg press to the Internet, has allowed us to achieve things our small brains still can hardly comprehend.

6

Why We Write: The Limbic System

Of course I stole the title of this talk ["Why I Write"], from George
Orwell. One reason I stole it was that I like the sound of the words:
Why I Write. There you have three short unambiguous words that
share a sound, and the sound they share is this:

I

I

I

In many ways writing is the act of saying I, of imposing oneself
upon other people, of saying listen to me, see it my way, change
your mind.

— Joan Didion, "Why I Write"

Why does my Muse only speak when she is unhappy?
She does not. I only listen when I am unhappy
When I am happy I live and despise writing
For my Muse this cannot but be dispiriting.

— Stevie Smith, "My Muse"

IF WRITING SKILL is primarily the domain of the cerebral cortex,
the motivation to write is primarily the domain of the limbic system.
The limbic system lies largely under the cortex, but also includes
some of the oldest parts of the cortex. Although the limbic system is
scorned by cortex snobs for being more primitive evolutionarily, it is
arguably much more important for happiness than the cortex is. The
limbic system controls the four *F*s (fear, food, fighting, and . . . sex),

but also more upscale functions such as social bonding, learning, and memory, that are important for writing. Some of its most primitive functions are intimately related to its more complex ones. Sleep-wake cycles, for instance, turn out to be tangled up with control of motivation — as anyone knows who has tried to stay up all night to finish a project.

The Brain's Control of Emotion

The limbic system is a slightly blurry category that includes different brain regions depending on which neuroscientist you ask. Most researchers would agree, however, that its primary components are the hypothalamus, deep in the midbrain, and several structures in the temporal lobe: the hippocampus and the amygdala (see Figure 2b in Chapter 1).

The hypothalamus is evolutionarily the oldest of the limbic structures, and its functions are the most primitive. It may nonetheless have some role in the drive to write. Perhaps our most basic emotions are arousal and quiescence, and the hypothalamus contains regions regulating those functions. Similarly, it has a role in sleep cycles, which both cause and are influenced by moods integral to writing, such as depression and hypomania. Regions near the hypothalamus, when electrically stimulated, produce pleasure or rage. They are the simplest components of a pleasure-displeasure system that extends up into limbic areas of the cortex. Functional MRI evidence suggests that these areas underlie not only such "primitive" pleasures as sex and drug addiction, they contribute to such high-level aesthetic pleasures as the appreciation of beautiful faces, the chill that runs down the spine when listening to certain music, and, perhaps, the delight that transported Keats "On First Looking into Chapman's Homer." The hypothalamus plays a role in primitive aspects of the mother-child bond, the joy of love and the grief of separation — two strong stimulants for writing.

Finally, the hypothalamus controls many housekeeping and endocrine functions of the body: appetite, blood sugar level, temperature regulation. When Yeats wrote "I went out to the hazel wood / Because a fire was in my head," how much of his poem was hypothalamic? Although literary-anatomical links such as these are in one sense facile, in another very practical sense they are not. If the food writer M. F. K. Fisher had damage to her lateral hypothalamus, she would become profoundly uninterested in food and probably food writing. If the lesion were ventromedial, she would become much more interested in food and probably food writing. (It may soon be possible to treat anorexia and obesity with permanent electrodes in the hypothalamus to stimulate or suppress activity in these areas.)

The hippocampus — Latin for seahorse because of the structure's coiled shape — is necessary for encoding new memories. Previously learned skills such as writing will not be lost, but amnesia from hippocampal damage may make the subject matter of the writing very odd indeed. For instance, Clive Wearing, the former conductor of the London Symphonietta, contracted a devastating cerebral infection that destroyed the hippocampus on both sides of his brain. From the time of his illness on, he could remember nothing from more than a few minutes before. It felt to him as if he were constantly awaking to consciousness in a world that was completely new. If his wife left the room for a few minutes, when she returned he would greet her with great joy. Although a degree of this freshness of perception might be useful in a writer, Wearing's amnesia triggered writing only to cripple it. He would often be found writing down a time, for example 3:10, and the note "I am now awake for the first time," only to cross out the 3:10 and add 3:15, followed by 3:20, and so on. Wearing was still able to conduct symphonies he knew well, even though after the fact he could not remember conducting them.

In rats, the hippocampus has many "place cells" that fire when the animal is in a particular location but not in others. Place memory is probably a function of the human hippocampus too. There have been several studies of London taxi drivers, people who in the course of their jobs must memorize thousands of places. When images of their brains are compared with the rest of us, they turn out to have significantly larger hippocampi, and the size increases the longer the person has been driving taxis. And knowing your place is crucial for more than not getting lost. The vivid moods we attach to places, and the evocative writing about place of William Faulkner's Yoknapa-tawpha or of Toni Morrison in *Beloved* reflect the limbic overtones that the hippocampus has added.

The amygdala (the name means almond shaped) seems to flag emotionally what should be encoded into memory by the hippocam-pus, and to discard what is boring enough to forget. It labels sensory inputs as important or unimportant, threatening or pleasant. The amygdala is required for negative emotional conditioning, such as the learned association between a swastika and fear. But it can confer positive emotions on sensations, too. It may thus be an organ of meaning in the emotional rather than the cognitive or linguistic sense of "meaning" that I discuss later in this chapter.

The rest of the temporal lobe, surrounding the amygdala and hip-pocampus, is primarily temporal cortex. The superior part contains the auditory and language centers mentioned in the last chapter. The inferior part is probably less relevant for language, but it contributes to visual object recognition (perhaps letter recognition, certainly face recognition). People with damage to the inferior temporal lobe often selectively lose the ability to recognize faces. (One French farmer, al-though still able to recognize humans after a stroke, lost the ability to recognize his cows.)

The medial part of the temporal cortex, along with its interactions with the amygdala and the rest of the limbic system, may play a role in the emotional volatility, philosophical and religious convictions, overinclusiveness, and altered sexuality of Geschwind's temporal lobe syndrome, but this involvement is not well understood. The right temporal lobe does seem to be critical for orgasm, at least in women. The evidence includes women who had spontaneous orgasms for years, often many a day, which turned out to be temporal lobe epilep-tic auras. Most of these women did not seek medical help quickly. Despite the literary prominence of the male orgasm (Miller's *Sexus*, Roth's *Portnoy's Complaint*), its brain source has been harder to pin down than that of the female orgasm. One case study points to an evolutionarily more, well, primitive location than the temporal cortex, in the hypothalamus.

Two areas in the frontal cortex are especially important for limbic function. The first, the orbitofrontal cortex, is one of the areas that is deliberately damaged in frontal lobotomies. Without it, people are calmer and less anxious — but are also more passive and have trouble with decision making. They often perseverate, making the same choice even when their choice is no longer correct. The second region, the cingulate cortex, is overactive in depression and chronic pain. It makes sense that it is overactive in writer's block as well, but this hypothesis has not yet been tested.

Do structures outside the limbic system play a role in emotion? Definitely. Because the brain is a complicated network, changes even in regions distant from the limbic system can cause emotional effects. We saw examples in the tendency of Broca's area lesions to cause depression, and of Wernicke's area lesions to cause mania. There also seems to be some specialization for mood in the left and right hemispheres. Left hemisphere activity tends to stimulate an energetic or positive mood, whereas right hemisphere activity is more likely to be associated with depression — another reason why it might not be wise to follow slavishly the pop-psych advice to increase your right brain's activity.

Finally, there is mounting evidence that another brain network, the basal ganglia, also contributes to motivation, both for simple movements, and for higher thought and emotion. Its role is most evident in the abnormal motivations seen in addiction to drugs such as cocaine. Drug addiction has close links to mood disorders. What about addiction other than to drugs, such as to compulsive gambling? There is initial evidence that gambling, and socially accepted variants such as stock trading, are controlled by a network that includes the inferior part of the basal ganglia. What about addiction to writing?

The brain regions described above depict a rough anatomical organization of the way the brain controls emotion and motivation.

Another way to look at the system is via its chemistry, its pharmacology. Neurons and clusters of neurons differ in which chemical neurotransmitters they use to communicate with other neurons. The neurotransmitters diffuse across the space from the first neuron to receptors on the synapses of the receiving neurons. The limbic system is especially rich in different neurotransmitters, and specific neurotransmitters are associated with specific aspects of emotion and motivation. Most psychiatric drugs, as well as street drugs such as cocaine and heroin, work by mimicking the effects of neurotransmitters on receptors. For instance, drugs in the Prozac class (the selective serotonin reuptake inhibitors, or SSRIs) influence mood by allowing serotonin to linger longer in the synapse. Heroin imitates endogenous opiates.

Perhaps the first neurotransmitter to be associated with mood was norepinephrine. It is closely associated with epinephrine, also known as adrenaline, the substance that makes our hearts pound and our hands shake when we are stressed. Like epinephrine, norepinephrine regulates alertness and arousal. When students writing term papers take amphetamines to stay awake, the drug is acting in part on norepinephrine systems. The neurotransmitter serotonin is also important in mood, as the success of drugs like Prozac will attest. Low brain serotonin levels are associated with depression, and also with aggression. Thus it is not surprising that serotonin levels are significantly lower in suicide victims, who combine both bleak mood and self-directed violence.

Dopamine is a neurotransmitter influential in stimulating motivation — to move, to seek rewards such as food, perhaps even to write. When subjects were asked to play video games for money in a PET scanner that allowed their brain to be indirectly monitored, dopamine release increased during the task and was proportional to how well the subject did in the game. Dopamine is important for states of abnormal motivation too, as in drug addictions. Changes in some aspect of the dopamine system may trigger schizophrenia, both its delusional motivations and its hallucinations. Large doses of drugs affecting dopamine can produce hallucinations even in normal subjects.

Dopamine's role in hallucinations may mean it underlies imagination as well. But hallucination is more than just very vivid mental imagery — there must also be some error in reality checking, so that the mental stimulus or visual illusion is interpreted as real. Many of my patients who receive dopamine-increasing medicines for Parkinson's disease have visual illusions that they know immediately to be unreal. One of them said to me: "I often see little ugly freckle-faced girls in plaid raincoats. But I know they are illusions because my daughter runs over them with her car without seeming to mind, and she probably wouldn't do that if they were real." It is only when the patient is also confused that he or she loses the ability to interpret these experiences as illusions. It is this grip on reality that separates a writer of hallucinatory intensity from a psychotic who is hallucinating.

One other neurotransmitter system that I will mention, in this emphatically incomplete list, is the endogenous opiates. Researchers studying the way in which drugs such as opium work not only located the brain receptors that mediate opium's actions, they also found that the brain already makes its own endogenous opiates and uses them to block pain and cause pleasure. Their role in reward means they also have a role in motivation. And they have a specific role in the rewards of social interaction and communication. I argue below that this connection underlies the pleasure of writing as well.

By looking at emotions and drives from the outside, the neuroscientific perspective notably neglects what they *feel* like. Another way to understand emotion is to start with what most agree is the simplest pair of emotions, pleasure and displeasure — or, in behaviorist terms, a predisposition to approach or avoid (sometimes called valence). Even at this simplest stage, cognitive inputs are crucial to determine whether an external stimulus is worthy of being approached or avoided, loved or hated. Many psychologists then introduce a second axis, independent of the pleasure-displeasure axis, along which to categorize emotion: arousal versus quiescence. On such a scheme, both rage and melancholic depression are unpleasant, but rage involves much more arousal than does melancholia, with its leaden apathy.

Recognizing arousal as a fundamental part of emotion has several advantages. For one thing, the biology of arousal is relatively understood. It is the province of the autonomic nervous system, which has two opposing halves. The first, the sympathetic nervous system, mediates arousal. It prepares the body for great effort: adrenaline is released into the blood, the heart rate increases, digestion is postponed for quieter times, and the pupils dilate. (The telltale tendency of the pupils to dilate when excited is why in some countries people prefer to wear dark glasses when negotiating a business deal.) The second half of the autonomic nervous system is the parasympathetic nervous system, which brings the body to a resting state and restarts housekeeping functions such as digestion. Sympathetic and parasympathetic reactions occur in a relatively stereotyped way, often regardless of whether they are useful — thus your heart races and your bowels clench when you contemplate how much of your writing project is still undone, even though you are only metaphorically running from your project.

Emphasizing the role of arousal in emotion has the advantage of pointing out the link between emotion and action. Arousal is usually directly proportional to action; a person who is aroused will often act even if no useful action is available. Thus someone who is ecstatic may jump or sing for no real reason, whereas someone who is in a blissfully unaroused state may not move even if there is reason to.

Arousal may be more important than valence in determining whether someone will pick up a pen and write. However, increasing arousal does not indefinitely increase writing, or indeed any action, because of the Yerkes-Dodson law described in Chapter 4. When arousal gets too high, it can overload the nervous system so that opposing impulses collide (metaphorically, but to some extent even physically) and the person freezes, pen in hand.

In certain circumstances action and emotion can come uncoupled. The most common example? Living in a society. After many years of training, a child learns not to push her sister to get what she wants. (Or so I hear.) When this societally induced emotion-action uncoupling goes too far, it can produce the many patients who are traditionally labeled neurotic, who feel the emotion appropriate to doing some action yet never do it. Such an explanation overlaps or complements the mechanisms for procrastination that are already described.

Rarer causes of emotion-action uncoupling are certain forms of brain damage that cause the expression of emotion without the sensation of emotion. A young patient I met several years ago first suspected something was wrong when he began laughing inappropriately, not just when he felt happy, but when he felt any strong emotion. His girlfriend broke up with him after he laughed all the way through her father's funeral, yet he was sure he had felt only grief during the ceremony. He entered psychotherapy, but his problem worsened. Only after he began slurring his words and having trouble with his right arm did neurologists order a brain scan. It revealed that he had a tumor in an area that controls, among other things, emotional behavior but not emotion. His laugh did not sound mechanical; it was charming and infectious. It was hard not to laugh along with him, even as he vividly described his suffering. By the time I met him, he was laughing every thirty seconds or so. Each laugh was followed by a fleeting look of torture. What happened to him? Surgery, tumor recurrence, radiation therapy, a second tumor. He was such an engaging boy, open-faced and brave. I sometimes worry that it was his laugh that made him seem brave, though, that it blinded us to the depths of his sorrow and fear.

Much more common are patients who cannot convey their suffering for less evident reasons. Some patients with chronic pain fall in this category. They look comfortable, they joke with you, but they tell you that they are having a "12 on a scale of 10" headache. Because they are so unconvincing, they generally don't receive much treatment. They then become angry at the doctors, and the doctors ignore them even more. Pain specialists often explain the apparently pain-free appearance of such patients by saying that people lose their autonomic responses to constant stimuli, even pain. Thus the behavior we normally look for in pain patients — pallor, restlessness, sweating — is absent.

I wonder if in at least some patients, the problem starts — rather than ends — with faulty pain behavior. Without such basic cues as these autonomic signs and appropriately inflected speech, some people are just not successful at engaging the sympathy of others. They tell you about their back pain or their mother's death, and you have trouble staying awake. If they then escalate their requests for help, doctors see them as needy or medication-seeking, and it becomes a vicious cycle. For people who are very inhibited behaviorally, writing is often a more effective way than speaking of making their emotional needs known.

Once past the first step of dividing emotions into pleasant and unpleasant (or mixtures of the two) and aroused and inactive, what comes next? There is considerably less agreement here. One question is whether drives such as (in rapidly decreasing order of instinctuality) hunger, the drive to communicate, and the drive to write count as true emotions. At least in the English school of the study of emotions, stimuli such as the taste of food are not said to trigger emotion. In other philosophical and psychological traditions, they do. My own inclination is to think of the drives as particularly goal-oriented emotions.

Researchers have generally supposed there to be a core set of primary emotions, such as anger, and a larger set of secondary emotions, such as envy or shame. Paul Ekman and others have looked at cross-cultural ability to recognize facial expressions and come up with a list of at least six universally recognized expressions: joy, sadness, anger, fear, surprise, and disgust. Evidence for the innateness of these expressions and the associated emotions comes from the fact that even children who are born blind can produce these expressions appropriately. Darwin, too, believed in the value of facial expression for understanding emotion. He performed many experiments on the subject, and described at great length and with almost hallucinatory intensity the minute changes in facial muscles that signal when an infant is about to burst into tears. Would it be shameless biographizing to propose that his fascination with the subject reflected the fact that he had eight children of his own?

Along with the list of primary emotions based on facial expression, at least a dozen competing lists base their categorizations not on expression but on other factors such as the existence of a neuroanatomically discrete brain system controlling the emotion. The surplus of emotional taxonomies made William James disillusioned with the project of categorizing emotions. He argued in 1892 that the literature on the emotions was as interesting as "verbal descriptions of the shapes of the rocks on a New Hampshire farm." Nevertheless, there is at least a rough correspondence between most of the different classifications.

Perhaps instead of making these lists of emotions, psychologists should figure out what makes people obsessed with such lists. What does it mean when someone, a researcher or a patient, is overly concerned with developing a taxonomy or record of emotions? Manic-depressive people sometimes keep obsessive mood graphs — graphs that during manic periods explode in complexity, with extra variables, four-dimensional vectors, and features that even the grapher does not understand. Do they help the patients or their doctors? Often they are merely graphical hypergraphia. Nonetheless, psychiatrists encourage patients to chart their moods, perhaps for the same reason they encourage diaries and basket weaving. It is safer than some of the other occupations their patients might take up. And occasionally the graphs do allow a pattern to emerge from the chaos of a person's life.

One thing on which most students of the emotions since the ancient Greeks have agreed is the opposition between emotion and reason, the irrational and the rational. This opposition has greatly influenced written genres, underlying as it does the distinction between literary and scientific prose. Plato, in the *Phaedrus*, described the soul as propelled on a chariot having three parts: a charioteer personifying reason, and two winged horses. One of the horses, white and easily controlled, represents the will; the other, dark and wild, represents the passions. This tradition of opposition between reason and emotion has continued through much of Western thought, especially Romantic thought. The same tradition is responsible for the way we speak of emotions as things that happen to us from outside ("I was overcome by rage"), as if there were a rational me separate from the emotional me, an ego distinct from its id.

An opposing strain in Western thought argues against too fine a distinction between reason and emotion. Darwin and his successors have pointed out that over the millennia the emotions have generally been rational, in the sense that they were evolutionarily advantageous. All else being equal, it is useful for an animal in a dangerous place to be frightened and run away. Even grief is a by-product of social bonds that help to hold a group together.

It is common to argue that emotion, while useful in our savage past, is something of a holdover — that heart pounding is more useful when we are confronted with bears than with bosses. It is true that we are less likely to be physically attacked than formerly — at least, if we are upper-middle-class Americans. We hear more of people who suffer from too much fear — phobias and panic attacks — than we hear of people with too little fear. But the latter certainly exist, for a short time anyway: a substantial proportion of modern accident victims may have been killed by their own carelessness, by being, in a sense, "fear deficient." Even today, emotions are evolutionarily adaptive.

The neurologist Antonio Damasio has outlined the anatomy underneath the usefulness of emotions, the rationality of the irrational. Emotional biases from the limbic system make possible quick decision making, paring down the array of choices the cortex generates to yield a more manageable list. Patients with brain lesions in areas of the limbic system essentially do not have enough emotions. They do not behave more rationally or intelligently than normal people, but actually are severely impaired when it comes to ordinary day-to-day decision making. For instance, they may waste hours ruminating over when to make a trivial appointment. Their choices are deeply flawed, despite their having normal IQs.

The moral philosopher Martha Nussbaum holds a similar view to these neurologists and evolutionary psychologists. For Nussbaum, a truly rational person will have certain emotions as the consequence of proper understanding — it would be irrational for an American not to feel grief on hearing of the destruction of the World Trade Center. Although the position blurs the distinction between reason and emotion, it avoids the corrosive skepticism of the stance held by certain literary theorists, who argue that the notion of rationality is fundamentally suspect.

Decreasing the exaggerated opposition between "rational" and "emotional" writing might make scientists write differently. An economist who cloaks his deeply felt personal beliefs in dry technical prose might be at once more honest and rhetorically more effective if he let some of his passion show through. Would the reverse cross-pollination help writing in the humanities? It might not benefit lyric poetry, with its explicit concern for "true for me" rather than "true." But in other genres, even the most devoted disciple of someone like Lacan (and I admit to a secret fondness for him) must sometimes wish for a thread of logical argument in his writing.

The Motivation for Language and Writing

What kind of an emotion is the desire to write? It is not a core emotion like joy or fear. Nor is it a biological drive in the sense that hunger or sexual desire is. But there are secondary emotions and secondary drives, made of a mixture of core emotions or drives, often in combination with certain beliefs. Secondary emotions include complicated states such as guilt, hope, and smugness. Secondary drives might include the urge to buy a house or to gamble. It is in this secondary category that the drive to write best fits.

The urge to write is a secondary drive that grows out of a more fundamental drive, the drive to communicate. How fundamental is the drive to communicate? Some researchers think it, too, is secondary, that we want to communicate solely because doing so gets us what we want: food, sex, permission to use the bathroom when we are in elementary school. The behaviorists were perhaps the prime proponents of the secondary drive position, arguing that we learn language because we are rewarded for doing so. Other researchers think that communicating is something hardwired into us — that we have, in Steven Pinker's term, a language instinct. This position does not deny that language is useful for getting things; indeed, it argues that language has been hardwired just because it is so useful.

Several lines of evidence indicate that the human brain insists that we speak. First, we have discrete brain regions controlling speech and little else. That is not true of skills that are less innate, such as tool-making or horseback riding. For instance, the brain's planum temporale, associated with Wernicke's area and speech comprehension, is bigger in the hemisphere controlling speech. And that asymmetry is present by the thirty-first week of embryonic gestation, even before a baby has been born and exposed to language.

The second line of evidence stems from the simple fact that every healthy person does speak. Tool use varies widely across cultures, but no culture gets along without a highly elaborate language.

A third line of evidence is the way that speech erupts in early childhood. The neurologist Frank Wilson points out, with his characteristic fizz, that the young child "behaves as if she has been given a labeling gun whose relentless operation compels her to take possession of the world by putting labels on everything she possibly can." Pinker supports the explosive quality of this behavior with the argument that from about eighteen months of age through about eighteen years, the average child learns a new word at a minimum of every two hours.

An aside: Linguists, when they describe the language ability that explodes in young children, often talk of children's effortless acquisition of speech. As a mother of young children, I find that statement inaccurate. Toddlers work hard around the clock to learn language, and they are frequently reduced to tears by the frustration of not being able to put their needs into words.

Followers of Noam Chomsky have made much of a fourth line of evidence for language's innateness: the ability of children to acquire elaborate grammars with only the sketchiest instruction, and to use the grammars to generate sentences that they have never heard before. A breathtaking example of children's ability to generate language more complex than what they have been exposed to is in the development of creoles from pidgins. Pidgins are degraded, agrammatic collections of vocabulary that result when speakers have to interact without the opportunity to fully learn each other's languages. When young children are exposed to pidgin, they turn it into a grammatically rich language called a creole, which far exceeds what they have heard from their parents.

This is not to say that language is independent of experience and education. Children must of course be exposed to language in order to learn it — they will, more or less, never speak unless spoken to. And culture determines what language we speak. A typical child can learn any of the world's languages regardless of his or her genetic background. (Imagine being excused from high school French on the grounds that you did not have enough French blood to understand it.)

In addition, clearly instinctual behaviors such as bird song are determined by environment. The social behavior of geese and swans, too, is influenced by the first few hours of life in a process called imprinting, during which they form their sense of what members of their species look like. If the first object a gosling sees is the ethologist Konrad Lorenz, then it will not only assume that Lorenz is its mother but will later try to mate with humans. (Does this concept have implications for literature? It does make it less likely that Hans Christian Andersen's ugly duckling and Rudyard Kipling's Mowgli were able to live happily ever after.)

So far what I have described focuses on the cognitive aspect of the drive to speak. This approach reflects the tendency of most linguists — they focus on semantics and syntax, and on sentences that transmit solely a logical proposition. In practice we often interpret sentences very differently, looking for the emotional or limbic aspects of speech, even before we bother with the semantic aspects. When a colleague bursts into your office ranting about some policy change, you may well store the entire fifteen-minute speech as a judgment about emotion, "Anne is angry," and dispense with the cognitive aspects of her argument. Traditional linguists may argue that the emotional aspect of language, transmitted as much by tone as by words, does not separate it from primitive nonlinguistic gestures such as giving someone the finger, and thus is not a fit subject for linguists. It is nonetheless an essential subject for understanding what drives us to speak and write.

The way emotion drives language becomes more evident when we look at the evolutionary origins of speech. Until recently, nearly everything that was said on this subject proceeded from a certain smugness about our role as the only species with language. It is true that nonhuman primate communication contains only a limited number of signals (sounds or gestures with innate meaning, such as laughing or screaming) and even fewer symbols (items whose meaning must be learned, as in the snake and eagle alarm calls of vervet monkeys). And there is little interchange in primate communication — primates make pronouncements rather than conversation. Finally, and crucially for the Chomskyites, primates have no grammar. Still, the communication of nonhuman primates, although it may not be language in a rigid sense, sheds light on the more complex constructions of human speech.

Primate signals such as grimaces and gestures always carry emotional content. Jane Goodall, based on her forty years of chimpanzee observation, argues that

the production of a sound in the *absence* of the appropriate emotional state seems to be an almost impossible task for a chimpanzee. . . .

Chimpanzees can learn to *suppress* calls in situations when the production of sounds might, by drawing attention to the signaler, place him in an unpleasant or dangerous situation, but even this is not easy. On one occasion when Figan was an adolescent, he waited in camp until the senior males had left and we were able to give him some bananas (he had had none before). His excited food calls quickly brought the big males racing back and Figan lost his fruit. A few days later he waited behind again, and once more received his bananas. He made no loud sounds, but the calls could be heard deep in his throat, almost causing him to gag.

This is not to say that nonhuman primate communication only expresses emotion — note that Figan was also signaling the location of food. The role of emotion is less overwhelming as the species becomes more complex. Monkeys produce only a few cognitively different alarm calls; apes have a greater range of gestures with more meaning, and humans can produce many sentences with no emotional content at all, as a chemistry text or the huge government documents section of any public library will attest. But most ordinary and literary human language has not yet had the blood drained out of it. It takes many, many years to learn how to write like a chemist or a government bureaucrat. It is still very difficult for us not to speak when we are strongly moved. When we bite our tongue to avoid crowing over our success, we are not much different from young Figan.

The existence of a strong link between emotion and language may explain some aspects of autism. The syndrome often begins with language difficulties, and people with autism also have a profound inability to interpret emotional states, both their own and those of others. Typical children, by contrast, compulsively narrate their experiences and desires. "That too loud in my two ears. I go up the stairs. I am da king of da all. Other baby, lie down." (For some time, my twins referred to each other dyadically as "other baby.") Some children even narrate their lives in the third person, as did a friend's child, Bina, who would run in from the garden calling "'Mama! Come out and see the gummy slug,' Bina said." There is an inner child after all, and it is a memoirist. Perhaps the sort of art that celebrates the objective beauty of the external world, independent of what it has done for the artist's mood, represents a higher stage of development. Perhaps it is simply a less natural behavior.

Most brain damage that causes language problems also causes changes in mood. In the case of Broca's aphasia, the inability to produce speech, the effect can be profound depression. In the case of Wernicke's aphasia, the inability to understand speech, the result is frequently manic. These moods can be interpreted psychodynami-cally as responses to the deficit: frustration in the case of Broca's aphasia, and freedom from having to make sense in Wernicke's apha-sia. The moods are also direct results of brain damage to those re-gions, because nearby lesions that do not cause language problems have the same mood effects. Interestingly, in aphasia the ability to read and write emotionally charged words is relatively preserved compared to nonemotional words. Does this support the role of emotion in language?

The psychologist Dylan Evans has argued that language was the first mood-altering substance. It can improve mood in several differ-ent ways: by consoling, by entertaining, and by venting. The first two ways benefit the hearer; the third, the speaker. Language can also worsen mood, of course, as in verbal abuse or the assertion of social dominance, or simply through boredom.

Consoling, although generally a service provided by one person to another, can also be done for oneself, as when we whisper silent words of encouragement to ourselves when we feel low. Cognitive-behavioral therapy attempts to create just such an internal mono-logue and it can be as effective as antidepressants in treating moder-ate depression. Consolation is not only an oral genre; it underlies the huge corpus of inspirational literature. Still, for many of us in this cynical age, consolation has become suspect. We have all experienced well-meaning or overly generic comfort that has trivialized the extent of our woe.

What about entertainment? Few of us are too cynical for that. And the most popular form of oral entertainment, except perhaps during the network sweeps, is gossip. Who hasn't had his woes temporarily washed away by learning of even a mild office scandal? Gossip may be one of the earliest forms of entertainment — some evolutionary psy-chologists have even argued that gossip is language's major function, because it helps to maintain group identity. Philip Lieberman has called this the Jewish *yenta* theory of language origin.

As a literary genre, entertainment includes not just escapist beach books, but all of great literature. Granting that it is controversial to allow that literature should be a source of pleasure, I will simply restate my thesis more baldly: if you are not reading literature for pleasure (among other things), then you are reading it wrong.

Evans's final linguistic technology for mood elevation is venting. To quote Lily Tomlin again, man invented language to satisfy his deep need to complain. Venting differs from consolation in that the listener provides much less feedback. Yet the listener's keen, if silent, attention is essential to venting's emotional relief. The psychoanalytic talking cure is the apotheosis of this approach; Freud claimed that speaking about negative emotions is sometimes the *only* way to get rid of them. In writing, where consolation is a benefit provided to the reader who receives the advice and sympathy of the author, venting is a benefit provided to the writer. In fact, the distance of the audience from the writer, the absence of well-intentioned voices saying "I know exactly what you're going through; it's just like when my father. . ." or "You wouldn't be in this boat if you hadn't sold your Thermogen stock," may make written venting more satisfying than oral venting to the wrong friend.

All the same, there may be situations in which talking or writing about a painful memory makes it worse. Some psychologists have argued that rehearsing a traumatic event, as in "debriefing" after a disaster, may simply engrave the pain more deeply in the mind. Indeed, a revolutionary study suggests that a simpler and more effective technique may be to give propranolol, the medicine that blocks the body's response to adrenaline, for a few days after a trauma. By decreasing the racing heart, tremor, and dry mouth that help alert the hippocampus to imprint the traumatic memory firmly on the brain, this simple technique may someday diminish the likelihood of posttraumatic stress disorder. Harmful or not, though, getting things off one's chest is a technique that has been around much longer than Freud. It is probably more ancient than language itself, as old as nonverbal behaviors such as weeping and screaming.

Evans's three-part role of emotion in language passes over the fact that the principal reason we complain or weep is to summon aid from others, not merely to vent. This point was brought home to me when I would sometimes go on daily rounds with the head research veterinarian of a laboratory animal facility. It was essentially an indoor zoo, with rats and chickens and frogs and monkeys and the occasional sheep. The veterinarian was concerned about the animals' mental as well as physical well-being, and one of his jobs in the monkey room was to go around with a lunchbox full of toys. Every day he would hand each of the monkeys a different toy to keep them from getting bored. They also had a TV to watch, often tuned to reruns of *Wild Kingdom* or *The Monkees*. I had a theory that part of the department's goal in avoiding monkey boredom was that when they were bored, they would just masturbate all day. This was no doubt thought to be bad for graduate student morale.

In the rhesus monkey room, the head veterinarian could easily tell when a monkey had a headache, because it held its head in its hands. In the squirrel monkey room, he warned me, the animals gave far fewer clues that they were in pain, so the veterinarians had to be careful to avoid undertreating them. Squirrel monkeys spend less time in social groups than rhesus monkeys do, so a pain behavior such as holding one's head tends not to be useful. It is less likely to attract the attention of a concerned tribe member, and more likely to signal to predators the presence of easy prey. In such intensely social primates as humans, on the other hand, holding your head in your hands is a great way to get everything from permission to stay home from school to painkillers.

How relevant to humans is nonhuman primate behavior? It certainly makes it easier to understand the bizarre research finding that patients rate their pain up to three times higher when their spouse is in the room. This initially chilling fact is somwhat tempered by learning that the effect is greatest with the most sympathetic spouses. It's not that our spouses make us miserable, but that we complain more if there is someone around who will help. How, then, can we explain crying in an empty room — and feeling relieved afterward? Most likely, all such private venting brings relief because of our long association of weeping with getting aid.

The theory that expressions of emotion are made in large part as expressions of need applies not just to weeping, but to other emotions. Angry shouting, for instance, attempts to intimidate the listener into meeting the shouter's needs. Surprise asks for an explanation. Even, perhaps especially, the expression of aesthetic appreciation is a need. When we see someone or something beautiful, we pursue it; our impulse is to stare, to keep it in our sight for as long as possible. (Once, when I was riding the gray London Underground with the painter Marcus Wood, he had me ride five extra stops with him because he couldn't take his eyes off the brilliant saffron of an elderly woman's sari.)

Why do people tell everyone when they are full of joy? In part, it is our need to announce success — concern for our all-important social ranking does not leave us even when we are elated. Further, people genuinely, if sometimes misguidedly, desire to make others happy with their own happiness. Laughter as an expression of amusement rather than delight may have a different origin. The neurologist V. S. Ramachandran explains amused laughter as a primate false-alarm call, a revocation of the need for assistance. If someone in your tribe slips on a banana peel and breaks a leg, no one laughs. But if he slips and gets up immediately, there is laughter — at least if you are a monkey, or a human with a taste for slapstick.

Is it too reductionist, then, to suggest that a major reason for creative writing is an abstracted version of the same biological urge that causes you to cry out in sorrow or anger? Let us call it the need theory of self-expression. It is perhaps a more inclusive formulation of Freud's description of literature, which he believed was driven mostly by unexpressed sexual needs. My theory also adds a dollop of more modern neuroanatomy and evolutionary biology.

There is admittedly a big step between nonlinguistic expressions of emotion and semantic propositions. Such an explanation need not fit all writing. It would not cover technical or impersonal writing — the medical journal *Prostate* and the book *How to Talk to Your Cat* come to mind. It would include most autobiographical writing, most fiction, most poetry, and most nonfiction in which the author had a strong personal stake in the subject. I was going to include my previous book, an apparently impersonal handbook of neurology, along with *Prostate* and *How to Talk to Your Cat*. Then I realized that it secretly was a record of three very happy years as a neurology resident, under the tutelage of two wonderful mentors — which is why I enjoyed writing it so much. Maybe the *Cat* author had similar personal motives.

Although my theory is perhaps better suited to modern writers, it fits earlier writers too, at least when we know enough about their lives to understand what drove them. Take Flaubert (*"Mme. Bovary, c'est moi"*), Dickens (*David Copperfield*'s exposé of the child labor that Dickens had suffered), Augustine's *Confessions*. My theory ignores the last fifty years of literary critics who have analyzed texts as if they were authorless, but it is not in opposition to that approach. It is just a different kind of theory; it has different uses.

On this view, how do we explain, say, my writing of this book? The answer is all too easy. The many quotations from literature and from scientific studies are simply an intellectualized scrim over my bewilderment at what wire in my brain snapped after the deaths of my first children. Whatever it was, it dragged me away from a happy career as a scientist toward an impractical compulsion to write. (My desire to practice medicine was not overwhelmed by writing; if anything, it has increased. Perhaps that is because of the limbic tug, the ache and the blood of being a doctor.)

Granted that I may have written down my thoughts in the process of trying to figure out what happened, why should I then try to inflict those thoughts on you? Apparently there is something I still need, something that still hurts. I cry out because some primitive part of me believes that when you cry out, someone warm and helpful comes. What do I need? It is not to have those tiny babies back. They were too small for me to remember; they have vanished like soap bubbles. I have two real children now. Nor do I want to return to the sunny, uniformly lit mental life I used to have, although there are aspects of that life that I miss.

In fact, during my postpartum break I discovered a mystery: I loved my sorrow. It was as if I had been preparing all my life for that event, that I had entered into my birthright. When I was in graduate school, my husband and I lived in an apartment over a ruined garden that had a grapevine as thick as a child's body, coiling up the fire escape to my window. At night I could lie in bed and reach out into the dark and pluck grapes to eat. My grief was like that, as if it had given me access to a shadowy world that lies so close to this one that when I concentrated I could push my arm into it and pluck dream fruit. It is a world where beauty cannot be separated from pain, and should not be, as when a scalpel is needed to expose the exquisite organs of the belly. A pen can be a scalpel too.

I no longer know whether it is my children that I long for, or my sorrow. I have an irrational belief, left over from my sensible past, that if I tell enough people about this knot that is always pulled tight, someone somewhere will be able to loosen it. But my new self needs it always to be pulled tight. I don't write to forget what happened; I write to remember. There are worse things in life than painful desire; one of them is to have no desire.

If language and writing grow out of a biological system for attempting to fill needs, then the notion of self-expression, so often invoked vaguely to explain the artistic urge, can be better understood. Self-expression is not simply a broadcasting of personal characteristics or tastes. It is generally, if subliminally, much more goal directed than that. Educators often justify art courses and creative writing courses on the grounds that self-expression can teach students about themselves. That may be true to some extent, but many creative writers have been quite capable of powerfully emotive writing while lacking insight into the internal conflicts that drive their suffering. While they may not gain insight, they still gain a sense of relief — and a sympathetic audience.

To the extent that self-expression does broadcast and reinforce a person's character, it clarifies a link between art, eccentricity, and mental illness. The more like ourselves we become, the odder we become. This is most obvious in people whom society no longer keeps in line: the eccentricity of the very rich, or of castaways.

Can any of this need theory of self-expression be tested? One group of studies by Alice Brand provides evidence that writing, at least on personally chosen subjects, satisfies some urge and has measurable mood effects. In both students and professional writers, the act of writing both intensified positive emotions and blunted negative ones. This outcome was something of a surprise to researchers in the field of composition studies, as the standard view of writing emphasized the anxiety induced in students by writing assignments. The findings were consistent with what has been described by many writers, from hypergraphic patients to Joyce Carol Oates, who said, "I have forced myself to begin writing when I've been utterly exhausted, when I've felt my soul as thin as a playing card . . . and somehow the activity of writing changes everything." Ernest Hemingway saw Oates's half-full glass as half empty: "When I don't write, I feel like shit." Some writers, such as the poet Tina Kelley, describe a physical sensation of unease or restlessness that torments them if they haven't written for a few days. For others, it is a sort of headache, a stuffy, swollen brain. Milton described feeling like a cow that needs to be milked. For many, there is the primal conviction that they should not do anything but write — because it is their vocation, in a nearly religious sense. Writing is what they are meant to do, and the headaches and the restlessness are their body's rebellion when it is kept from fulfilling its destiny.

Brand's studies did show some writing-induced anxiety, but it was outweighed by the pleasure or sense of relief the subjects had while writing. It is perhaps not a surprise that the anxiety increased with the amount of education the subject had; it was highest among professional writers. In more naive subjects, writing satisfied something. The positive effect of writing was stronger, the more personal the writing.

Being a physician biases me, of course, toward the theory that a principal role of language and of writing is to express need. Most of my patients are suffering, and they use their words to try to get me to help them. But the idea that art arises from suffering is not just the province of doctors with literary pretensions. "What is a poet?" asked Søren Kierkegaard. "A poet is an unhappy being whose heart is torn

Figure 8. A self-portrait by Frida Kahlo, drawn after a miscarriage (1932). Longing drives art. The arm that holds a palette is overseen by a weeping moon, reminiscent of Sylvia Plath's cyclic *Ariel* imagery. The blood of Kahlo and her fetus fertilizes the growth of strange new creatures, half plant, half organ.

by secret sufferings, but whose lips are so strangely formed that when the sighs and cries escape them, they sound like beautiful music. . . . And men crowd around the poet and say to him: 'Sing for us soon again'; that is as much to say: 'May new sufferings torment your soul, but may your lips be so formed as before; for the cries would only frighten us, but the music is delicious.'" Or consider Gide, in his retelling of Philoctetes, the Greek tragedy of a man exiled because of an incurable wound: "I have learned to express myself better, now that I am no longer with men — and I took to telling the story of my sufferings, and if the phrase were very beautiful I was so much consoled, I even sometimes forgot my sadness in uttering it."

My theories about art, language, and pain are shaped more by getting hit by a truck than by being a doctor. (Admittedly there aren't many truck collision–based art theories, but there is at least one other: Stephen King's book *On Writing* tells how being struck by a van gave him his first episode of writer's block.) In my case, a truck hit me when I was bicycling to daycare to pick up a sick daughter. My twins were then one year old. The truck did something to my leg that has the graphic name of "degloving injury." (Imagine peeling off a rubber glove.) I lay on the ground and screamed. Later, a friend asked how long I had to lie there — she had once been injured and people had just stepped over her as she was stretched out on the sidewalk. With me, people came running and stood over me, dialing madly on their little cell phones. The difference, I think, was the loudness of my screams. Did you ever have the dream in which you try to scream and nothing comes out? It was a relief to find out that in real life I could make a great deal of noise. I didn't mean to scream; the sound just arrived. When the ambulance came, my screams stopped spontaneously. They were vocalizations that, like the distress calls of primates, had done their job.

In the emergency room at the hospital where I work, I became very chatty because talking distracted me from my pain. I talked until my jaw hurt. I talked to anyone, even the anxious premedical volunteers who sit around waiting for something to happen that they can put in their medical school application essay. I found that it helped my pain more to talk to someone who was emotionally important to me, such as my husband or my chairman, than just to some orthopedist or medical student.

After surgery, I was in my room; it was two in the morning and my leg hurt and there was no one left to talk to. I started to write and didn't stop for three days. Whenever I paused for a minute, the pain surged up again. As a painkiller, writing didn't work as well as talking, but I could do it without waking the other patient in the room, a lovely French woman as thin as parchment who was dying of pancreatic cancer. My writing was interspersed with injections of opiates, which temporarily decreased my desire to write — although the vivid reveries they induced (none of which I am going to repeat here) gave me even more to write about the next time the pain came back. Their effects made me think about the opiate-addicted writers such as Coleridge and de Quincey. In fact, my writing was laced with feverish theories about opiates and communication and pain. One of them still seems to me worth repeating.

The experience of human contact is a great joy. In Walt Whitman's description,

> I have perceiv'd that to be with those I like is enough,
> To stop in company with the rest at evening is enough,
> To be surrounded by beautiful, curious, breathing, laughing
>   flesh is enough, . . .
>
> I do not ask any more delight, I swim in it as in a sea.
> There is *something* in staying close to men and women and
>   looking on them,
> And in the contact and odor of them, that pleases the soul well,
>
> All things please the soul, but these please the soul well.

This transcendent phenomenon is also a brain state, probably caused largely by opiate neurotransmitters. And bereavement, when

the social interaction is taken away, is a brain state of opiate deple-
tion. It has many of the same physical symptoms as morphine withdrawal, including tearful eyes, restlessness, and insomnia.

A few scientists studied the neurochemistry of bereavement in unpleasant experiments in which they took a baby animal away from its
mother and then counted the number of whimpers as an index of the
infant's grief. The researchers then tried various drugs to treat the bereavement. Alcohol, a traditional favorite of humans in mourning,
turned out to be fairly ineffective. It didn't calm the whimpering until the baby animal was nearly asleep. The results were similarly dis-
mal for tranquilizers such as diazepam (Valium). But very low doses
of opiates were startlingly effective. They quickly eased the infant's
whimpering and let it resume its normal activities. Opiates also take
the place of social interaction in normal unbereaved animals and
make them less interested in contact with others. And drugs that
block endogenous opiates make both animals and humans more so-
ciable.

The opiate theory of social bonding explains why talking to others
helped my pain: as I was talking, presumably my brain was releasing
endogenous opiates that made me feel better. Writing was a stand-in
for talking — not as good, but a passable substitute when I was alone.
The opiate hypothesis also shows one reason that opiates temporarily
decreased my drive to write — and presumably that of Coleridge and
de Quincey. The theory explains why so much of literature is about
loss, why people write when they are in love and their lover is absent,
when someone they love dies.

Julia Kristeva has argued that one of language's first functions is to
help a child create a mental image of his mother, one that can soothe
him when she is absent. Opiate addicts from Coleridge to William S.
Burroughs describe how vividly their drug can bring back soothing
memories of the past — the "minutest incidents of childhood," in de
Quincey's words. (There is a trade-off, however: opiate addicts seem
to have trouble learning new memories.) Sometimes, in what the es-
sayist Nancy Mairs calls the literature of personal disaster, the person
the writer is mourning is herself, the person after a calamity mourn-

ing the loss of the person before. And sometimes, as in Proust, the writer is trying to re-create an entire world that has died.

Unfortunately, we all know from experience that literary imitations of people or worlds that we long for never release quite as much internal opiate as we would like. Writing took the edge off my pain, it didn't cure it. As Flaubert wrote, "No one, ever, can give the exact measure of his needs, his apprehensions, or his sorrows; and human speech is like a cracked cauldron on which we bang out tunes that make bears dance, when we want to move the stars to pity."

How does the literature of suffering interest anyone but the sufferer? Mel Brooks has argued that it doesn't: "Tragedy is if I cut my finger. Comedy is if you walk into an open sewer and die." Nonetheless, the problems of others do, sometimes, interest us — through empathy, through style, and through content that is only indirectly related to the pain that triggered the work. Thus Keats could write sonnets about beauty as he died of tuberculosis, and Vermeer could paint jewel-like domestic scenes after the horrors of the Thirty Years' War.

You may reasonably argue that such an emphasis on suffering in literature falsely downplays the joy of writing, and of reading. In response I invoke the ancient psychological and literary truth that suffering and joy are inseparable, the opposites not of each other but of blandness. Stephen King described the way happiness emerged from pain after his van accident:

> On some days that writing is a pretty grim slog. On others — more and more of them as my leg begins to heal and my mind reaccustoms itself to its old routine — I feel that buzz of happiness, that sense of having found the right words and put them in a line. It's like lifting off in an airplane; you're on the ground, on the ground, on the ground . . . and then you're up, riding on a magical cushion of air and prince of all you survey. That makes me happy, because it's what I was made to do.

There are places where literature and science come to similar conclusions, and the difficulty of separating joy and suffering may be one of them. Evidence mounts that joy from widely different causes activates the same brain systems, many of them the opiate systems; different causes of suffering also seem to activate a unified pain pathway. The two pathways seem to have a push-pull relationship; chemicals such as morphine that potentiate the opiate system increase pleasure, chemicals such as naloxone that hinder the opiate system increase pain. Yet the pleasure and pain systems do not entirely cancel each other out, supporting our introspective sense that it may not be possible to feel great joy without recently having felt great pain (the "food tastes better when you're hungry" school of aesthetics). Far more important, a life chosen to maximize joy may be very different from one chosen to minimize pain.

And joy is inextricably intertwined with creative inspiration. Joy can even give a sense of being inspired when no real inspiration exists. Today, for instance, I was unreasonably happy. Happiness fizzed on and off behind my solar plexus; it ticked my stomach and made me smile despite myself, although it was unrelated to the terribly serious meeting to which I was supposed to be paying attention. The tickle felt significant. Every time it occurred I would stop and listen to it. Perhaps it was a vibration I was picking up from the ether. I felt an idea was coming. Perhaps I was too happy; perhaps it was mania. Perhaps I should have described myself as a psychiatrist would: "The patient was inappropriately giddy during a meeting." Perhaps I should step back even farther from normal discourse and describe myself as a neurologist would: "An episodic sense of visceral stimulation was experienced by the patient, similar to that in some seizure auras. Afterward the left corner of the patient's mouth would be drawn upward in a stereotypic manner." (Why is scientific and medical writing always in the passive voice? Is it because science is the mouthpiece of determinism, and literature the last holdout of free will?)

The idea never came — or perhaps it did; it was these paragraphs. Here is the thing. I think there was actually something odd and neuropsychiatric about my happiness. It really felt as if the corner of my mouth was being pulled up without my conscious control. But I was still the one who pulled it up, and what I felt was still an important human emotion — even more important for being spontaneous, a gift from somewhere. And the same is true of "rational" happiness too, and of all emotions.

What Writers Desire

Chapter 1 identified a number of neurological, perhaps "patholog-ical," conditions that can produce driven creative writing. In this chapter I am trying to present creative writing as something healthy, arising from the useful evolutionary drive to communicate needs. Is it possible for both explanations to be true? Of course. That paradox is one of the things that pains the caring parents of a college student who says that he is no longer going to apply to law school because he wants to become a poet. "Don't get us wrong; we love literature," they say to their friends. "And of course we want him to express himself — that's important. But poets are all so unhappy. And it's a stage kids go through, like experimenting with drugs. Ten years from now he'll wish he had a real job." (A writer I know, whose parents objected strongly when both their sons became writers, pointed out drily that upper-middle-class parents who work hard to expose their children to the arts shouldn't be surprised when some of them end up wanting to be artists.) Art as recreation, art as therapy, art as sign of illness, art as highest proof of health — these are concepts that battle, if uncon-sciously, in the minds of everyone from an MFA student's parents to the most sophisticated art critic.

The doctrine of literature as cry of need is not very restrictive; people need so much. What do writers themselves say about why they write? It sometimes seems that nearly all of them have written an es-say on the subject, ranging from George Orwell's "Why I Write," to Joan Didion's "Why I Write," to Ben Jonson's "Why I Write Not of Love" (1616), to such Web sites as "Why I Write Romances About Wrestlers" and "Why I Write About Web Services." The kaleidoscope of reasons why writers think they write remains hard to fit into any one theory, although all fit the needs theory of self-expression to some extent. At the end of this chapter, though, I will try to show that most of their reasons have another common factor as well.

Writers are often explicitly motivated by the desire for fame and money. Evolutionary psychologists see fame as an aspect of position in the dominance hierarchy, that structure crucial to the life of all primates. In such a scheme, status is valuable because it makes material resources available. As Chekhov put it: "The main thing is — father and mother must eat. Write." There are many better ways than writing to gain status and autonomy, but for a certain sort of person (introverted, hyperlexic) it may be the best shot. Orwell called the drive for status "sheer egoism," and argued that it was the fundamental incentive for writing. He did, however, concede that three other factors entered in: aesthetic enthusiasm (the desire to propagate beauty), the historical impulse (the drive to discern true facts and store them for the use of posterity), and the political impulse (the desire to push the world in a particular direction).

In fact, the more you look, the more reasons writers give for being writers. Many writers say that they became writers because they simply could not do anything else. Nathaniel Hawthorne wrote: "I don't want to be a doctor, and live by men's diseases; nor a minister to live by their sins; nor a lawyer to live by their quarrels. So I don't see there's anything left for me but to be an author." T. S. Eliot, who had been a boxer in college, noted: "I was too slow a mover. It was much easier to be a poet." And George Bernard Shaw pointed out a practical advantage of the writing life that still largely holds true: "My main reason for adopting literature as a profession was that, as the author is never seen by his clients, he need not dress respectably."

A desire for self-transformation often motivates writers. In some cases it is to exorcise a neurosis — William Faulkner argued that "an artist is a creature driven by demons. . . . He has a dream. It anguishes himself so much he must get rid of it." Writing, like psychotherapy, is often the modern, guilt-free replacement for confession, in which a memoirist writes the way a snake sheds its skin, to put a former self behind him. Franz Kafka described this paradoxical way in which putting something down in writing can be putting it out of your mind: "I write in order to shut my eyes." Coleridge's "Rime of the Ancient Mariner" exemplifies the more old-fashioned, guilt-ridden urge to confess and be shriven:

> Forthwith this frame of mine was wrench'd
> With a woful agony,
> Which forced me to begin my tale;
> And then it left me free.

If I understood the desire to confess, it would have saved me a great deal of unhappiness. After I was discharged from my psychiatric hospitalization, I had the feeling, common after such experiences, of being no longer quite human. Although I had long before spoken with my job supervisors, who assured me that my work was fine, I nonetheless developed a fear that everyone was being too easy on me. The only way to relieve my fear, for a short time at least, was to tell someone new about my diagnosis. Then I could be reassured when that person looked surprised and said, "Really? You've always seemed perfectly normal to me."

That success, however, would make me doubt what had happened to me. If everyone I worked with thought I had been normal, then probably I hadn't been depressed but merely tired and malingering. Because that possibility horrified me too, I would find a new listener and tell my tale in a more heightened manner; that person would back away and look uncomfortable, and I would have to find yet another listener to whom I could tell the story in a more boring way, and the process would begin again. The more I tried to confess, the more confused I got. After I ran out of people to tell, I turned to writing down alternate views of what was true, and the next thing I knew I was writing a book. Although I was no longer sure I could tell an accurate story, at least I could tell one that was consistent, that would save me from the vortex of possibilities. Creating consistency is one thing writing is good for, and one reason it is dangerous.

Even more fruitless than my desire to admit my mental illness was my desire to confess to my role in the deaths of my first children. Feeling responsible for unavoidable death is a common delusion — even my obstetrician, who was blameless and had worked overtime to try to save the twins, clearly had an unnecessary sense of guilt. I knew the medical decisions I made had contributed to their deaths only to a very minor extent. But that sort of rational argument was irrelevant to me. My body had not kept my children alive. I began to think that there was not much difference between me and Andrea Yates, the woman who at about that time had killed all five of her children during a postpartum psychotic depression. What made my desire to confess my feelings of guilt even more painful was that I had to keep from doing so. When I spoke out, people were horrified; they dismissed what I was saying almost angrily. And when they didn't? No one could absolve me of such a crime except God, and I was an atheist. So I wrote to keep from speaking.

Why, why do I have to tell of these things, especially here? They will only upset people. Perhaps I am not seeking aid, but to hurt myself with these disclosures. As for you, the audience, I know you cannot help me with my dead children, or with my guilt. Not even your sympathy would do much. An audience is a shadowy thing; the hands of ghosts cannot soothe.

Sometimes I think of Midas, who felt his secret would rip him in half unless he told someone. He did not dare to tell a human about his ass's ears, so he dug a hole and whispered his secret into the ground. But reeds grew there, and their whispering spread his secret to the world. Reeds, papyrus, the first paper. We write instead of speak when we are ashamed to look our audience in the eye.

(I was pleased with my Midas metaphor until I remembered that it was his barber who had whispered to the reeds. Even Midas, partly an ass, could keep his mouth shut.)

Writers sometimes write for an even odder reason than to confess: they write to prove that they or the rest of the world is real. For Anne Lamott, "the . . . the thrill of seeing oneself in print . . . provides some sort of primal verification: you are in print; therefore you exist.

Who knows what this urge is all about, to appear somewhere outside yourself, instead of feeling stuck inside your muddled but strobo-scopic mind, peering out like a little undersea animal — a spiny blenny, for instance — from inside your tiny cave?" In some cases, it may be a desire for the poet's world to live forever, as in Shakespeare's sonnets:

> Nor shall Death brag thou wand'rest in his shade
> When in eternal lines to time thou grow'st.
>> So long as men can breathe or eyes can see,
>> So long lives this, and this gives life to thee.

Narrating the world into existence can reflect our need for contact with what psychoanalysts chillingly call the Object, and the rest of us call other people. "Over the years I've come to realize that my greatest fear in life is a dread of a certain kind of solitude, of abandonment," wrote Francine du Plessix Gray. "And I've come to know that by writ-ing I'm creating a presence which fills that solitude, which takes the place of some ideal Other." The novelist Milan Kundera described the same situation more bleakly. In the process, he coined the useful term "graphomania":

> The reason we write books is that our kids don't give a damn. We turn to an anonymous world because our wife stops up her ears when we talk to her. . . . Let us define our terms. A woman who writes her lover four let-ters a day is not a graphomaniac, she is simply a woman in love. But my friend who xeroxes his love letters so he can publish them someday — my friend is a graphomaniac. Graphomania is not a desire to write let-ters, diaries, or family chronicles (to write for oneself or one's immedi-ate family); it is a desire to write books (to have a public of unknown readers).

Graphomania, the desire to be published, thus exists in partial dis-tinction from hypergraphia, which is merely an excessive desire to write. Kundera argued that graphomania arises from emotional isola-tion and ennui, and takes on the proportions of a mass epidemic whenever a society develops to the point where it can provide three basic conditions:

1) A high enough degree of general well-being to enable people to devote their energies to useless activities;
2) An advanced state of social atomization and the resultant general feeling of the isolation of the individual;
3) A radical absence of significant social change in the internal development of the nation. (In this connection I find it symptomatic that in France, a country where nothing really happens, the percentage of writers is twenty-one times higher than in Israel.)

For Kundera, mass graphomania threatens the meaning of the written word because the resulting flood of words drowns out the chance for anyone to be heard. Yet he was writing in 1980, even before the tidal wave of the Internet. After Kundera's marvelous cynicism, it would perhaps be banal to be optimistic. In fact, though, the Web's flood has so far been surprisingly well channeled with powerful search engines (again, technology helping writing) and has successfully allowed isolated people to connect to one another. It is perhaps not the *existence* of Web diaries or blogs, but the fact that many other people read them that is the marvel.

How do writers hope words will bridge isolation? Simply by transferring facts to their readers? Sometimes at least the more sophisticated of them also try to communicate that which falls between the facts. "The role of the writer is not to say what we can all say," wrote Anaïs Nin, "but what we are unable to say." And the writer is often not only struggling to say it to others, but to herself. To quote E. M. Forster's well-known phrase, "How do I know what I think until I see what I say?"

The need for narrative, the need to place events in stories, shapes much of our writing and speech. Linking facts into cause-and-effect chains makes them easier for our brains to absorb, making them more memorable for readers and even for the writer. Creating narrative links gives a sense that there are causal chains that will allow us to predict and control events in the future, a sense that is not always true. My obstetrician felt responsible for my children's deaths; I thought they were my fault. A sense of guilt as a way of fleeing from randomness, or as a delusion of grandeur.

Narratives can provide spin for both the writer and the reader, as in the stories that some Serbians told to justify their country's actions — or that we tell to justify ours. Life stories, often touted as the basis for our sense of self, can also lock us into a self that is too rigid. Sometimes the goal of psychotherapy is not to help people make sense of their lives, but to help them make less sense of them — to break a few links in the narrative chain so that behavior can be more unpredictable and creative.

Some literary critics and therapists present narrative, in the sense of long causal chains, as a primary biological urge. I admit, despite my own obsession with narrative, to being a little suspicious of this largely unsubstantiated claim. Such critics and therapists tend to base their observations on reading and on patients from a narrow slice of socioeconomic and cultural backgrounds; outside that slice, people's needs for and use of explanations vary widely. It may be, for instance, that pat causal self-narratives are not so useful if your life has been as chaotic as a Cambodian refugee's.

Causal reasoning is also to some extent learned. Young children link ideas associatively rather than causally. ("Does your grandmother live nearby?" "Oh, no! She's very big.") When they ask their strings of "why" questions, they learn not only specific answers but more generally what are acceptable answers to "why" questions, what count as causal links. The modern narrative may have been an invention that caught on because it was useful. It is perhaps no coincidence that novels, with their tight plots and neat conclusions, arose at the same time as the scientific method and the steam engine.

I became a scientist, paradoxically, because of the seductiveness of literary narrative. When I read a novel, I lost myself in it; when I made up an elaborate story about why I was late for Girl Scouts, I wasn't sure whether it was true or not. (They soon kicked me out anyway; the facts — there was a brook nearby and I always arrived muddy up to the knees — were more coherent than any of the stories I told.) I hoped the narratives of science could make my grip on reality firmer.

Once I became hypergraphic, though, I started to wonder whether squeezing reality as tightly as science does deforms it too.

In the end, using writing to give cognitive meaning to events may parallel an equally deep human need, the need to give emotional meaning to an existence that is opaque. The universal desire to feel that life has some purpose is perhaps stronger in writers, whose occupation instills in them a mania for meaning — a desire, as Paul Valéry put it, "to erect a minor monument of language on the menacing shore of the ocean of gibberish." This noncognitive notion of meaning, a sense of emotional importance or ultimate goal, is independent of the more traditional semantic notion of meaning as definition or intellectual content. The emotional sense of meaning is what worries adolescents, and the mentally ill, late at night. Sometimes even normal folk worry, although the ability to suppress thinking about questions like the meaning of life could — arguably — be part of the definition of mental health.

Is there any scientific content to the notion of meaning in this noncognitive sense? After all, "What is the meaning of life?" was the question notoriously ridiculed by the logical positivists as being itself meaningless. At the risk of oversimplifying something subtle and significant, I propose that meaning in the sense of importance has a great deal to do with valence, the pleasure-displeasure, good-bad dichotomy that I argued earlier is the most basic aspect of emotion. This sense of meaning has its origins in the limbic system, as opposed to the linguistic meaning encoded primarily in the cerebral cortex's temporal lobe. Within the limbic system the amygdala, with its ability to label stimuli as good or bad, is especially important. The interaction between temporal lobe meaning and limbic meaning reflects what has been called the tension in language between the dictionary and the scream. Without the former, we would have no ability to communicate; without the latter, the need to express our needs, we would have no drive to communicate.

Limbic meaning includes as one aspect the psychological feeling of meaning. It is the feeling that is present when hearing speech that makes sense, a feeling uncomfortably absent when hearing a foreign language or nonsense. It is what is lacking in depressed patients who say that words have lost their meaning (even though they can still understand them semantically), or in blocked writers who watch their thoughts shrivel as they hit the paper. Conversely, when the feeling is intense it literally forces people to write, to communicate what is pressing to get out. Narrative not only ties events into a chain that makes cognitive sense, it is also an important way of creating a feeling of meaning. Goals, which are common answers to meaning-of-life questions ("to raise my children to be happy and strong," "to be part of something bigger than myself"), add a sense of meaningfulness in the same way.

Why some people find life meaningful and others do not is, of course, complicated. Some psychiatrists would argue that there is simply an imbalance in such people's limbic systems. People with a lack of interest in life that is easily helped by antidepressants may be in this category. In other people, perhaps the problem is that random events have disrupted their lives so that they can never assign clear value to events, no matter how many medicines they are on. Feeling that meaning exists may not be a more accurate position than feeling its absence. We know only that it is usually more pleasant.

Obviously, people write for reasons other than a desire to create meaning. They write to give tips on how to do a spinal tap or use a particular computer spreadsheet; they write for money, for the thrill of saying "I'm an author" to strangers at dinner parties, for all the reasons discussed above and more. But the sort of writing that is driven by the desire to make meaning — limbic meaning — is arguably the most closely related to making literature as opposed to merely making text.

Usually, cortical and limbic meaning are interdependent: facts affect our emotions, and our emotions affect not only our perception of the facts, but the facts themselves. The two aspects of meaning can come apart, though, not only in pathological circumstances, but in appreciating nonlinguistic art forms. The limbic sensation of meaning may be the feeling that makes music seem to be not words without meaning, but meaning without words.

Writers are often explicit that they are not writing to clarify the world of factual meaning. In his well-known passage describing negative capability, Keats argues that to try too hard for cognitive truth may be restrictive: "I had not a dispute but a disquisition with Dilke on various subjects: several things dove-tailed in my mind, and at once it struck me what quality went to form a Man of Achievement, especially in Literature, and which Shakespeare possessed so enormously — I mean Negative Capability, that is, when a man is capable of being in uncertainties, mysteries, doubts without any irritable reaching after fact and reason."

This equation of meaning with emotional rather than semantic content helps explain why writers are especially vulnerable to mood disorders. On the one hand, mild manic states, with their sense of a world suffused with meaning, trigger writing in an attempt to preserve or broadcast that meaning. They may also heighten the sharpness of the writer's sensations. On the other hand, melancholic depressions, with their drab meaninglessness, their absence of both joy and sorrow, trigger a search (after the sufferer's depression has resolved somewhat) for a framework of words to ward off the emptiness that had pressed in on all sides. Finally, in mixed states such as agitated depression, features of mania and depression do not cancel each other out to produce a normal state; instead, they add up to tormented states of frozen or unsatisfiable desire. Mixed states produce the most painful form of writer's block. Manic, depressed, and mixed states are related to states that all humans feel to some extent; they are merely exaggerated in creative writers, and perhaps especially in writers with mood disorders.

Reuniting language with screams and cries goes against the emphasis of traditional linguistics on language as semantics, as a way of making statements about truth. But the huge popularity of fiction, in which the majority of the "events" are not true, tells us that something more is going on with language than the symbolization of truth, at least truth narrowly defined. If chimpanzees use utterances for emotional expression, if toddlers are compulsive memoirists, it may be that these are merely the most primitive facets of language.

That is not a reason to neglect them, however. Their very primitiveness fits with what we feel about language and writing, that it is fundamental to our nature. Emotional meaning is deeper than cognitive meaning, both literarily and literally, anatomically. In thinking about language we need to broaden our scope from mastering syntax and constructing tight paragraphs, to looking also at gains and losses of significance, at the afflictions of writers who write too much or hold back from writing, and at our primal desire for our words to mean something to someone else, somewhere.

7

Metaphor, the Inner Voice, and the Muse

Ordinary words convey only what we know already; it is from metaphor that we can best get hold of something fresh.

— Aristotle, *Rhetoric* 1410b, X, trans. W. Rhys Roberts

A novelist at work hears many voices in her head.

— Rebecca Goldstein

Me too the Muses forced to write verse.

— Virgil, *Eclogue*, ix.32, trans. Katharina Trede

Metaphor as Mediator Between Thought and Emotion

SO FAR, I have argued that genius truly is, in Edison's words, 99 percent perspiration or drive. Now at last, I turn to the last 1 percent, inspiration. What makes readers feel that an image, an interpretation, a theory is inspired? The two-part understanding of meaning presented in the last chapter, in which meaning has both a temporal lobe or semantic component and a limbic or emotional component, can help us understand this sensation of inspiration. It can also help us understand something about the nature of metaphor — and not coincidentally, since metaphoric thought probably has a great deal to do with the imaginative leaps that characterize inspiration.

Metaphor, broadly and prosaically defined as any use of a word for one thing to describe another thing, is nonetheless one of the most magical aspects of language. Yet metaphor's value has been controversial since Plato, who explicitly disapproved of it (despite using it constantly), and Aristotle, who praised it. The idea that metaphor is merely a rhetorical trick, a misleading figure of speech, was perhaps first proposed in Plato's notoriously antipoetical *Phaedrus*. But it was with the British empiricists, including Thomas Hobbes and John Locke, that antimetaphorical writing reached its apotheosis. The empiricist Samuel Parker, for instance, condemned metaphors as "meer products of Imagination, dress'd up (like Childrens babies) in a few spangled empty words. . . . Thus their wanton and luxuriant fancies climbing up into the Bed of Reason, do not only defile it by unchaste and illegitimate Embraces, but instead of real conceptions and notices of Things, impregnate the mind with nothing but Ayerie and Subventaneous Phantasmes." What a shamelessly juicy use of metaphor to attack metaphor, and what an intriguing word "Subventaneous," although it turns out to mean merely windy.

When we think of metaphor, most of us think of virtuosic literary examples such as this interchange from *A Midsummer Night's Dream,* when Hermia insults Helena: "Thou painted maypole!" and Helena replies, "Get you gone, you dwarf; you minimus, of hindr'ing knotgrass made; you bead, you acorn." But more prosaic forms of metaphor permeate human language. For instance, the metaphor "permeates." Even the word "metaphor" was originally a metaphor, meaning, in Greek, "transfer." One study found that English speakers produced an average of three thousand novel metaphors per week. A metaphor databank on the Internet tries to list the major classes of metaphors for mental phenomena (for example, under "mind parts as separate beings," a butler in a cereal ad says, "I can't deny that *part of me desires* frosting.") The database is very, very large. Even a short time browsing it will convince you that you can never rid your mind of metaphors, that nearly everything is a metaphor.

The lack of metaphor — or figures of speech, more broadly — may at first glance seem the cardinal stylistic difference between scientific and literary writing. But if metaphors are ubiquitous, those of us engaged in either genre, or in unhealthy hybrids of the two, may have to rethink what differentiates them. There is subject matter, but then some literature is about true events, some scientific articles are entirely false, and if Auden could write a poem on neuroanatomy called "Ode to the Diencephalon," anything is possible. There is the stylistic importance of logical argument and testability in science. Literature is often trying to prove something too, but characteristically convinces us by evocation of emotion and aesthetic response — limbic functions — along the lines of Keats's "Beauty is truth, truth beauty." (Keats, who had medical training — and, contrary to the received view of his dreaming through class, excelled in it — wrote poetry strongly influenced by medical theories of his day. But Keats was not, of course, interested in proposing testable hypotheses.)

Another characteristic that sets scientific prose apart from literary prose is that it is stylistically so bad. "Broken English," as Nobel laureate Sir Peter Medawar said, "is the universal language of science." Why is it, and is this inevitable? The question is of particular relevance to the neurosciences, which more and more are trying to provide descriptions of mental states formerly essayed only by poets. And it is, of course, of interest to the many poets and novelists who have grappled with the strangeness of being at once humans and collections of organs and DNA. My question is not quite the same as the one that C. P. Snow asked in his 1959 essay "The Two Cultures," which asked whether scientists and scholars in the humanities had lost the ability to understand one another. Nor is it the revised question that E. O. Wilson asks in *Consilience;* namely, whether science can help us understand problems traditionally thought to be the province of the humanities.

Rather, it is the question of why Wilson's popular writing engages us when his scientific writing — although also excellent — does not. Is it chiefly because we don't know enough about the final instar larvae of *O. longinoda,* or minor-to-major worker ratios in *Pheidole* species, to understand his scientific journal articles? No; a lack of scientific background is not the primary block to enjoying scientific prose. Even most scientists who are fluent in their discipline prefer (if secretly) to read novels or magazines. Scientific writing's rejection of style as a decorative scrim obscuring the truth not only breaks fundamental rules of human communication (such as "Don't be boring") but is itself a style that can speciously add the appearance of weight to arguments. The passive voice of much scientific writing both gives it a false objectivity and dehumanizes it by removing all the actors. It is never "We injected the patients," but rather "The patients were injected," as if, in the eventuality of a lawsuit, this would somehow protect the shadowy injectors.

The atomization of scientific writing, perhaps necessary in fields that have grown too large for any individual to comprehend, is excruciating even for scientists. It produces papers on topics so constrained and abstruse that their implications, if any, can only be traced through an extended network of associations — sometimes metaphorical — with many other papers. Before my postpartum break, my brain was calm enough to hold within it pieces of this glimmering network that W. V. Quine called the web of belief. I saw that my work in a small branch of a single field could support a theory that would help disprove another theory, which could eventually lead to drugs that could directly help living people, perhaps my patients. After I became excited and hypergraphic, I found the web a tangle that often distracted me from the real human beings who came to my clinic.

The final reason why scientific writing dehumanizes is of course its studied pretense of emotionlessness — the apparent absence of the limbic, the tyranny of the cortical. Yet Antonio Damasio's arguments that emotion is essential for decision making apply here. The choice to do any experiment is packed with value judgments. Should we bother to fight AIDS? Send someone to the moon? Before my postpartum break I saw the unnaturalness of scientific thought as beautiful, a way to escape the limitations of the messy brain not only by the discoveries that the brain generates, but through the way the very activity changes the brain's shape, like a dancer going *en point*. Now that my limbic system stands up for its rights more, I suppose the same image still applies, but part of me draws the opposite conclusion. Who would want to do that to her poor feet?

Of course, despite this antiscience rant, the moment I come up against someone who acts on emotion rather than evidence, I rant in the opposite way.

Scientific prose does not differ from literary prose by the absence of metaphor, but it does have a much higher frequency of a particularly codified and rigid type of metaphor: the scientific model. Metaphor and model differ primarily in the tightness of fit between the object and the item to which it is being compared. Thus, from a poetic metaphor like "Juliet is the sun," we conclude that her presence (metaphorically) warms Romeo, that he needs her to live, but we should go no further — not, for example, concluding that she is 96 million miles away from Romeo, or that she emits radiation that can cause DNA damage to Romeo's skin cells.

From a scientific model we need the ability to predict accurately the behavior of the object from our knowledge of the model. "Wave" is a metaphor in "a wave of emotion" but a model in "light waves." The metaphor-model continuum is fluid, however. When Newton first introduced the word "vibrations" to describe sound, his readers interpreted it as a metaphor, and a rather awkward one at that. Since then, because of its excellent predictive power, the metaphor has been used so often that it became first a model and finally an identity.

A model can also turn back into a metaphor when people become disillusioned with it. Thus we say that medical practice was formerly dictated by metaphor, as when in the eighteenth century the heart in fever was modeled as a boiling pot and bloodletting was prescribed to reduce its fuel. These days, when we say that in a fever the hypothalamus's thermostat is set too high, and that Tylenol turns the thermostat down, we are still making metaphors — they just work better. Although not always. The model of conception in which the sperm manfully approaches and then penetrates the passive egg hindered modern biologists for decades from acknowledging the egg's active role in this process.

Psychologists have long believed that metaphorical thinking — realizing similarities between disparate objects — underlies creativity in both artistic and scientific creation. Metaphor unites reason (because metaphor involves categorization and inference) and imagination (because metaphor requires a novel leap from one object to another). For creativity researcher Colin Martindale, creativity *is* metaphor formation:

> To create, then, involves the realization of an analogy between previously unassociated mental elements. On the verbal level, creativity involves production of novel statements of the form "A is like B" or statements involving novel modifiers for V. Hugo's image, "I climbed the bitter stairs" is more creative than, say, "I climbed the steep stairs." The only real difference at this level between poetry and science or technology concerns what — if anything — is concluded from such analogies. The poet writes a poem. The technologist builds a machine. The inspiration for McCormack's reaper was the idea that grain is like hair. Not being a poet, McCormack went on to reason that clippers cut hair and that, therefore, something like clippers could cut grain.

For scientists, a model's ability to predict a phenomenon is, nearly by definition, proof that they understand the phenomenon. Literature, on this account, tends to use metaphors to create a subjective feeling of understanding, and for readers of literature, there is sometimes not a clear difference between feeling you understand a phenomenon (Romeo's pain at Juliet's seeming death) and actually understanding it. Perhaps in literature there is actually no distinction? In the real world, however, the distinction is crucial — and is one reason why telling someone in mourning that "I know just how you feel" is unwise.

In practice, what I am calling the literary and scientific aspects of metaphor, like the limbic and cortical aspects of meaning, are not usually found in isolation. The typical scientific metaphor used to help us understand the age of the earth — that if the entire history of the earth fit in a day, humans would exist for less than the last second — does not add any predictive power to our understanding; it gives us a feeling of understanding that is primarily emotional. Similarly, we might use metaphor to make a model of Romeo's love for Juliet that is, at least within the world of the play, predictive of his individual actions toward her.

Thus, rather than splitting the predictive and subjective aspects of metaphor, I might say more accurately that metaphors are useful, perhaps even necessary, to unite the cognitive and emotional meaning of a proposition. The way the two are integrated has everything to do with the way our brains work. Metaphor's resonance comes from its ability to activate not only the cerebral cortex's cognitive and sensory networks, but also the limbic system's affective and motivational networks. That both systems are necessary for what we would call understanding, in science and in literature and in life, is clear from instances in which only one is engaged. Someone you love dies and you have trouble believing it has happened — this is not your cortex being slow, but your limbic system. Conversely, when a customs official berates you in a foreign language, your limbic system is perfectly engaged in his anger, although your cortical speech areas are spinning their wheels. And when a book describes waves crashing against a bulkhead as enraged, the writer is, in psychiatrist George Murray's words, adding limbic music to the cortical drone.

George Lakoff and Mark Johnson, among others, argue that metaphors are cognitively useful because they rephrase an abstract concept in more physical terms. This engages the cortex with its visual, auditory, tactile, and olfactory maps, and the limbic system with its emotional charge. The synesthetic metaphors discussed in Chapter 5 do so especially vividly. As we all know from trying to memorize facts in school, the more senses that are involved, the more fully the memory is encoded. Metaphors enliven a text and create a sense of understanding by an analogous mechanism. By giving abstract concepts tastes, colors, smells, and emotional resonance, metaphors fix them in our minds and make us feel we understand them.

Or should I say, *feel* we understand them — we should still somewhat mistrust these iridescent creatures that hold us in thrall. And metaphors can breed quickly, especially in the work of hypergraphics. Some aspiring writers use so many that they create the jangling sensory overload of being in Times Square on New Year's Eve. The excess metaphor problem recalls Murray Kempton's advice, "Don't try to kill them with every paragraph, because you might succeed."

If metaphors contribute to a sense of understanding by increasing the number of brain regions active in processing an idea, we can explain phenomena that the traditional theories cannot. The common theory mentioned above, that metaphors take concepts and express them in more physical or familiar terms, does not fit many literary metaphors in which the comparison is less familiar than the original idea. In Yeats's poem "For Anne Gregory," for example:

> Never shall a young man,
> Thrown into despair
> By those great honey-colored
> Ramparts at your ear,
> Love you for yourself alone
> And not your yellow hair.

Surely we, and even Yeats — despite his living in a tower — are more familiar with blondes than with castle ramparts. The metaphor works not by making Gregory's hair more easily imagined, but by a vivid exaggeration of her sexual impregnability, and of the massy thickness of her hair. Thus it is complicating limbic and sensory overtones, not simplifying them.

What of the special case of metaphors for mental states? It is crucial for anyone interested in the neurosciences, and also for clinicians who want to maximize the relief their patients get through unburdening themselves. Why does it help someone in an extreme emotional state to find a vivid metaphor for what he or she is feeling? One reason is clearly the limbic drive to communicate our pain to others who might be able to help us. We choose metaphors to engage the listener's limbic system more strongly than nonfigurative language would.

Some deserving people, though, are incapable of telling an engaging story about their suffering. Often, these people are also alexithymic. Alexithymia, literally the inability to read one's own emotions or the loss of words for one's feelings, was first discussed in Chapter 2 as being linked to low creativity. Alexithymia is an interesting concept, at once useful and personally threatening. We can all think of other people who don't understand their emotions, but surely that is never true of *us*. The concept of alexithymia brings up unpleasant memories of others explaining us to ourselves, the primal case being a parent saying, "You're not angry, dear, you're just tired." To be told that we don't know how we feel offends our sense of identity, of having privileged access to our own mental states. It would seem that if we have just experienced something, then we must know how it feels.

Nonetheless, alexithymia is very common. It is perhaps most frequent in cases where a person blurs the distinction between physical and mental pain or fatigue. Psychiatric sophistication is not always protection. I know of one thoughtful man, a psychotherapist from Europe whose doctors were investigating his severe weight loss for everything from cancer to worms. It was only when his mentor visited and pointed out how miserable he was in his new job, that he moved back to his former country and began to recover.

Biological psychiatrists have proposed that alexithymia is an inadequacy of the limbic system, because monitoring internal states is preeminently a limbic function. Psychoanalysts would say, equally usefully, that the sufferer represses conscious — linguistic — access to his or her suffering. What is left is often only the physical aspects of a mood: headache, back pain, fatigue, weight loss, constipation, heart palpitations, increased susceptibility to infections.

Should we think of the alexithymic's physical complaint as a metaphor for his mental anguish? Alexithymics complaining of these physical symptoms are not hypochondriacs — their symptoms are real because conditions such as depression are diseases that affect the rest of body as well as the brain. It is simply that the symptoms of alexithymics respond to treatments such as therapy and antidepressants better than they respond to migraine drugs, back surgery, and the other interventions to which they are often, unfortunately, subjected. At the same time, doctors should admit they are often guilty of a sort of reverse alexithymia, attributing pain to depression simply because the pain does not respond to the treatment the doctor thinks should work.

Perhaps one way of understanding the possibility of alexithymia in ourselves is to realize that "I know how it feels" is not the same thing as "I can describe what it feels like." The simile or latent metaphor in the latter statement points to our need to say how a mental state relates to other mental states, both in ourselves and in others. Thus reading someone else's description of a state like ours can help intensely, because it translates a direct sensation into words that have links to other mental phenomena. A depressed patient once described to me what a relief it was simply to read the sentence "The world looked as if it were at the wrong end of a telescope." Even a Latinate medical label for a mental state can sometimes be a comfort. So the patient knows it is not "all in his head." So he knows others have suffered in the same way.

I described in Chapter 5 the evidence that metaphor requires an intact temporal lobe. What if excessive metaphor is one of the processes that goes wrong in delusions? Metaphor lies on a continuum between fact and delusion, and exactly where it lies is crucial. Simile becomes metaphor, the "as if" disappears; "I suffer like Jesus" becomes "I am Jesus." Other slides into the delusional are less obvious: "'I shall behave, for my own gain, toward that person over there *as if* she were less human, less real, than I am' is rapidly shortened to 'That person *is like* an object,' and again to 'That person *is* an object.'"

During my postpartum hypergraphia, metaphors ruled. Not quite delusions, not quite hallucinations, but with the flavor of both, they illuminated their subjects so brightly that the rest of the world was thrown into shadow. I saw a truck with construction equipment on it: a huge pitted excavator, its jaws dripping dirt. Suddenly, it appeared animate. I knew it was not alive, but — limbic music having been added to its cortical drone — it was as interesting as if it were the living plesiosaur it resembled. For the next few days excavators entranced me. I stopped to ask questions at construction sites and browsed Web sites about them (most turned out to be aimed at six-year-old boys). Even now, when I pass an excavator, I am captivated. Although I try to convince myself that excavators are an unwholesome fetish, that I should be more interested in preparing my taxes, I cannot. I think you should be amazed by excavators too.

During that period, vivid images began to swarm around my head like bees. Rooftops reminded me of Psalm 121: "I will lift up mine eyes unto the hills." My psychiatrist's yellow blanket was as warm as the sun; conversely, the actual sun penetrated me like x-rays. Were the images metaphors or hallucinations? They distracted and tormented me. Metaphor as illness, to misquote Susan Sontag. Yet when medications managed to rid me of them, the world became so dead that my psychiatrist and I lowered the doses until I could have at least some of my tyrannical metaphors back. I am very grateful for her skill in doing this — and for her understanding, rare among physicians, that there are sometimes worse things than being ill.

Later, when I was hospitalized for depression, the admitting resident asked me a rote question about my self-image, and I described how my hands seemed alien, how they looked like leather claws, but how I knew this was a fancy; none of it actually real. I told him how I had once found excavators unnaturally beautiful, alive. Here is another place where the limbic, primitive, tortured desire to communicate only caused problems. The admitting resident was not interested — perhaps understandably? — in the nice distinctions I was making between my metaphor-riddled state and what I considered true hallucinations and delusion. He wrote "psychotic" on the intake form and put me on a locked ward.

Perhaps he was right; perhaps it was a distinction without a difference to say that I was speaking metaphorically, not psychotically. Perhaps any sane person would have had the sense to keep quiet in such a situation. On the other hand, it may just have been that twenty-something male residents are not particularly aware of what back-to-back twin pregnancies can do to your skin. Now that I am recovered from my depression, my hands still look like leather claws; I am just more resigned to the fact.

Sometimes I think the hospital psychiatrist judged my thoughts too strictly because I was a physician. If doctors' thoughts are not perfectly linear, they need — what else? — medicine. Metaphors and heightened imagery are permissible only for poets. Before my post-partum break I believed that too, and even now I miss the days when I had the kind of faith in the scientific method that a nun has in her vows. But now my skull is more permeable to metaphors than it was before. That makes it easier for me to see that, although science is still powerful, it is not always strong enough to keep from being misdirected by metaphor — and also by lack of metaphor, the inability to jump to something new. And now I know there is something the scientific method is missing — something I can no longer do without. The deliberate bloodlessness of scientific writing now seems less a necessary imperfection in the search for objectivity than a crime against humanity.

At other times, I wonder whether the psychiatrist was right to hospitalize a doctor who had gone over to the dark side, who had stopped taking her medicines because she thought her illness was less of a torture than the treatment, maybe even than health. Perhaps that is what delusion feels like; perhaps my belief then that my metaphors were important was psychotic. If so, it is psychotic today, too. Although the lines that used to appear to meet at right angles in my head — science and literature, mind and body, health and disease, creativity and psychosis, truth and falsehood — are now notably wavy, when I press other people, the lines become wavy for them too.

The only way we know we are not delusional, of course, is to see if other people approve of our thoughts. How melancholy. In some ways I liked it better when metaphors were supreme, when truths were self-evident and other people's approval was only dimly relevant. If a cloud was threatening or an idea important, I could see it vibrate with meaning; I did not have to look over my shoulder to see if anyone else was impressed.

Psychotics tend to share this indifference to public opinion with a rather different group, visionaries. On occasion, they share another, more peculiar characteristic: the belief that ideas are being put into their minds or dictated to them by another being. In psychotics, psychiatrists call this thought insertion or auditory hallucination. Artists call it the muse.

The Muse and the Inner Voice

The notion of the muse has been attacked for slowing down scientific research on the creative process. Indeed, outside of New Age spirituality, almost no one takes the poor muse seriously anymore. A few psychologists, however, are beginning to study the mental sensation of visitation by the muse. The muse is more than a poetic device. Their work suggests that personifying inspiration as an external being is an attempt to say something about what inspiration actually feels like, about the way it seems to come from the outside just as the air you breathe does during respiratory inspiration.

Although the nine Greek Muses are of only historical interest, it is hard to resist naming them anyway. Over the centuries they have sometimes traded jobs, but the current standard is that Calliope is the epic Muse; Clio, the Muse of history; Erato, of love poetry; Euterpe, of lyric poetry; Melpomene, of tragedy; Polyhymnia, of sacred poetry; Terpsichore, of choral song and dance; Thalia, of comedy and idyllic poetry; and (out in left field) Urania, of astronomy. Once in a while a reference to the Tenth Muse shows up, sometimes as the deity responsible for some disreputable new genre — Web pages, the talk show. Although the Muses are described as virgins, they somehow managed to become the mothers of several sons, most famously Orpheus.

Widely different writers have invoked the muse or other independent inspirational being in a way that seems to be more than convention or figure of speech. While the girl in a white gown is still a popular model, the more important features are the otherness of the being and its independence of authorial control. Jean Cocteau's film *Orphée,* for instance, has a haunting image of a contemporary Orpheus who neglects his wife to return night after night to his car, where his muse, his car radio, transmits fragments of poetry. Accounts of the muse's influence are matched by complaints of its fickleness. An example is Donald Justice's poem "The Telephone Number of the Muse":

> I call her up sometimes, long distance now.
> And she still knows my voice, but I can hear,
> Behind the music of her phonograph,
> The laughter of the young men with their keys.
> I have the number written down somewhere.

Such personification is on a continuum with accounts in which there is simply a force rather than a being. "A man cannot say, 'I will compose poetry,'" said Shelley. "The greatest poet even cannot say it; for the mind in creation is as a fading coal, which some invisible influence, like an inconstant wind, awakens to transitory brightness . . . and the conscious portions of our natures are unprophetic either of its approach or its departure." The phenomenon of feeling an external presence is not restricted to poets or great writers, but exists in the general population as well. It has even been the subject of a scientific study, one which provided data that those who are most likely to receive a sense of meaningfulness from reading or writing are also the most likely to report a felt muse-like presence.

The experience of being inspired by the muse is not restricted to literature. Here is the painter Henri Matisse, describing what happened when, after having to take a leave of absence from his occupation in the legal profession, he took up painting as a hobby: "I had become possessed by painting and could not abstain. When I started to paint, I felt transported to a kind of paradise. . . . Something drove me, I do not know what, a force, something alien to my normal life as a man." Mozart reportedly wrote down symphonies as quickly as if he were listening to them and transcribing. Nor is the idea of the muse especially Western. The Indian mathematical genius Srinivasa Ramanujan said that his equations were whispered to him by the Goddess Namagiri.

Some professional writers are firm that they have never been visited by the palest shadow of the muse. They may simply be trying to emphasize the importance of hard work, and warning of the danger of relying on gifts from above. Some writers, though, may truly write without ever getting lost in their work, without ever feeling as if it just flows out of them, let alone flows into them from an external source. Certainly most of them are writing for some reason other than the pleasure of writing. The psychologist Mihaly Csikszentmihalyi, known for his work on peak experiences and creativity, argues that true happiness in work almost always involves such a feeling of flow. If writers who deny the importance of such states in their writing prefer to write that way, that is of course their choice. It is my proposition, however, that such sensations of flow or inspiration or the muse — however irrational they may be — are so highly motivating that they drive people to do their best work.

Why would artists attribute their best ideas to something outside themselves? The fact that so many do raises questions about the nature of our sense of agency and how we identify our inner voice. I will anxiously pass by the simplest and historically most popular hypothesis — namely, that the ideas really are coming from a being outside the artist. Yet the sense that the ideas are foreign underlies something crucial about the nature of creative ideas: they surprise and baffle even the creator. T. S. Eliot argued that "if the word 'inspiration' is to have any meaning, it must mean just this, that the speaker or writer is uttering something which he does not wholly understand — or which he may even misinterpret when the inspiration has departed from him." Inspiration is a submission to "the voice of language," wrote the poet Octavio Paz, "the voice of no one and of all. Whatever name we give this voice — inspiration, the unconscious, chance, accident, revelation — it is always the voice of *otherness*."

A common hypothesis to explain why creativity seems, as psychiatrists would put it, ego-alien is that creative ideas come from the unconscious and, when they erupt into consciousness, they surprise that surface dweller, the ego. The muse would thus be a personification of the unconsciousness. Ernst Kris and more recently Roy Shafer argued that believing the muse is an external force is useful for creators with novel or shocking ideas because it helps the creator deny responsibility for those ideas. Even writers whose ideas are not especially shocking but who are resisting social pressure to, say, be a doctor rather than a writer may be soothed by the belief that they are driven to their artistic destiny by a force beyond their control.

Since Freud, most psychiatrists have thought that being alienated from our unconscious makes us neurotic, but being too much in touch with our unconscious makes us psychotic. This book and many others have touched on the possible links between creativity and psychosis. I would rather focus here on the smaller question of just how mad it is to have a muse or, more broadly, to feel inspired. I would argue that these creative states are extreme variants of the inner voice, that constant monologue which fills us from when we first learn language as toddlers until we lose it in nursing homes and intensive care units.

When we write, we feel as if we are setting down what our inner voice is saying. Whether that is really what we are doing is in question — preliminary evidence tells us that the inner voice telling us to move occurs after a decision to move, and is just an epiphenomenon. Our experience of the inner voice is nonetheless a crucial aspect of our mental health. The inner voice may be absent in dreams or hypnotic states. But in general, everyone has an inner voice that lulls us with its familiar chatter or keeps us amused with daydreams on long plane rides. It can get more foreign simply by becoming more intense, as when it starts shrilly, going on about our failings, intrusively announcing that the plane might crash, or merely singing the same song over and over.

In more extreme states, the inner voice can seem even more alien to the listener. Many sane people have experienced this in times of stress. Freud himself (paragon of sanity?) wrote that "I remember having twice been in danger of my life, and each time the awareness of the danger occurred to me quite suddenly. On both occasions I felt 'this was the end,' and while otherwise my inner language proceeded with only indistinct sound images and slight lip movements, in these situations of danger I heard the words as if somebody was shouting them into my ear, and at the same time I saw them as if they were printed on a piece of paper floating in the air."

The spectrum of alienation from one's inner voice continues into psychosis. The most prominent theory of schizophrenic auditory hallucinations explains them as a more extreme process of such dissociation, as a misattributed inner voice rather than a sensory or perceptual illusion. When schizophrenics wear a simple device that prevents them from subvocalizing (mumbling under their breath) their hallucinations dramatically decrease. This may be because the device blocks them from the perception of their own inner voice, and thus from interpreting it as coming from outside themselves. The sense of one's voice being outside one is parallel to the sense of being outside one's body, induced by temporal lobe electrical stimulation, described in Chapter 1.

On this view, proposed by Julian Jaynes, Michael Persinger, and others, the experience of receiving instruction from the muse lies somewhere on the spectrum ranging from the normal inner voice to the completely ego-alien voices in auditory hallucinations and, perhaps, religious experience. I am certainly not implying that an artist who feels he or she has been visited by the muse is merely hallucinating. Rather, all these phenomena have at least some similarities that may help us understand them.

Nonetheless, the similarities do make this spectrum of relations to one's inner voice blurred. For instance, at the start of my hypergraphia, my inner voice became unusually entrancing and writing was almost an effortless process of taking down dictation. As my illness progressed, however, my voice was more clamorous. It gave a great deal of advice. "Why can't you concentrate?" it would shout, disrupting my concentration. "You're not ill, you're making it up." And "You can do anything you want, so why don't you?" It got louder, and suggested (rather unselfishly) that if I had my brain surgically removed, I could rid myself of its clamor.

Did my inner voice cross the line into psychosis? Most of my sane friends say they have had similar experiences, differing only in intensity. Most psychiatrists I saw, by contrast, recommended trying a neuroleptic, a class of medications prescribed for delusions and excessive ruminations. It seemed like overkill, but it helped. The voice stopped yelling. Once my head was quiet, my writing returned, evidence that too strong an inner voice is not always useful for a writer. Perhaps the neuroleptic worked by bringing the voice back into a range where I could listen to it. At the same time, I soon learned that staying on the neuroleptic was not good for my writing either; it flattened me out so that my inner voice had nothing to say. (A relevant Cajun proverb says: "If you ain't talking to yourself, you talking to the wrong people.")

Neuroleptics like the one I tried block the effects of dopamine in the brain. Dopamine may be a major part of the neurochemistry of the inner voice, for drugs that block dopamine tend to decrease its intensity, whereas drugs that increase dopamine's action can increase its intensity. These outcomes occur more strongly in susceptible people, such as those with mental illness. Dopamine agents have less effect on normal people, perhaps because normal brains have powerful homeostatic mechanisms that can fight the drugs and keep dopamine levels constant.

I wouldn't argue, however, that we should aim for some happy medium in our relationship with the inner voice. The truth is more complicated. The days when I was most ill were usually terrible writing days, but they were also the days when I had what seemed my best ideas — even if the ideas had later to be reworked on more rational, editorially minded days. Often the productive writing days were during transitions between moods, not during stable moods. The genesis of this book, for instance, occurred during one of my most exaggerated transitions. The morning bristled with a threatening significance. The way a crow flapped its wings as it rose heavily off the ground was a semaphore signaling something just past my understanding. I couldn't shake the feeling that some ominous question pressed on the world.

Later, as I bicycled back from my lab, life began to invert. The patterns that had seemed ominous now reflected the secret harmony of the universe, and I was filled with happiness. Suddenly, by the Charles River Dam, the phrase "the opposite of writer's block" came into my head. I was immediately convinced that I had to write a book about hypergraphia. The words of my revelation, which must sound comically anticlimactic, seemed to me as if they came from some higher power. "As if" — even at the time, I knew they did not. Or my cortex knew it. Some limbic force still believes it absolutely and has driven me to work on the manuscript nearly every day for the past four years, with a singlemindedness that seems abnormal even to me.

Many readers will be put off by this odd story. My friends say I am exaggerating the effects of a few minutes of nuttiness, that my book is the product of many different motivations. I know that ideas don't usually arrive via psychiatrically suspect revelations, because even mine usually don't. My illness taught me, however, that the sensation of inspiration can help us understand the milder, if still pleasurable, "aha!" reactions to problems such as finding the right adverb. The satisfactions that drive day-to-day writing can be better understood by looking at inspiration in its more exaggerated form.

Of course, on its own the sensation of inspiration is not enough. Many such sensations come to nothing and are soon forgotten, or perhaps suppressed out of embarrassment (like experiences of "love at first sight," which on second sight morph into disinterest). Perhaps the feeling of inspiration is merely a pleasure by which your brain lures you into working harder. From an evolutionary standpoint, it is not surprising that creative activity should be so intensely rewarding, given that the innovations that are its fruits have been so useful for human survival. But inspiration is still one of life's highest pleasures, even if also one of its most pragmatic. And it is wrapped up in the strange question, with practical importance for psychiatry and perhaps for the nature of religious experience, of why one's inner voice sometimes seems alien.

Before my illness I had never experienced this sort of internal-external presence, one which, for lack of a proper scientific word, I started calling the muse. I knew my "revelations" came from me; at the same time, they seemed too beautiful and true to come from me.

Ideas flooded me, so entrancing that the world around melted away. They sometimes choked or crushed me too. If I were objective, I would have to admit that the bad days outnumbered the good. But it would be wrong to be objective about it. The moments when everything made sense, if only to me, made the suffering irrelevant. And my writing at the height of my excitement, mostly cryptic sentence fragments, nonetheless contained nearly all the ideas that I later, more ploddingly, fleshed out into this book.

In severe psychotics, the inner voice can become so powerful that words can preposterously be made flesh and the boundaries between speech and speaker become fluid. Perhaps the most literate example lies in the writing of Daniel Paul Schreber, arguably the most famous schizophrenic ever (aside from a few dictators). His *Memoirs of My Nervous Illness* was the basis of a case history by Freud that shaped Freud's theories of paranoia, and a huge secondary literature has evolved. Schreber's paradoxically lucid description of his delusions show how language can become an almost physical force — in his case through compulsive writing, hallucinations of voices commanding him to recite, and a "bellowing miracle" that forced him to emit involuntary screams. (This last habit reminded me of both my own post-truck screams and young Figan with his bananas.)

Nonsensical sentence fragments and snatches of music tormented Schreber. Poignantly, he attempted to use the language of others to fight his intrusive voices: "Playing the piano and reading books and newspapers is — as far as the state of my head allows — my main defense, which makes even the most drawn-out voices finally perish; at night when this is not easily done or in day-time when the mind requires a change of occupation, I usually found committing poems to memory a successful remedy."

Schreber's battle is another instance of mental illness being like sanity, only much much more so. Many normal people get a tune stuck in their heads, a tune Germans call an *ohrwurm*, or "earworm." Many use the trick of singing another tune to block the intruder. When I took a neuroleptic, I was startled to find that as a side effect it rid my brain of *ohrwurmen*. It made me realize that when looked at from a neuropsychiatric perspective, such songs are being sung by an ego-alien voice, just as auditory hallucinations are. While hearing voices is probably a function of Wernicke's area in the left temporal lobe, hearing songs is likely to be a function of the analogous region in the right temporal lobe. Although verbal hallucinations are more dangerous than musical ones because the former can have suicidal or homicidal content, I suspect that some of the most annoyingly catchy top-ten tunes pose a health risk of their own.

The phenomenon of being alienated from one's inner voice may have even more implications for ancient literature, as Julian Jaynes has argued brilliantly, if eccentrically. Taking the Greek epics as his primary texts, he maintains that only recently did humans recognize their inner voices as coming from within, instead attributing them to gods. This approach may explain why ancient texts often baffle us with their protagonists' lack of a sense of personal agency. Seductions, rampages, suicides frequently occur without explanation or are ascribed to the influence of Athena or Zeus.

Jaynes offers a tentative neurological hypothesis for why the ancients' inner voices may have gone unrecognized as self. He proposes that this alienation arose from an imperfectly educated brain in which the left and right hemispheres did not operate in complete coordination. Thus linguistic or cognitive commands from the right hemisphere, specifically from its analogue of Wernicke's language area, may have been seen as alien by the dominant left hemisphere. (Despite the left dominance for language, the right hemisphere is not completely devoid of linguistic ability.) In times of stress, modern people, whose brains have been trained to recognize the origin of the inner voice, may revert to this primitive way of thinking, as Freud did in his "this was the end" quotation. For Jaynes, religious experience too may originate in ego-alien right hemisphere voices. Not all religious people reject this out of hand. Some have even argued that God may well speak to us through the right hemisphere.

Jaynes's hypothesis fits intriguingly with the proposals of other psychologists; for instance, with Melanie Klein's view that infants — and neurotic or stressed adults — cannot identify internal states such as rage or fear as their own, and therefore project them outward onto others. While Jaynes's hypothesis is by no means proven, it is supported by at least a sprinkling of experimental evidence. Schizophrenics, the chief modern examples of people with profoundly alien inner voices, do seem to have a defect in interhemispheric communication. And patients after split-brain surgery are profoundly alexithymic. Nor is such a deficit restricted to pathological situations. Children initially have hemispheres with relatively unsynchronized electrical activity. Only as they mature does the corpus callosum effectively coordinate activity between the left and right sides of the brain. Finally, interhemispheric communication may have a role in the sensation of an alien presence even in normal people.

Jaynes went on to propose that music and its wordful but still tonal and rhythmic relative, verse, first originated in the right hemisphere. The early literature of all languages was in poetry, not prose — and this poetry was probably chanted or sung. As civilization thickened and the brain's hemispheres became both more integrated and more specialized, he speculated that the right hemisphere progressively lost its power to generate poetry. To revive the original poetry-generating mechanism, ancient — and to some extent modern — poets have resorted to trance states, drugs, and other attempts to return the right hemisphere to its full linguistic power. For Jaynes, who like Harold Bloom sees verse as inexorably in decline, modern consciousness has been the death of poetry.

Although our modern brains can now usually localize the inner voice, it is still remarkable how often they don't. Consider the parallel between the psychotic Schreber and Anne Lamott in their use of language to keep their ego-alien voices at bay. I am not arguing that Lamott's imagery — the imaginary "vinegar-lipped Reader Lady," or, as Lamott describes later, "the dogs in their pen who will surely hurtle and snarl their way out if you ever stop writing" — is psychotic or even protopsychotic in any meaningful way. She knows that the

Reader Lady doesn't exist, and that makes all the difference. But the continuum on which both Lamott and Schreber and all of us live allows us to make some predictions. Taking a narrow, pharmacological perspective, we could forecast that Lamott would find (as she did) alcohol to be little help in quieting these voices, just as alcohol does little to help actual hallucinations. It would be interesting to know whether a neuroleptic, blocking the effects of dopamine, would have stifled her Reader Lady.

Let me ask one more time: what would make one's inner voice start to seem as if it were first involuntary and then alien? An analogy with a simpler system, voluntary movement, might help. Sometimes you move and feel that you intended to; at other times, as in a startle reaction or a tremor, you ("you") feel you did not intend to move. The difference may depend in part on which brain region initiated the movement, or on the ratio of activities in different regions. For instance, if electrical current is passed into your premotor cortex, important for planning movement, you will move your arm and feel as if you chose to move it. When current is passed through the motor cortex, an area of cortex more directly encoding the nuts and bolts of movement execution, your arm will move without your feeling that you chose to move it.

Initial evidence suggests that the sensation of volition or intention occurs after the movement is already planned. Therefore, the sensation may be an epiphenomenon without causal role in movement planning. I am not going to discuss what neuroscience has to say about whether free will exists. Instead, I'll focus on a more interesting and more practical question: the neuroscience of the *sensation* of free will. That sensation is critical for human happiness. For neurologists who study movement disorders, the sensation of free will varies with motor behaviors ranging from idly choosing whether to move your finger to the left or to the right, through being pressured by your advisor to write yet another thesis on the Bloomsbury group, through having a strong desire to scratch your poison ivy, through having Tourette's syndrome with an irresistible urge to curse, through hav-

ing a tremor that starts with no intention at all whenever you are under stress, through having a limb that flails constantly and so wildly
that you sometimes break it. How complicated a behavior is and how
voluntary it feels are not always well correlated.

The sensation of free will is especially relevant to psychiatric problems. It is diminished in procrastination, writer's block, and depression, and in psychotic auditory hallucinations where a person is com-
manded to do something by an apparently alien voice. In manic
patients it is greatly increased, and they feel they can do anything. The
sensation of free will often determines whether people seek medical
help for their behavior. I once consulted on a young woman who had
been admitted for mania. Medication quickly made her more rational
and suppressed all her symptoms except one, hypersexuality. For
her husband and physicians, that remaining symptom was reason
enough to keep her in the hospital. She argued, now very coherently,
that she wanted to be hypersexual, and that if NBA players could behave that way, why couldn't she?

A psychiatric *eminence grise* was called in to mediate. In the con-
ference room he leaned back with the look of pleasure that a certain
type of doctor has when faced with a really difficult case. "She reminds me of a woman I treated in the 1950s," he said, "but that
woman was tortured by her hypersexuality — perhaps because the
culture was so different then. White gloves that went above your el-
bows and so on. Eventually she had a frontal lobotomy to get rid of
it." (Lototomies were one of the few psychiatric treatments available
for anything in those days.) We gulped, and asked if the surgery had
helped. "It was such a shame; we never found out," he said. "She died
under the knife." As if not finding out were the shame.

My patient, faced with the choice between legal hearings and taking her medications, did what most patients do in that situation: she
took the pills long enough to get discharged and then decreased the
doses again. Perhaps the only unusual aspect of her story was how eloquently she defended her right to choose her illness. But her experience, and that of her more tragic predecessor, has stayed with me be-

cause of the way it illustrates how little distance there can be between feeling that your whole being chooses to do something, and feeling that you are compelled to do it.

Luckily, hypergraphia causes less pain to my family than hypersexuality would. It makes me wonder about the gray zone between desire and addiction, however. Some days I feel as if I choose to write, and it is my greatest pleasure. Some days the urge drags me, panicked, away from activities I think are more important. Addiction experts usually argue that a compulsive behavior isn't an addiction unless it is harmful, and that hypersexuality is undesirable because it is self-destructive — "Think of the risk if she goes to bars, she could get AIDS. . . ." But doctors, because of their occupation, are biased to see as immoral any behavior that endangers the health. Is the rest of the world so sure? Astronauts and tightrope walkers and soldiers feel differently. And Winston Churchill, on being told he would live twenty years longer if he did not drink, smoke, or eat so much, said "It would only seem twenty years longer."

Feeling powerless in the face of a compulsion is often distressing, but not always. Experiences of being forced by the muse to write, for instance, seem by most reports to be intensely pleasant, perhaps even because they are involuntary. It may be that in whatever way muse-driven writing is less willed, it gains the fluidity of unselfconscious tasks, or of flow states in Csikszentmihalyi's term. In general, involuntary experiences of inner voices are probably experienced as pleasant when they command you to do something you already want to do (for some people, write a book), but not when the command is something you don't want to do (for most people, kill yourself).

To argue by analogy from limb movement to speech, perhaps the inner voice only feels volitional when an appropriate balance exists between the activities of certain brain areas. When one area's activity changes too much, or is disorganized, it may create the impression that one's voice is not one's own. Where might that area be? Several lines of evidence point to the temporal lobe, for it contains the auditory cortex (the area of cortex most important for hearing) and

Wernicke's area (the region most important for speech comprehension). When brain surgeons electrically stimulate the temporal lobe near Wernicke's area, even people with no history of hallucinations report hearing voices coming from outside themselves, and when schizophrenics are hallucinating voices, the superior temporal lobe is the area that is most active on functional imaging scans. Finally, student poets are more likely than nonpoets to have had the experience of "hearing inner voices," and they also have altered temporal lobe EEG activity. Thus the area most directly involved in the inner voice seems to be the same as the area most important for hypergraphia, and perhaps for literary creativity in general.

Up to now I have been talking about voices and auditory experiences. Don't people have visual hallucinations as well? False visions are common in drug intoxication and in people with senile dementia, but rare in psychosis. One reason may be that abnormal activity in the mood and semantic regions of the temporal lobe can easily spill over into the nearby auditory cortex, but does not usually spread all the way to the visual cortex.

What about people who have never heard sounds? Once I examined a twenty-year-old woman, Angela, deaf from birth because of prenatal German measles. A gangly, bright-eyed woman, she was brought to the hospital by her parents because of unusual, although not dangerous, behavior. On questioning through a sign interpreter she admitted calmly that her television set was telling her to do things. The most likely cause of these command hallucinations was a first episode of schizophrenia. Getting messages from the TV is a common form of command hallucination — TV and radio waves being the modern equivalent of the spirits and demons to whom earlier schizophrenics attributed their symptoms. In Angela's case, there was another diagnostic possibility: she may have had a rare late complication of prenatal German measles that causes brain degeneration and hallucinations.

So there was a diagnostic dilemma, but there was also a more theoretical puzzle. How was the TV communicating with Angela? She had never heard speech. What could she possibly have been imagining? Close-captioned commands? Were the messages being telepathically inserted into her head without any imagined physical vehicle? Although Angela was too disoriented to tell me, the nature of deaf command hallucinations turns out to be merely a special case of the nature of the inner voice of the deaf. Which, of course, is closely linked to the nature of the inner voice in all of us.

Functional brain imaging and studies of deaf patients who grew up with hearing but later lost it show that their language areas have essentially normal locations, and that they probably continue to think to some extent in "sound." Congenitally deaf people seem to think in sign language instead. When congenitally deaf signers are asked to grip building blocks tightly in their hands while memorizing a list of words, the request has the same disruptive effect as asking hearing people to repeat the nonsense phrase "Jack and Jill, Jack and Jill" during memorization tasks. Signers also tend to make mistakes such as confusing the word "vote" for the word "tea" — words that look quite different in print but are almost identical in sign. Further proof that signers think in sign language comes from the way deaf people sign in their sleep or "think aloud" with fluttering hands when struggling to answer a difficult test question.

It is likely that for all of us, deaf and hearing alike, our inner voice (whether sound or visual sign) becomes more or less sensory depending on the situation. When we are rehearsing a proposal of love, we may hear the words and even the intonations in our head. ("'I *love* you.' No — 'I love *you*.' No — '*I* love you.'" . . .) When we are thinking abstractly, though, we seem to be doing so prelinguistically, both because the speed of our thoughts seems faster than words and because of the difficulty we often have in putting fleeting thoughts into real words. By contrast, in both the experience of the muse and in psychotic hallucinations, the voice heard has more of a sensory quality as well; it is more like a voice, less like an idea.

This notion fits with our sense that voices, whether spoken or signed, in some way are more primitive than silent thoughts. Just as two-year-olds say aloud much of what goes through their heads, just as six-year-olds subvocalize when they read, so people in the throes of creation, as well as people hallucinating, may be thinking more primitively. Not necessarily more simplistically, but primitively in the sense of the primary-process thought discussed in Chapter 2: more vividly, more concretely, more associatively, less constrained by societal convention.

The Experience of Inspiration

If it is controversial to compare literary or creative inspiration to psychotic hallucination, how much more so is it to compare either to religious inspiration? On one level, the similarities are marked. There is the visitation from and control by a higher power, the decreased sense of self, and the sense of self-evident truth of the received vision. Many mixed states are simultaneously religious and creative. This description by Abiezer Coppe, one of the seventeenth-century radical English preachers known as the Ranters, makes God sound very like the muse: "The Word of the Lord came expressly to me, saying, write, write, write. And ONE stood by me, and pronounced all these words to me with his mouth, and I wrote them with ink in this paper."

The overlap between religious and creative inspiration has been remarkably persistent over time and across religions. Compare these two passages. From Philo of Alexandria, a Greek philosopher born before Christ: "Sometimes, when I have come to my work empty, I have suddenly become full; ideas being in an invisible manner showered upon me, and implanted in me from on high; so that . . . I have been conscious of a richness of interpretation, an enjoyment of light, a most penetrating insight, a most manifest energy in all that was to be done." From Albert Einstein: "In my view, it is the most important function of art and science to awaken this [cosmic religious] feeling and keep it alive in those who are receptive to it. . . . I maintain that the cosmic religious feeling is the strongest and noblest motive for scientific research."

Religious inspiration makes the world look fresh. Billy Bray, whom William James describes in his inimitable way as "an excellent little illiterate English evangelist," charmingly recorded his sense of seeing the world clearly for the first time: "In an instant the Lord made me so happy that I cannot express what I felt. I shouted for joy. I praised God with my whole heart . . . I think this was in November, 1823, but what day of the month I do not know. I remember this, that everything looked new to me, the people, the fields, the cattle, the trees. I was like a new man in a new world." Similarly, the products of artistic and scientific inspiration, whether literary metaphors or scientific models, make us see familiar objects as if we have never seen them before.

The original meaning of "inspiration," which we apply to both literary creativity and religious grace, was "breath" — breath being both the most obvious symptom of life and a requirement for language. The word for "life force" means "breath" in Greek *(pneuma)*, Hebrew *(ruach)*, Chinese *(chi)*, Japanese *(reiki)*, Hindu *(prana)*, Algonquin *(manitou)*, East Africa *(mulungu)*, and many other languages.

One notable exception to equating the life force with breath is Freud's entry in the life-force-naming contest. "Libido" has a sexual rather than a respiratory basis. Despite his revolutionary emphasis on oral, anal, and genital drives, psychoanalysis (and indeed most schools of psychiatry) barely discuss the most fundamental drive: to breathe. The psychiatrist Mark Epstein has pointed out that keeping respiration in mind as a model for our give-and-take relationship with the external world, and especially with our creative work, would have a very different effect from thinking of the world as something (on the oral, anal, or genital models) to be consumed, expelled, or penetrated.

Not all breathing is equal, as I learned while examining a Russian patient's lungs. I proudly used one of my few Russian words and told her, I thought, to inspire. She gasped with horror and amusement — it turned out that the word I used meant expire in the sense of "take your last breath." Even though we all need to do both, in nearly every culture inspiring is good and expiring is bad. Yet for certain aspects of literary or artistic creation, the image of expiration may be more appropriate. Jean Cocteau attempted to redefine the relationship be-

Figure 9. William Blake's frontispiece to *Europe: A Prophecy* (1794) is often praised as a moving image of Creation in which God using calipers to introduce rationality into the world. In fact, it shows Blake's invented anti-God, Urizen, dividing the divine from the logical. Blake justified his unusual theology and hatred of Newtonian science as stemming from mystical instructions by the Virgin Mary, Gabriel, and various historical figures.

tween breathing and creativity: "It is not *in*spiration; it is expiration (the gaunt, fine hands on the thorax; evacuation of the chest; a great breathing out from himself)."

The image is not of the artist enriched by the spirit of art, but exhausted by its leaving his body. Finishing a project successfully is, paradoxically, a not uncommon cause of clinical depression. We might explain this phenomenon on a number of levels: as the loss of a goal around which the artist has organized his days, or as a fear that the work is not good enough, or as an exaggerated period of rest and withdrawal after a vigorous effort. I think that when you work hard enough on any work, everything of value in you goes into that work. When you finish it, it leaves you, and you are empty. I think this partial suicide of giving birth caused my postpartum depression. Yet I think estrogen and progesterone shifts did too. I think until it makes me dizzy.

Just as creative and religious inspiration share at least some characteristics, so do religious and psychotic visions. Again, I do not mean to imply that religious visions are psychotic. Yet asserting the reverse, that many psychotic visions have religious content, is uncontroversial. Even among psychotic people who were not originally religious, the number who have primarily religious hallucinations and delusions — who speak daily to the Virgin Mary, or are tormented by voices accusing them of sins they did not commit — is extraordinarily high.

Sometimes a single delusion is isolated in an otherwise nearly normal person. One patient of mine, a gentle homeless man, had a fixed belief that the pope should pay for his chemotherapy. He refused to have his cancer treated until that happened. Luckily, his tactful oncologist managed to convince him that the pope's check was in the mail and that he could begin treatment immediately — the hospital's free care program picking up the tab until the pope's check arrived.

I was not brought up in a very religious family. Except for a tendency to read theology that I kept hidden (except for some excellent conversations with my pope-obsessed patient), the closest I came to religion was the huge park around a convent where in high school my friends and I used to trespass in the middle of the night. The nuns kept the sacred offices at matins, prime, tierce, sext, nones, vespers, compline. Were they using sleep deprivation as an aid to mystical experience? Their nocturnal restlessness allowed us to play a game, Touch the Convent, in which we got as close as we dared before we saw their habits begin to flit across the lighted windows in preparation for the next office.

The convent sat at the top of a ravine with a lake at the bottom, where we would splash until the nuns called the police to sweep their headlights across the water. This became another game, Escape the Nazis; with each sweep we would hold our breath under water until the police got bored and went away. After that there was a statue garden to run through, two rows of nude figures representing the arts gleaming dimly in the moonlight. The nudes didn't seem especially appropriate for a convent, but then the mansion had been built by a high liver during Prohibition. It was full of chandeliers with clusters of crystal grapes as large as fists and a mural representing Dionysian revels.

The convent took in upper-class ladies who were "fragile," which is to say mentally ill or unduly artistic. Religion, creativity, mental illness — how complex a triad. The willingness of religious organizations over the ages to extend charity to the mad is both admirable and evocative. In a sense, the arts have done something similar. What is remarkable is how well some psychiatric patients can do in such settings. How much can religion be seen as one of the original attempts to relieve mental distress? And how much is mental illness the product of incompatibility between a sufferer's nature and the sort of environment that civilization has produced outside convent walls? In some less-developed countries, despite a similar incidence of the major mental disorders and despite far less access to psychiatric drugs, the rate of suicide and violence from mental illness is much lower than in the West.

If religious and creative inspiration share several features, their absence does the same. Writers often describe writer's block or creative failure as analogous to losing grace or being abandoned by God. In this mood they sometimes talk of the "the dark night of the soul," a reference to the book of that name by the sixteenth-century mystic Saint John of the Cross. The analogy offers blocked writers hope by interpreting their suffering as a necessary stage that will ultimately help them become better writers, just as religious trials, periods of doubt, and wrestling with inner demons firm a convert's convictions and bring him closer to perfection. Many episodes of religious inspiration have immediately followed periods of melancholy or tortured loss of faith, a pattern similar to the alternation of writer's block and hypergraphia, depression and hypomania.

Trusting in a favorable outcome is a delicate business for both writers and believers. For Christians, it is a sin to presume on God's grace. For writers, perhaps the equivalent mistake is to confidently wait for the next spasm of inspiration before starting to write. At the same time, vigorous attempts to induce inspiration are equally harmful. Perhaps one reason many writers prefer quiet, inflexible writing schedules that do not depend on inspiration is that they have some similarity to the strict lifestyles of contemplative monks and nuns. The daily practice prepares and calms the artist, creating more fertile soil for whatever seed lands.

At least at first glance, the most telling difference between religious and literary inspiration is the fact that the former so often feels inexpressible, a characteristic that seems antithetical to literary creation. On second glance, the distinction between the ineffable and the effable becomes more complicated. Recipients of indescribable spiritual favors often write copiously in their attempts to describe them. Saint Teresa of Avila's long autobiography is a classic example. Many who have mystical experiences become preachers, driven by the ineffable to transmit their worldview to others. The incommunicable seems paradoxically to be a linguistic state too. Certainly it seems to create the drive to communicate.

Why would descriptions of creative and mystical states be similar? One hypothesis is that it is merely because both are pleasant and culturally esteemed, so we freely use metaphors from one pleasure to describe another, just as one might describe love as sweet.

A second hypothesis is that the similarity reflects the fact that all writing is driven by God. This is certainly possible — although, to have inspired agonized works such as Picasso's *Guernica,* it would have to be a God with rather more complicated tastes than the God we usually hear about.

A third hypothesis is that literary and religious inspiration use similar language because art and religion have long had a historical link. For thousands of years, most art has been sacred art. Literature was perhaps the earliest of the arts to break away from religious themes, giving us, for instance, Aristophanes' satirical play *The Frogs* and Pietro Aretino's pornographic sonnets. Yet ultimately, even one of modern literature's fundamental goals, the attempt to find meaning in experience, still has religious undertones.

A fourth hypothesis, which complements but does not replace the first three cultural explanations, proposes that the two activities may come from similar brain regions. The temporal lobe's roles in hypergraphia and the inner voice point to its importance in the drive to write. There is evidence that the temporal lobe underlies mystical experience as well.

Some scientists have argued that the universality of religious beliefs and experiences makes it likely that there is a specialized region in the brain that processes them. Mystical and spiritual beliefs appear to occur worldwide. The archaeological evidence that even Neanderthals performed ritual burial suggests that religious or magical beliefs have been among us for more than one hundred thousand years. In the United States, 95 percent of the population believe in God and more than 40 percent say they have had at least one mystical experience. The neurologist V. S. Ramachandran has called the thesis that there is a neuroanatomical center for religion the God module argument. The existence of a God module would not disprove the existence of God, just as the existence of the visual cortex does not disprove the existence of visual objects. Ramachandran points out, however, that while every culture knows how to cook — "even the English" — no one would argue that there is a specialized cooking region in the brain.

Nevertheless, a significant scientific literature has postulated that religious experience really does stem largely from a God module, and that this module is based in the temporal lobe. The first line of evidence is that what we know of the function of temporal lobe structures — the amygdala, hippocampus, and temporal cortex — fits with what an "organ of religion" would require. Theologians have argued that the predominant emotion in mystical experience is awe, or a mixture of joy and fear. And the amygdala generates both joy and fear in intensities worthy of mystical experience. Its connections with the hypothalamic regions controlling the sympathetic nervous system (which stimulates arousal) and the parasympathetic nervous system (which stimulates relaxation) would explain the strange mixture of excitement and release produced by mystical experience. The amygdala seems also to function at least in part as the organ of emotional meaning, labeling certain states as significant (tigers, mother, an exam, being one of the Elect), and others as lacking interest. Thus the amygdala might be preeminent in activities intended to give life meaning, whether religious or artistic.

For those who believe, as many psychiatrists do, that our ideas of God are heavily influenced by our infant memories of those giant, all-powerful beings, our parents, the hippocampus, encoder of those memories, must also be important for religious experience. The special role of the hippocampus in memory of places may be relevant to its religious function too, since sacred places have been crucial to both early and modern religions. Besides the role the temporal cortex plays in hearing spirits or gods, its face recognition area probably mediates the rarer occasions when a believer actually sees a religious figure, as in the visions at Lourdes or Guadeloupe.

A second line of evidence for the temporal lobe's importance in religious states is the experience of some people with temporal lobe epilepsy. Many have had vivid mental events that they describe as religious, including repeated conversions, revelations, and visions. Dostoevsky described his seizures as a "holy experience." In *The Idiot,* he wrote of Prince Myshkin having seizures like his own:

There was always one instant just before the epileptic fit . . . when suddenly in the midst of sadness, spiritual darkness and oppression, his brain seemed momentarily to catch fire, and in an extraordinary rush, all his vital forces were at their highest tension. . . . His mind and his heart were flooded with extraordinary light; all his uneasiness, all his doubts, all his anxieties were relieved at once; they were all resolved in a lofty calm, full of serene, harmonious joy and hope, full of reason and ultimate meaning.

Epileptic religious behavior is not restricted to seizure auras. Between seizures, many people with epilepsy remain much more interested in religion and philosophy than the general population. Ramachandran has studied this phenomenon empirically in patients with temporal lobe epilepsy and strong religious sentiments. He showed them pictures and words ranging from ordinary objects, familiar faces and names, to sexually explicit, violent, and religious words and images. He found that their galvanic skin resistance, an index of emotional agitation that is measured by skin electrodes, changed greatly for religious items but changed little for the rest, even the sexual and violent images that would produce a strong change in galvanic skin resistance in most people. This research suggests that the temporal lobe seizures have not been enhancing the sense of meaning indiscriminately, but that the enhancement is selective for religious ideas and images at the expense of other stimuli.

Ramachandran points out that if religious interests arise in the temporal lobe, then patients who have had their temporal lobes removed should have less interest in religion — a "Godectomy." There are few examples, in part because few patients who have religious seizures are willing to undergo the surgery.

One thoughtful, if fictional, account of a nun with a temporal lobe tumor that caused both religious seizures and an overpowering urge to write poetry is described in Mark Salzman's novel *Lying in Wait*. Paradoxically, or perhaps not, Salzman himself endured six years of writer's block while struggling with his book. In an attempt to avoid the distractions of his home office, he spent one of those years writing in his parked car with a towel wrapped around his head — although even then he was troubled by the noise of his cats jumping on the roof. The towel links him to a literary tradition that includes Proust, with his cork-lined room, and Jonathan Franzen, who wrote parts of *The Corrections* wearing a blindfold and earmuffs in a room with double-glazed windows, blackout blinds, and soundproofed walls and ceiling. These writers may have been using a womb-like sensory deprivation to induce literary vision the way some religious traditions use it to induce religious visions. (Other writers find such sensory deprivation unbearable, and do better "writing against resistance," surrounded by the noise of a café or a droning lecturer.)

Neurologists and others have attributed the behavior of many famous religious leaders directly to temporal lobe epilepsy. Sometimes the attribution smacks of circularity: a religious leader is called a temporal lobe epileptic because he has religious visions and is "hyperreligious," and then his existence is taken as evidence that the temporal lobe underlies religious experience. Nonetheless, a striking number of religious personages have had what appear to be frank seizures, Geschwind syndrome, or postseizure deficits such as temporary paralysis or loss of language.

Moses, for instance, reportedly had convulsive fits starting at age three, speech problems suggestive of aphasia or dysarthria, unusually prolific writing, episodes of sudden rage, and religious visions. One neuropsychologist has even speculated that his epilepsy was caused by his being left in that basket among the bullrushes for several days and sustaining a brain injury from heatstroke. Saint Paul's event on the road to Damascus, after which he was blind for three days, make him perhaps the most likely candidate for a seizure among the major religious figures. (If we take the biblical record as being reliable enough to make such a diagnosis, however, we also have to explain why, when Saul heard the voice cry from the light of heaven, his companions heard the voice as well.) Other religious leaders who may have had temporal lobe epilepsy include Mohammed, who wrote the Koran after having spells; Black Elk, with his grand "buffalo" vision;

Joan of Arc; Saint Teresa of Avila; and Joseph Smith, who wrote the Book of Mormon by taking dictation from the angel Moroni.

Most religious believers vigorously contest such diagnoses of epilepsy. Mormons, for instance, point out that many other Mormons have said they had visions like those of Joseph Smith, many more than could possibly have had temporal lobe epilepsy. But religious experience may arise from more subtle forms of temporal lobe activity that need not progress to frank seizures. The psychologist Michael Persinger, who has investigated religious experience in the general population, argues that temporal lobe epilepsy is the extreme end of a continuum of temporal lobe activation, that lesser degrees of activity occur during strong religious feeling, and still lesser degrees during "early morning highs" or when we find reading a text or viewing a work of art deeply meaningful.

Meditation seems to enhance this temporal lobe activity. So does communication between the two hemispheres, a finding that is consistent with the decreased creativity of split-brain patients. Low-frequency transcranial magnetic stimulation (TMS) temporarily decreases brain activity. When aimed at the temporal lobe, it can decrease hallucinated voices in schizophrenic patients. High-frequency TMS, on the other hand, can increase rather than decrease brain activity, and when placed over the temporal lobe can in normal people cause the experience of a sensed presence. Different subjects interpret the presence in different ways: as a ghost, a religious visitation, an absent friend. In a paper engagingly entitled (at least for a scientific paper) "The Feeling of a Presence and Verbal Meaningfulness in Context of Temporal Lobe Function: Factor Analytic Verification of the Muses?" Persinger and his collaborators provide experimental evidence that some subjects interpret that sensed presence as the muse.

The controversy over attributing Joseph Smith's experiences to temporal lobe activity highlights how deeply offensive some believers in any denomination find the possibility that a leader has epilepsy. Some of this sentiment, of course, reflects only the stigma that epilepsy still unfortunately bears. But there are other reasons for the controversy. A neuroscientific concern about this temporal lobe model of religious experience, as about the localization of literary drive, is that complicated behaviors seem unlikely to have such narrow neural localizations. If even sneezing requires activation of regions throughout the brain, could the complex task of perceiving God be squeezed into the temporal lobe?

One research group has reported evidence for the relevance to mystical experience of at least one area outside the temporal lobe. Their subjects were nonepileptic people who are highly practiced in religious meditation, such as Tibetan Buddhist monks. They used a low-resolution imaging technique called a SPECT scan to measure brain activity. Preliminary experiments showed a decrease in brain activity in the temporal cortex — but also in a region of the parietal cortex. The researchers believe that region to be important for the self's orientation to the world, and thus for the sense, imparted by some meditation, of union with the divine. If other experimenters can confirm this finding, it may be evidence that the parietal lobe is important for all mystical experience. Or it may be that the oceanic peace of meditation is a different brain phenomenon from the more personalized and more emotionally extreme mystical experiences traditionally associated with temporal lobe activity.

Another objection to localizing religious activity in the brain is the reductionist "nothing but" argument — that if religious states are brain states, they are nothing but brain states, and the experience of God is simply a neurological disorder. This argument is popular among believers and atheists alike, believers contending that the argument disproves the possibility of localizing religious experience, atheists contending that it disproves the existence of God.

All the same, a number of moderate thinkers from both religious and scientific backgrounds have maintained that states can be both neural and religious, and have proposed that certain temporal lobe brain states may even be the way God talks to the believer. Most religions have long acknowledged that the physical state of the body can shape religious experience. They have traditionally used psychoactive drugs — mescaline among Mesoamericans, hashish among Sufis, wine among early Christians — or they have used other physiological ways of altering consciousness — meditation, fasting, sensory deprivation, physical pain — to induce mystical states. Here again is a parallel between religious and creative inspiration. Over and over, writers and other artists have attempted to use drugs and alcohol to induce creative states.

When scientists use the "nothing but" argument against their religious opponents, it can turn and sting them too. Scientific and literary insights are the product of the same soggy mass of neural tissue that produces religious experience. As William James put it a hundred years ago, "There is not a single one of our states of mind, high or low, healthy or morbid, that has not some organic process as its condition. Scientific theories are organically conditioned just as much as religious emotions are; and if we only knew the facts intimately enough, we should doubtless see 'the liver' determining the dicta of the sturdy atheist as decisively as it does those of the Methodist under conviction anxious about his soul."

The fact that science rests on a questionable assumption of ourselves as rational observers was not news even in Hippocrates' time. He himself noted, not incidentally in a study of epilepsy, that "men ought to know that from nothing else but the brain come joys, delights, laughter and sports, and sorrows, griefs, despondency, and lamentations. And by this, in an especial manner, we acquire wisdom and knowledge, and see and hear, and know what are foul and what are fair, what are bad and what are good, what are sweet, and what unsavory." Why, after five thousand years, do we still have trouble accepting this concept in anything more than a superficial, intellectual way? Because it is a deeply disturbing fact.

During my postpartum mood disorder, my mistrust in science and my own brain was paradoxically most irrelevant and most painful when I had experiences of bathing in a divine warmth — as the remnants of my scientific self looked on with horror. Sometimes I wonder whether it was my scientific training that drove those religious feelings away. If I had not taken so many damned biochemistry courses in college, could I have hung onto that sense of inspiration, had a true conversion, still be pinned down, filled, lifted up by that illumination? I suspect that my training was a minor part of the problem. There was something in my brain that, when it swelled, no amount of education could stop. And now that it has ebbed away, I think I will feel its loss for the rest of my life.

After my postpartum illness resolved, my doctor and I started gradually lowering my mood stabilizers. Their vise grip had been a necessary part of my treatment, I know, like those steel halos into which head injury patients are sometimes screwed. Still, it was a relief to have the screws loosened a little. The world started mattering more again, not in the constant, placid way it had before my illness, but in occasional brilliant flashes. Sometimes they felt like aesthetic experiences because the sense of revelation had a clear external stimulus: a phrase of music, a 220-foot crane towering over Boston, the heraldic image of a black dog on a green field, the sight of my children asleep with their limbs tangled together.

What about those moments not triggered by any external stimulus, when suddenly I want to go still, reorient, and listen for those vibrations in the ether? Is this inspiration, something separate from the aesthetic response? Is it psychosis? Virginia Woolf described the same blur in *Mrs. Dalloway,* when Septimus Warren, experiencing intensely the beauty of the objects around him, felt that "the pattern" was beckoning him to interpret: "The sparrows fluttering, rising, and falling in jagged fountains were part of the pattern; the white and blue, barred with black branches. Sounds made harmonies with premeditation; the spaces between them were as significant as the sounds."

I know more now than I used to about what aesthetic and scientific inspiration states share with religious revelation and even psychosis, all subjects that I was able to keep in neat compartments before my break. How did I gain my knowledge? Because of the research described in this book — but also because my viscera and my heart and my midbrain know it — and they have more influence over my cortex than they used to. This is not, of course, how scientists are supposed to think. It fills me with sorrow, although it also animates me, that I no longer feel entirely like a scientist, although I try hard to think in the sober way I used to (note all those references). Whether most scientists are as objective as I dream I used to be — well, that is a position that many philosophers and historians of science and even working scientists dismiss. Even I, my head still spinning from whatever disease or decision suddenly propelled me from my old understanding of science into a world where science and literature are not far apart, even I am fairly sure that the real problem is not my new lack of rationality but my new awareness of my — of our — old lack of rationality.

One reason I wrote this book was to show that science can help us create and understand literature, that by thinking of problems like writer's block as something more than a failure of willpower, by testing treatments systematically, we can help people more effectively. Yet literature can also help us to understand science, the way it is both driven and sometimes misdirected by metaphors and emotion.

Using literature to help us understand science is, of course, as dangerous as using science to understand literature. The risk is of explaining away something powerful and precious. Scientists are often, rightly, derisive of papers by deconstructionists who had trouble getting through college physics but who claim, for example, that the theory of natural selection is merely capitalist dogma. Science may be riddled with metaphors, but it is still better to consult a civil engineer than a citizens' committee (or a group of deconstructionists) when building a bridge.

Yet there are times when it might be better to have the citizens' committee than the scientist, because there are times when what appear to be scientific or medical judgments are primarily moral ones. Medicine may fairly tell you that taking a pill will rid you of a symptom, and in this book I have tried to extend this line of thinking to ever stranger territory. But medicine may not fairly tell you that you *should* take it, although doctors, including myself, usually can't resist doing so: "You should stop smoking, lose weight, take your antidepressant so that you will write more and be a more productive member of society," or "You should stop your antidepressant because it has made your writing bland." Often decisions about such treatments have strong family and societal implications, but individuals should, as much as possible, have control over what happens in their own brains. As treatments develop for problems with creativity, I hope their existence will not trigger a requirement that they be used, or increase pressure on people to medically tame or to augment their creativity.

And yet, and yet. I know, and I presume most of the people reading this book know, how much joy the feeling of creativity brings. It is 5:30 A.M. and I have already been typing long enough that my legs are numb, but this discomfort is many miles away. Most people come by their love of writing in a healthier way, but for me it was an illness that makes me associate writing with this joy that makes my heart race, yet at the same time makes my head quiet enough that I can hear vibrations in the ether.

The scientist in me worries that my happiness is nothing more than a symptom of bipolar disease, hypergraphia from a postpartum disorder. The rest of me thinks that artificially splitting off the scientist in me from the writer in me is actually a kind of cultural bipolar disorder, one that too many of us have. The scientist asks how I can call my writing vocation and not addiction. I no longer see why I should have to make that distinction. I am addicted to breathing in the same way. I write because when I don't, it is suffocating. I write because something much larger than myself comes into me that suffuses the page, the world, with meaning. Although I constantly fear that what I am writing teeters at the edge of being false, this force that drives me cannot be anything but real, or nothing will ever be real for me again.

REFERENCES

Important references are indicated in boldface. Italicized numbers indicate fleeting references, whereas numbers in parentheses refer to mere implications or unwarranted extrapolations. Asterisks are used to identify particularly distasteful passages.

— Peter Schickele, *The Definitive Biography of P. D. Q. Bach, 1707–1742*

The inevitable outcome of unrestrained growth, whether of references or of tissues, is death.

— Ramzi Cotran, M.D., lecture on oncologic pathology (1989)

Introduction

PAGE

4 *I read a passage:* C. S. Lewis, *Surprised by Joy* (New York: Harcourt, Brace, 1956).
a face so beautiful: E. Scarry, *On Beauty and Being Just* (Princeton: Princeton University Press, 1999).

7 *"little man":* A. R. Luria, *The Mind of a Mnemonist: A Little Book About a Vast Memory* (New York: Basic Books, 1968).

8 *prodigious memory:* L. MacFarquhar, "The Prophet of Decline: Harold Bloom's Anxiety and Influence," *New Yorker,* Sept. 30, 2002, 85–97.

9 *despite the complexity:* P. Hoban, "A Couch for Authors in Need of One," *New York Times,* Aug. 31, 2002.

13 *pregnancy-induced mood disorders:* B. McEwen, "Estrogen Actions Throughout the Brain," *Recent Progress in Hormone Research* 57 (2002):357–384.

16 *problems such as procrastination:* T. A. Pychyl, Richard W. Morin, and Brian R. Salmon, "Procrastination and the Planning Fallacy: An Examination of the Study Habits of University Students," *Journal of Social Behavior and Personality* 15 (5) (2000):135–150.

1. Hypergraphia

17 *Consider a young man:* J. L. Rice, *Dostoevsky and the Healing Art: An Essay in Literary and Medical History* (Ann Arbor: Ardis, 1985); P. H. Voskuil, "The Epilepsy of Fyodor Mikhailovitch Dostoevsky (1821–1881)," *Epilepsia* 24 (6) (Dec. 1983):658–667.

18 *"Again, what is my object":* F. Dostoevsky, "Notes from the Underground," in *Three Short Novels* (Garden City, N.Y.: Anchor Books, 1960).

19 *In the 1970s:* S. G. Waxman and N. Geschwind, "Hypergraphia in Temporal Lobe Epilepsy," *Neurology* 24 (1974):629–636; H. H. Sachdev and S. G. Waxman, "Frequency of Hypergraphia in Temporal Lobe Epilepsy: An Index of Interictal Behaviour Syndrome," *Journal of Neurology, Neurosurgery, and Psychiatry* 44 (1981):358–360.

a typical page: Waxman and Geschwind, "Hypergraphia."

22 *cognitive and emotional behaviors:* J. D. Schmahmann, ed., *The Cerebellum and Cognition* (San Diego: Academic Press, 1997).

24 *a spectrum of:* M. A. Persinger and K. Makarec, "Temporal Lobe Epileptic Signs and Correlative Behaviors Displayed by Normal Populations," *Journal of General Psychology* 114 (1987):179–195; K. Makarec and M. A. Persinger, "Electroencephalographic Correlates of Temporal Lobe Signs and Imaginings," *Perceptual and Motor Skills* 64 (1987):1124–26.

25 *work driven by:* T. M. Amabile, "Motivation and Creativity: Effects of Motivational Orientation on Creative Writers," *Journal of Personality and Social Psychology* 48 (2) (Feb. 1985):393–397.

greater on girls: J. Baer, "Gender Differences in the Effects of Extrinsic Motivation on Creativity," *Journal of Creative Behavior* 32 (1) (1998):18–37.

Yeats's wife: B. Maddox, *Yeats' Ghosts: The Secret Life of W. B. Yeats* (New York: HarperCollins, 1999).

26 *Lewis Carroll:* E. LaPlante, *Seized* (New York: HarperCollins, 1993).

27 *The eminent neurologist:* F. Lhermitte, B. Pillon, and M. Serdaru, "Human Autonomy and the Frontal Lobes. Part I: Imitation and Utilization Behavior: A Neuropsychological Study of 75 Patients," *Annals of Neurology* 19 (4) (Apr. 1986):326–334; F. Lhermitte, "Human Autonomy and the Frontal Lobes. Part II: Patient Behavior in Complex and Social Situations: The 'Environmental Dependency Syndrome,'" *Annals of Neurology* 19 (4), (Apr. 1986):335–343.

The emotional symptoms: K. Dewhurst and A. W. Beard, "Sudden Religious Conversion in Temporal Lobe Epilepsy," *British Journal of Psychiatry* 117 (1970):496–507; D. M. Bear and P. Fedio, "Quantitative Analysis of Interictal Behavior in Temporal Lobe Epilepsy," *Archives of Neurology* 34 (1977):454–467; Giriguotta et al., "Temporal Lobe Epilepsy with Ecstatic Seizures (So-Called Dostoevsky Epilepsy)," *Epilepsia* 21 (1980):705–710.

28 *"a whirlpool of ideas":* LaPlante, *Seized.*

Edward Lear, for instance: J. Wullschlager, "Edward Lear," at www.penguin classics.com.

29 *temporal lobe abnormalities:* J. G. Small et al., "Topographic EEG Studies of Mania," *Clinical Electroencephalography* 29 (1998):59–66; L. Gyulai et al., "I-123 Iofetamine Single-Photon Computed Emission Tomography in Rapid Cycling Bipolar Disorder: A Clinical Study," *Biological Psychiatry* 41 (1997):152–161.

30 *the anticonvulsant drugs:* R. M. Post, "Sensitization and Kindling Perspectives for the Course of Affective Illness: Toward a New Treatment with the Anticonvulsant Carbamazepine," *Pharmacopsychiatry* 23 (1990):3–17.

A surprising proportion: K. R. Jamison, *Touched with Fire* (New York: Free Press, 1993), 88; N. C. Andreasen, "Creativity and Mental Illness: Prevalence Rates in Writers and Their First-Degree Relatives," *American Journal of Psychiatry* 144 (1987):1288–92; K. Makarec and M. A. Persinger, "Temporal Lobe Signs: Electroencephalographic Validity and Enhanced Scores in Special Populations," *Perceptual and Motor Skills* 60 (1985):831–842; J. Ratey and C. Johnson, *Shadow Syndromes* (New York: Doubleday, 1998).

32 *This belief was written down:* Aristotle (or a follower of Aristotle), "Problems Connected with Thought, Intelligence, and Wisdom," *Problems,* c. 2nd century B.C.E., as cited in J. Radden, ed., *The Nature of Melancholy: From Aristotle to Kristeva* (New York: Oxford University Press, 2000).

So many writers: N. Casey, *Unholy Ghost: Writers on Depression* (New York: Morrow, 2001).

This link between writing: T. J. Mayne, "Negative Affect and Health: The Importance of Being Earnest," *Cognition and Emotion* 13 (1999):601–635; C. S. Tang, "Predicting Accuracy of Judgment of Contingency," *Journal of Social Psychology* 130 (1990):703–705.

33 *Many psychiatrists argue:* E. Kraepelin, *Manic-Depressive Insanity and Paranoia* (Edinburgh: Livingstone, 1921); H. S. Akiskal, "Mood Disorders: Clinical Features," in B. J. Sadock and V. A. Sadock, *Kaplan and Sadock's Comprehensive Textbook of Psychiatry* (Philadelphia: Lippincott Williams and Wilkins, 2000), 1338–77.

37 *The scientist in me:* M. Schou, "Artistic Productivity and Lithium Prophylaxis in Manic-Depressive Illness," *British Journal of Psychiatry* 135 (1979):97–103.

EEG studies show: J. G. Small et al., "Topographic EEG Studies of Mania," *Clinical Electroencephalography* 29 (2) (Apr. 1998):59–66.

40 *"oh hear":* J. Rhawn, *Neuropsychiatry, Neuropsychology, and Clinical Neuroscience* (Philadelphia: Lippincott Williams and Wilkins, 1996), 140.

41 *One psychiatrist and historian:* E. F. Torrey, *The Roots of Treason: Ezra Pound and the Secret of St. Elizabeth's* (New York: Lucas Books, 1999).

As in the writing: M. E. Shenton et al., "A Review of MRI Findings in Schizophrenia," *Schizophrenia Research* 49 (1–2) (Apr. 2001):1–52; S. M. Lawrie et al., "Reduced Frontotemporal Functional Connectivity in Schizophrenia Associated with Auditory Hallucinations," *Biological Psychiatry* 51 (12) (June 15, 2002):1008–11; R. E. Hoffman et al., "Transcranial Magnetic Stimulation of Left Temporoparietal Cortex in Three Patients Reporting Hallucinated 'Voices,'" *Biological Psychiatry* 46 (1) (July 1999):130–132.

46 *phenomena so acceptable:* N. Baker, *Room Temperature* (New York: Vintage, 1995).

descriptions of driven writing: M. Cowley, ed., *Writers at Work: The Paris Review Interviews*, vol. 1 (New York: Viking Press, 1958).

47 *"The extraordinarily prolific writer":* V. Nelson, *On Writer's Block* (Boston: Houghton Mifflin, 1993), 141.

"Coming back to the question: L. S. Dembo, ed., *Interviews with Contemporary Writers, 2nd series, 1972–82* (Madison: University of Wisconsin Press, 1983), 352–353.

48 *Dostoevsky rejected this position:* F. Dostoevsky, *The Idiot* (New York: Oxford University Press, 1998).

2. Literary Creativity and Drive

50 *Even social scientists:* T. M. Amabile and E. Tighe, "Questions of Creativity," in J. Brockman, ed., *Creativity* (New York: Simon and Schuster, 1993), 8; S. Freud, "Dostoevsky and Parricide" (1928), in J. Strachey and others, eds. and trans., *The Standard Edition of the Complete Psychological Works*, vol. 21 (London: Hogarth Press, 1957–74); H. Gardner, *Frames of Mind: The Theory of Multiple Intelligences* (New York: Basic Books, 1983).

51 *The definition of creative work:* M. Csikszentmihalyi, "Implications of a Systems Perspective for the Study of Creativity," in. R. J. Sternberg, ed., *Handbook of Creativity* (New York: Cambridge University Press, 1999), 313–338.

52 *For instance, researchers find:* E. P. Torrance, "Creativity Research in Education: Still Alive," in I. A. Taylor and J. W. Getzels, *Perspectives in Creativity* (Chicago: Aldine, 1974), 278–296; N. C. Andreasen, "Creativity and Mental Illness: Prevalence Rates in Writers and Their First-Degree Relatives," *American Journal of Psychiatry* 144 (10) (Oct. 1987):1288–92.

The psychologist: D. K. Simonton, *Origins of Genius: Darwinian Perspectives on Creativity* (New York: Oxford University Press, 1999); J. Swafford, *Johannes Brahms: A Biography* (New York: Knopf, 1997).

53 *As the poet:* W. H. Auden, ed., *Nineteenth Century British Minor Poets* (New York: Dell, 1965), 15.

55 *While strong instrinsic motivation:* E. L. Deci, "Effects of Externally Mediated Rewards on Intrinsic Motivation," *Journal of Personality and Social Psychology* 18 (1) (Apr. 1971): 105–115; T. M. Amabile, "Motivation and Creativity: Effects of Motivational Orientation on Creative Writers," *Journal of Personality and Social Psychology* 48 (2) (Feb. 1985):393–397; H. A. Simon, *Administrative Behavior: A Study of Decision Making Processes in Administrative Organizations* (New York: Free Press, 1976).

This implies that: Plato, in E. Hamilton and H. Cairns, eds., L. Cooper and others, trans., *The Collected Dialogues of Plato, Including the Letters* (New York: Pantheon Books, 1961), 218–221;. Amabile and Tighe, "Questions of Creativity."

59 *The first theory:* S. Freud, "The Relation of the Poet to Day-Dreaming," *Collected Papers* (London: Hogarth, 1908–59), vol. 4, pp. 173–183.
    It may help: F. W. Nietzsche, *Thus Spake Zarathustra,* trans. T. Common (New York: Modern Library, 1917), ch. 64.

60 *Extending the Freudian model:* E. Kris, *Psychoanalytic Explorations in Art* (New York: International Universities Press, 1952).
    For Segal: H. Segal, "A Psycho-Analytical Approach to Aesthetics," in M. Klein, P. Heimann, and R. E. Money-Kyrle, eds., *New Directions in Psycho-Analysis: The Significance of Infant Conflict in the Pattern of Adult Behavior* (New York: Basic Books, 1955), 390.

61 *He described a life:* M. Proust, *Remembrance of Things Past,* trans. C. K. Scott Moncrieff and T. Kilmartin (New York: Vintage Books, 1981), 51.

62 *Modern researchers:* C. Martindale, "Biological Bases of Creativity," in R. J. Sternberg, ed., *Handbook of Creativity* (New York: Cambridge University Press, 1999), 138.

63 *Plato even thought:* Plato, 245a, unknown trans., cited in P. Sandblom, *Creativity and Disease,* 10th ed. (New York: Marion Boyars, 1997), 50.
    The eighteenth century: www.trp.dundee.ac.uk/research/glossary/hermitce.html.

64 *One complication:* F. Barron and D. M. Harrington, "Creativity, Intelligence and Personality," *Annual Reviews of Psychology* 32 (1981):439–476; K. R. Jamison, *Touched with Fire* (New York: Free Press, 1993); A. M. Ludwig, "Creative Achievement and Psychopathology: Comparison Among Professions," *American Journal of Psychotherapy* 46 (3) (1992):330–356; N. C. Andreasen, "Creativity and Mental Illness: Prevalence Rates in Writers and Their First-Degree Relatives," *American Journal of Psychiatry* 144 (10) (Oct. 1987):1288–92.
    Clear examples of such genes: See F. K. Goodwin and K. R. Jamison, *Manic-Depressive Illness* (New York: Oxford University Press, 1990), 169, ch. 14; R. Richards et al., "Creativity in Manic-Depressives, Cyclothymes, Their Normal Relatives, and Control Subjects," *Journal of Abnormal Psychology* 97 (3) (Aug. 1988):281–288.

65 *The James siblings:* J. L. Karlsson, "Creative Intelligence in Relatives of Mental Patients," *Hereditas* 100 (1) (1984):83–86; Richards et al., "Creativity in Manic-Depressives"; Jamison, *Touched with Fire;* D. Steel, *His Bright Light* (New York: Delta, 2000); J. Groopman, "The Doubting Disease," *New Yorker,* Apr. 10, 2000, 52–57.
    Other researchers have suggested: L. J. Webb, "The Byron Menagerie," www.saqnet.net/users/kuranda/menagerie.htm; J. Rothfuss, "Joseph Beuys: A Brief Biography," www.walkerart.org/beuys/gg3.html.

66 *One study comparing:* A. Rothenberg, *Creativity and Madness: New Findings and Old Stereotypes* (Baltimore: Johns Hopkins University Press, 1990).

67 *In the nineteenth century:* S. Plant, *Writing on Drugs* (New York: Farrar, Straus, and Giroux, 1999); J. Morgan, "The William S. Burroughs Interviews," *Creem Magazine,* 1978, quoted at www.artdamage.com/wsb/medical.htm.
    the oracle at Delphi: W. J. Broad, "Fumes and Visions Were Not a Myth for Oracle at Delphi," *New York Times,* Mar. 19, 2002.

68 *"I once inhaled"*: O. W. Holmes, *Mechanism in Thought and Morals: An Address Delivered Before the Phi Beta Kappa Society of Harvard University, June 29, 1870* (Boston: James R. Osgood, 1871).
the equivocal ability of drugs: Jamison, *Touched with Fire.*

69 *most people's left hemisphere:* C. Martindale et al., "EEG Alpha Asymmetry and Creativity," *Personality and Individual Differences* 5 (1) (1984):77–86; K. D. Hoppe and N. L. Kyle, "Hemispheric Specialization and Creativity in Psychotherapy," *Psychotherapy Patient* 4 (1) (1987):139–151; N. Jausovec and K. Jausovec, "Differences in Resting EEG Related to Ability," *Brain Topography* 12 (3) (Spring 2000):229–240.

70 *Right-brain enthusiasts:* W. H. Calvin, *The Throwing Madonna: Essays on the Brain* (New York: McGraw-Hill, 1983), 103; K. D. Hoppe, "Hemispheric Specialization and Creativity," *Psychiatric Clinics of North America* 11 (3) (Sept. 1988):303–315.

72 *frontal lobe activity:* I. Carlsson, P. E Wendt, and J. Risberg, "On the Neurobiology of Creativity: Differences in Frontal Activity Between High and Low Creative Subjects," *Neuropsychologia* 38 (6) (Mar. 2000):873–885.
A subset of people: B. L. Miller et al., "Emergence of Artistic Talent in Frontotemporal Dementia," *Neurology* 51 (4) (Oct. 1998):978–982.

74 *Vincent van Gogh:* P. Sandblom, *Creativity and Disease,* 10th ed. (New York: Marion Boyars, 1997), 99; www.geocities.com/CapeCanaveral/2612/vangogh. htm.
"Sometimes I draw": E. LaPlante, *Seized* (New York: HarperCollins, 1993), 6.

75 *Van Gogh's direct comparison:* C. Lambert, "Seizures of Genius: Van Gogh's Malady," *Harvard Magazine* (Jan.-Feb. 1999); Matt. 18:9.
Besides van Gogh: A. Panico, A. Parmegriani, and M. R. Trimble, "Compulsive Painting: A Variant of Hypergraphia?" *Behavioural Neurology* 9 (3–4) (Fall-Winter 1996):177–180.

77 *TMS over the temporal:* M. A. Persinger and K. Makarec, "The Feeling of a Presence and Verbal Meaningfulness in Context of Temporal Lobe Function: Factor Analytic Verification of the Muses?" *Brain Cognition* 20 (2) (Nov. 1992): 217–26. L. Osborne, "Savant for a Day," *New York Times,* June 22, 2003, 38. A. Conca et al., "Transcranial Magnetic Stimulation: A Novel Antidepressive Strategy?" *Neuropsychobiology* 34 (4) (Nov. 1996):204–207.

3. Writer's Block as State of Mind

79 *In professional writers:* M. Rose, *Writer's Block: The Cognitive Dimension* (Carbondale: Southern Illinois University Press, 1984); P. Monaghan, "Some Fields Are Reassessing the Value of the Traditional Doctoral Dissertation," *Chronicle of Higher Education* 35 (1989):A1; G. Eliot, *Middlemarch* (New York: Modern Library, 1994), 190; A. Camus, *The Plague,* trans. S. Gilbert (New York, Knopf, 1948); Margret and H. A. Rey, *Whiteblack the Penguin Sees the World* (Boston: Houghton Mifflin, 2000).

81 *I sit down religiously:* J. Conrad to E. Garnett, Mar. 29, 1898, in F. R. Karl and L. Davies, eds., *The Collected Letters of Joseph Conrad* (New York: Cambridge University Press, 1983–96), vol. 2, p. 49.

Defining block: Z. Leader, *Writer's Block* (Baltimore: Johns Hopkins University Press, 1991).

82 *Such times may:* J. Keats, "To J. H. Reynolds," Feb. 19, 1818, in R. Gittings, ed., *Letters of John Keats* (Oxford: Oxford University Press, 1970), 65–66.

Thus, some writers: F. Kafka to F. Bauer, Nov. 29, 1912, in E. Heller and J. Born, eds., *Letters to Felice,* as quoted in Leader, *Writer's Block,* 21.

83 *One poet has said:* W. Stafford, *Writing the Australian Crawl: Views on the Writer's Vocation* (Ann Arbor: University of Michigan Press, 1978).

Yet when he tried: S. T. Coleridge to R. Southey, July 19, 1802, in E. L. Griggs, ed., *The Collected Letters of Samuel Taylor Coleridge* (Oxford: Clarendon Press, 1956–71), vol. 2, p. 814.

Oliver Sacks tells: O. Sacks, personal communication, June 29, 2001.

84 *The phrase "writer's block":* E. Bergler, *The Writer and Psychoanalysis* (New York: Doubleday, 1950).

"Trollope's calmly professional attitude": R. Pack and J. Parini, eds., *Writers on Writing* (Middlebury, Vt.: Middlebury College Press; Hanover, N.H.: University Press of New England, 1991), 203–204.

One literary critic points out: Leader, *Writer's Block.*

85 *"What a waste":* G. Flaubert to L. Colet, 1846, as quoted in P. Sandblom, *Creativity and Disease,* 10th ed. (New York: Marion Boyars, 1997).

Fitzgerald was one: F. S. Fitzgerald, "An April Letter," in E. Wilson, ed., *The Crack-Up,* (New York: J. Laughlin, 1945).

"Writing at such a time": N. Mailer, *Cannibals and Christians* (New York: Dial Press, 1966), 124.

86 *Even literary critics:* A. Hickey, *Impure Conceits: Rhetoric and Ideology in Wordsworth's Excursion* (Stanford: Stanford University Press, 1997), 1.

87 *The Hungarian composer:* Unsigned liner notes from a Kurtág recording at www.ecmrecords.com/ecm-cgi-bin/background/1619.

88 *The writing researcher:* Rose, *Writer's Block.*

The literary critic: Leader, *Writer's Block.*

90 *"a rifle hanging":* A. Chekhov, *The Seagull,* trans. D. French (Toronto: Playwrights Co-op, 1977).

91 *"Of all mental systems":* L. Trilling, "Freud and Literature," *The Liberal Imagination: Essays on Literature and Society,* in *The Works of Lionel Trilling: Uniform Edition* (Oxford: Oxford University Press, 1981), 33–55.

"Analysis shows": S. Freud, "Inhibitions, Symptoms, and Anxiety" (1926), in *The Complete Psychological Works* (London: Hogarth Press, 1957–74), vol. 20, pp. 89–90.

92 *"Some procrastinate":* C. Ducey, personal communication, Sept. 2000.

93 *One systematic:* A. Lipson and D. Perkins, *Block — Getting Out of Your Own Way: The New Psychology of Counterintentional Behavior in Everyday Life* (New York: Carol Publishing, 1990).

94 *Whereas in fact:* "Folly and Female Education," in G. K. Chesterton, *What's Wrong with the World* (New York: Dodd, Mead, 1910), iv.14.

95 *Anecdotal evidence tells us:* D. Bayles and T. Orland, *Art and Fear: Observations on the Perils (and Rewards) of Artmaking* (Santa Barbara, Calif.: Capra, 1993). *Several trials:* K. Szymanski and S. G. Harkins, "Self-Evaluation and Creativity," *Personality and Social Psychology Bulletin* 18 (3) (June 1992):259–265; E. Weisskopf-Joelson and T. S. Eliseo, "An Experimental Study of the Effectiveness of Brainstorming," *Journal of Applied Psychology* 45 (1961):45–49; M. Diehl and W. Stroebe, "Productivity Loss in Idea-Generating Groups: Tracking Down the Blocking Effect," *Journal of Personality and Social Psychology* 61 (1991):392–403.

96 *That brainstorming is:* L. Börne, "The Art of Becoming an Original Writer in Three Days," quoted in A. Phillips, *Equals* (London: Faber, 2002), 100. Ferenczi discussed in Phillips, *Equals,* 23.

insecure people: C. See, "Making a Literary Life: Advice for Writers and Other Dreamers," quoted in D. Garner, "A Heartbreaking Work of Staggering Genius," *New York Times Book Review,* Aug. 11, 2002; L. Slater, "The Trouble with Self-Esteem," *New York Times,* Feb. 3, 2002.

"First there's the": A. Lamott, *Bird by Bird* (New York: Pantheon, 1994), 21–26.

97 *One writing coach:* B. Goldberg, *Beyond the Words: The Three Untapped Sources of Creative Fulfillment for Writers* (New York: Tarcher, 2002), quoted in Garner, "Heartbreaking Work."

99 *"W. Somerset Maugham's day":* H. A. Mulligan, "Travis McGee's Creator Takes On TV Evangelists," *St. Louis Post-Dispatch,* May 15, 1983, quoted in R. T. Kellog, *The Psychology of Writing* (New York: Oxford University Press, 1994), 185.

Habit is a phenomenon: E. R. Kandel, "The Molecular Biology of Memory Storage: A Dialogue Between Genes and Synapses," *Science* 294 (2001):1030–38; S. Corkin, "What's New with the Amnesic Patient H.M.?" *Nature Reviews — Neuroscience* 3 (2002):153–160.

100 *Writers such as:* S. Kunitz, quoted in G. Plimpton, ed., *The Writer's Chapbook: A Compendium of Fact, Opinion, Wit, and Advice from the Twentieth Century's Preeminent Writers* (New York: Viking, 1989), 80.

Writers are more vocal: T. Olsen, *Silences* (New York: Delacorte Press/Seymour Lawrence, 1978).

101 *"The intellect of man":* W. B. Yeats, *The Collected Poems of W. B. Yeats* (New York: Scribners, 1997).

"Balzac, you remember": Olsen, *Silences,* 18

104 *The Romanticists' view:* Leader, *Writer's Block.*

"A grief without a pang": S. T. Coleridge, "Dejection: An Ode," lines 21–24, 39–41, in E. H. Coleridge, ed., *The Poems of Samuel Taylor Coleridge* (London: Oxford University Press, 1917).

105 *Modern critics:* W. J. Bate, *The Burden of the Past and the English Poet* (New York: Norton, 1972); W. Shakespeare, Sonnet 26, *The Riverside Shakespeare* (Boston: Houghton Mifflin, 1997); M. Twain, *Mark Twain's Notebooks and Journals* (Berkeley: University of California Press, 1997).

105 *Harold Bloom made more explicit:* H. Bloom, *The Anxiety of Influence: A Theory of Poetry,* 2nd ed. (New York: Oxford University Press, 1997).

106 *They can inspire:* J. Keats, "On First Looking into Chapman's Homer," *The Complete Poems of John Keats* (New York: Modern Library, 1994).

107 *For Roland Barthes:* R. Barthes, "What Is Writing?" in *Writing Degree Zero* (New York: Noonday Press, 1990).
     "Writing/not writing": V. Nelson, *On Writer's Block* (Boston: Houghton Mifflin, 1993), 162; J. Thurber quoted in M. Cowley, ed., *Writers at Work: The Paris Review Interviews,* vol. 1 (New York: Viking Press, 1958).

4. Writer's Block as Brain State

110 *tortured by indecision:* W. James, *Diary,* Apr. 30, 1870.

111 *"I went one evening":* W. James, *The Varieties of Religious Experience: A Study in Human Nature* (New York: Modern Library, 1994), 179.

114 *"the thoughts rise":* L. Sterne, *Tristram Shandy* (New York: New American Library, 1960), 501–502, as quoted in Z. Leader, *Writer's Block* (Baltimore: Johns Hopkins University Press, 1991), 125, 287.
     Samuel Johnson's essay: S. Johnson, *The Rambler,* no. 134 (Sat., June 29, 1751), in W. J. Bate, ed., *Samuel Johnson: Selected Essays from the Rambler, Adventurer, and Idler* (New Haven: Yale University Press, 1968), 176–181.

117 *Attempts to improve:* T. A. Pychyl, R. W. Morin, and B. R. Salmon, "Procrastination and the Planning Fallacy: An Examination of the Study Habits of University Students," *Journal of Social Behavior and Personality* 15 (5) (Spec 2000): 135–150.
     deadlines hinder creativity: T. M. Amabile, "How to Kill Creativity," *Harvard Business Review* (Sept.-Oct. 1998), pp. 77–87.

118 *Shakespeare fills Hamlet:* W. Shakespeare, *Hamlet,* in *The Riverside Shakespeare* (Boston: Houghton Mifflin, 1997), 2.2.295–309, 1.2.133.

119 *The French psychoanalyst:* J. Kristeva, *Black Sun* (New York: Columbia University Press, 1989), 3.
     "Whenever I read Kafka": L. Wieseltier, *Kaddish* (New York: Knopf, 1998).

121 *When the patient's depression:* A. L. Brody et al., "Brain Metabolic Changes in Major Depressive Disorder from Pre- to Post-Treatment with Paroxetine," *Psychiatry Research* 91 (3) (Oct. 11, 1999):127–133; P. Videbech, "PET Measurements of Brain Glucose Metabolism and Blood Flow in Major Depressive Disorder: A Critical Review," *Acta Psychiatrica Scandinavica* 101 (1) (Jan. 2000):11–20; S. D. Martin et al., "Brain Blood Flow Changes in Depressed Patients Treated with Interpersonal Psychotherapy or Venlafaxine Hydrochloride: Preliminary Findings," *Archives of General Psychiatry* 58 (7) (July 2001):641–648.

124 *Producer Joseph Papp:* N. Shange, "The Dark Room," in J. Shinder, ed., *Tales from the Couch* (New York: HarperCollins, 2000).
     "The intensest light": H. Melville, *Pierre, Or: The Ambiguities* (New York: HarperCollins, 1995).

125 "It's been almost": L. Slater, Prozac Diary (New York: Random House, 1998).

126 Dawn simulators: M. J. Norden and D. H. Avery, "A Controlled Study of Dawn Simulation in Subsyndromal Winter Depression," Acta Psychiatrica Scandinavica 88 (1) (July 1993):67–71.

128 Its crossover: J. Groopman, "Eyes Wide Open," New Yorker, Dec. 3, 2001.
    The artist: D. Bayles and T. Orland, Art and Fear: Observations on the Perils (and Rewards) of Artmaking (Santa Barbara, Calif.: Capra, 1993).

130 On average, people: K. R. Jamison, Touched with Fire (New York: Free Press. 1993).

131 Sylvia Plath's poetry: K. Moses, "The Real Sylvia Plath," www.salonmag.com/ books/feature/2000/06/01/plath2/.

132 Late in life: H. C. Margolese, "The Male Menopause and Mood: Testosterone De-cline and Depression in the Aging Male — Is There a Link?" Journal of Geriatric Psychiatry and Neurology 13 (2) (Summer 2000):93–101; A. Sullivan, "The He Hormone," New York Times Magazine, Apr. 2, 2000; S. N. Seidman and B. T. Walsh, "Testosterone and Depression in Aging Men," American Journal of Geri-atric Psychiatry 7 (1) (Winter 1999): 18–33.

136 the Hemingway defense: S. King, On Writing (New York: Scribner, 2000), 94.
    Ultimately it is likely: A. M. Ludwig, "Alcohol Input and Creative Output," British Journal of Addiction 85 (1990):953–963; E. P. Noble, M. A. Runco, and T. Z. Ozkaragoz, "Creativity in Alcoholic and Nonalcoholic Families," Alcohol 10 (4) (July-Aug. 1993):317–322; T. Dardis, The Thirsty Muse: Alcohol and the American Writer (Boston: Houghton Mifflin, 1989).

137 In a relevant parable: A. Lipson and D. Perkins, Block — Getting Out of Your Own Way: The New Psychology of Counterintentional Behavior in Everyday Life (New York: Carol Publishing, 1990).
    As Franz Kafka wrote: F. Kafka, Diaries, Nov. 7, 1921.

139 One physiological technique: D. S. Shannahoff-Khalsa, M R. Boyle, and M. E. Buebel, "The Effects of Unilateral Forced Nostril Breathing on Cognition," Inter-national Journal of Neuroscience 57 (3–4) (Apr. 1991):239–249.
    sixteen studies of the Mozart effect: C. F. Chabris et al., "Prelude or Requiem for the 'Mozart effect'?" Nature 400 (Aug. 1999):826–828.

140 In a recent: D. G. Amen, "The Temporal Lobe," www.brainplace.com/bp/brain system/temporal.asp.

5. How We Write

156 Here a patient with Broca's: M. C. Linebarger, M. F. Schwartz, and E. M. Saffran, "Syntactic Processing in Agrammatism: A Reply to Zurif and Grodzinsky," Cog-nition 15 (1983):215–225.

157 In the following example: M. Coltheart, "Acquired Language Disorders," rosella. bhs.mq.edu.au/~max/Language/ (1998).

158 Such a medicalized look: R. Ochsner, Physical Eloquence and the Biology of Writing (Stony Brook: State University of New York Press, 1990).

158 *The linguist:* R. Jakobson and M. Halle, "Two Aspects of Language and Two Types of Aphasic Disturbances," in *Fundamentals of Language* (Paris: Mouton, 1971).

160 *Functional brain imagining:* H. H. Brownell et al., "Appreciation of Metaphoric Alternative Word Meanings by Left and Right Brain-Damaged Patients," *Neuropsychologia* 28 (4) (1990):375–383; G. Bottini et al., "The Role of the Right Hemisphere in the Interpretation of Figurative Aspects of Language: A Positron Emission Tomography Activation Study," *Brain* 117 (6) (Dec. 1994):1241–53; M. Faust and S. Weisper, "Understanding Metaphoric Sentences in the Two Cerebral Hemispheres," *Brain Cognition* 43 (1–3) (June-Aug. 2000):186–191.
Besides Broca's: M. J. Farah and M. A. Wallace, "Semantically-Bounded Anomia: Implications for the Neural Implementation of Naming," *Neuropsychologia* 7 (1992):609–621.

161 *The neurologist:* O. Sacks, *The Man Who Mistook His Wife for a Hat* (New York: Simon and Schuster, 1985), 76; N. L. Etcoff et al., "Lie Detection and Language Comprehension," *Nature* 405 (2000):139.

162 *"Since the fragment":* Sacks, *The Man Who Mistook His Wife*, 134.

163 *tally marks:* D. Schmandt-Besserat, *How Writing Came About* (Austin: University of Texas Press, 1997).
In hieroglyphs: S. Pinker, *The Language Instinct* (New York: HarperCollins, 1995), 186.
"The grand jury thing": Watergate transcripts, Committee on the Judiciary, U.S. House of Representatives, 1974, quoted in Pinker, *Language Instinct*, 221.

164 *"Some people":* Pinker, *Language Instinct*, 223.

165 *"Usually the entries":* www.lion-schools.co.uk/marketing/exam/hughes/art.htm.

166 *Actually, reading silently:* P. Saenger, *Space Between Words: The Origins of Silent Reading* (Palo Alto: Stanford University Press, 2000); J. Gold, *The Story Species* (Markham, Ontario: Fitzhenry and Whiteside, 2002), 47.

167 *"'Ah' is something":* A. R. Luria, *The Mind of a Mnemonist* (New York: Basic Books, 1968), 25. The original vowels were Russian.
"It was on a June morning": B. Blood, "The Poetical Alphabet," quoted in J. Rasula and S. McCaffery, *Imagining Language* (Cambridge, Mass.: MIT Press, 1998).

169 *Scientists propose:* E. Paulesu et al., "The Physiology of Coloured Hearing. A PET Activation Study of Colour-Word Synaesthesia," *Brain* 118 (pt. 3) (June 1995):661–676.

170 *"A black":* A. Rimbaud, "Vowels," in *Collected Poems* (New York: Oxford University Press, 2001).

171 *One patient:* N. Del Grosso Destreri et al., "Selective Uppercase Dysgraphia with Loss of Visual Imagery of Letter Forms: A Window on the Organization of Graphomotor Patterns," *Brain and Language* 71 (3) (Feb. 15, 2000): 353–372.
In a rare side effect: K. Baynes et al., "Modular Organization of Cognitive Systems Masked by Interhemispheric Integration," *Science* 280 (5365) (May 8, 1998):902–905.

172 *If reading and writing:* H. J. Bischof, "Imprinting and Cortical Plasticity: A

Comparative Review," *Neurosciences Biobehavioral Review* 7 (2) (Summer 1983):213–225; N. W. Daw et al., "Factors That Are Critical for Plasticity in the Visual Cortex," *Ciba Foundation Symposium* 193 (1995):258–276, discussion 322–324.

172 *Are second languages:* N. Gordon, "The Acquisition of a Second Language," *European Journal of Paediatric Neurology* 4 (1) (2000):3–7.

178 *Most dyslexics are denied:* M. Habib, "The Neurological Basis of Developmental Dyslexia: An Overview and Working Hypothesis," *Brain* 123 (12) (Dec. 2000):2373–99.

Postmortem studies: J. Stein and V. Walsh, "To See But Not to Read; The Magnocellular Theory of Dyslexia," *Trends in Neuroscience* 20 (4) (Apr. 1997):147–152.

179 *The first theory proposes:* G. Eden et al., "Abnormal Processing of Visual Motion in Dyslexia Revealed by Functional Brain Imaging," *Nature* 383 (1996):66–69; M. S. Livingstone et al., "Physiological and Anatomical Evidence for a Magnocellular Defect in Developmental Dyslexia," *Proceedings of the National Academy of Sciences, USA* 88 (18) (Sept. 15, 1991):7943–47.

As attractive as: I. Lundberg, J. Frost, and O. Peterse, "Effects of an Extensive Program for Stimulating Phonological Awareness in Preschool Children," *Journal of Experimental Child Psychology* 18 (1988):201–212.

A third theory: R. H. Fitch, S. Miller, and P. Tallal, "Neurobiology of Speech Perception," *Annual Review of Neuroscience* 20 (1997):331–353.

Supporting the temporal: M. M. Merzenich et al., "Temporal Processing Deficits of Language-Learning Impaired Children Ameliorated by Training," *Science* 271 (5245) (Jan. 5, 1996):77–81.

180 *If dyslexia emerges:* J. M. Rumsey et al., "A Positron Emission Tomographic Study of Impaired Word Recognition and Phonological Processing in Dyslexic Men," *Archives of Neurology* 54 (1997):562–573; K. R. Pugh et al., "Functional Neuroimaging Studies of Reading and Reading Disability (Developmental Dyslexia)," *Mental Retardation Developmental Disability Research Review* 6 (3) (2000):207–213.

181 *At the same time:* E. Uta Frith Paulesu et al., "Dyslexia: Cultural Diversity and Biological Unity," *Science* 291 (5511) (Mar. 16, 2001):2165–67.

6. Why We Write

185 *London taxi drivers:* E. A. Maguire et al., "Navigation-Related Structural Change in the Hippocampi of Taxi Drivers," *Proceedings of the National Academy of Sciences, USA* 97 (8) (Apr. 11, 2000):4398–403.

186 *The amygdala:* A. Bechara et al., "Double Dissociation of Conditioning and Declarative Knowledge Relative to the Amygdala and Hippocampus in Humans," *Science* 269 (1995): 1115–18.

One French farmer: G. Assal, C. Favre, and J. P. Anderes, "Nonrecognition of Familiar Animals by Farmer: Zooagnosia or Prosopagnosia for animals," *Revue Neurologique (Paris)* 140 (10) (1984):580–584.

186 *the evidence includes:* P. J. Reading and R. G. Will, "Unwelcome Orgasms," *Lancet* 350 (9093) (Dec. 13. 1997):1746.

187 *Two areas:* A. Bechara, H. Damasio, and A. R. Damasio, "Emotion, Decision Making and the Orbitofrontal Cortex," *Cerebral Cortex* 10 (3) (Mar. 2000):295–307.

    Finally, there is: G. F. Koob, "The Role of the Striatopallidal and Extended Amygdala Systems in Drug Addiction," *Annals of the New York Academy of Sciences* 877 (June 29, 1999):445–460; H. C. Breiter et al., "Functional Imaging of Neural Responses to Expectancy and Experience of Monetary Gains and Losses," *Neuron* 30 (2) (May 2001):619–639.

188 *Low brain serotonin levels:* J. R. Kaplan et al., "Assessing the Observed Relationship Between Low Cholesterol and Violence-Related Mortality. Implications for Suicide Risk," *Annals of the New York Academy of Sciences* 836 ((Dec. 29, 1997):57–80.

192 *Researchers have generally:* P. Ekman, "Facial Expression and Emotion," *American Psychologist* 48 (4) (Apr. 1993):384–392.

193 *Along with the list:* "Basic emotions," www.personalityresearch.org/basic emotions.html; W. James, *Psychology: The Briefer Course* (New York: Harper and Row, 1892), 241.

194 *The neurologist:* A. Damasio, *Descartes' Error* (New York: Avon, 1995).

195 *The moral philosopher:* M. Nussbaum, *Love's Knowledge* (New York: Oxford University Press, 1992).

196 *a language instinct:* S. Pinker, *The Language Instinct* (New York: HarperCollins, 1995).

    And that asymmetry: M. Habib and A. M. Galaburda, "Biological Determinants of Cerebral Dominance." *Revue Neurologique* 142 (12) (1986):869–894.

    A third line: F. Wilson, *The Hand* (New York: Vintage, 1998), 192; Pinker, *Language Instinct,* 267–271.

    Followers of: N. Chomsky, *Reflections on Language* (New York: Pantheon, 1975), 9–11; D. Bickerton, "The Language Bioprogram Hypothesis," *Behavioral and Brain Sciences* 7 (1984):173–221.

198 *"the production of a sound":* J. Goodall, *The Chimpanzees of Gombe: Patterns of Behavior* (Cambridge, Mass.: Harvard University Press, 1986), 125.

200 *The psychologist:* D. Evans, *Emotion: The Science of Sentiment* (New York: Oxford University Press, 2001), 75.

    some evolutionary psychologists: P. Lieberman, *Eve Spoke: Human Language and Human Evolution* (New York: Norton, 1998), 30.

201 *Indeed, a revolutionary study:* R. K. Pitman et al., "Pilot Study of Secondary Prevention of Posttraumatic Stress Disorder with Propranolol," *Biological Psychiatry* 51 (2) (Jan. 15, 2002):189–192.

202 *It certainly makes:* H. Flor et al., "Spouse Presence Alters Brain Response to Pain," *Society for Neuroscience Abstracts,* 2002; H. Flor, R. D. Kerns, and D. C.

Turk, "The Role of Spouse Reinforcement, Perceived Pain, and Activity Levels of Chronic Pain Patients," *Journal of Psychosomatic Research* 31 (2) (1987):251–259.

203 *Laughter as an expression:* V. S. Ramachandran and S. Blakeslee, *Phantoms in the Brain* (New York: Morrow, 1998), 206.

206 *One group of studies:* A. Brand, *The Psychology of Writing: The Affective Experience* (New York: Greenwood, 1989).

"What is a poet?": S. Kierkegaard, *Either/Or* (Princeton: Princeton University Press, 1987); A. Gide, *My Theater: Five Plays and an Essay* (New York: Knopf, 1952); P. Sandblom, *Creativity and Disease.*

209 *"I have perceiv'd":* W. Whitman, "I Sing the Body Electric," in *Leaves of Grass* (New York: Metropolitan Books, 2001).

210 *the neurochemistry of bereavement:* J. Panksepp, *Affective Neuroscience* (New York: Oxford University Press, 1998), ch. 14.

Opiate addicts: S. Plant, *Writing on Drugs* (New York: Farrar, Straus and Giroux, 1999).

211 *"No one, ever":* G. Flaubert, *Madame Bovary* (New York: Modern Library, 1982).

"Tragedy is": K. Tynan, *New Yorker,* Oct. 30, 1978.

"On some days": S. King, *On Writing* (New York: Scribner, 2000), 269.

216 *Writers sometimes write:* A. Lamott, *Bird by Bird* (New York: Pantheon, 1994), xiv; W. Shakespeare, Sonnet 18, *The Riverside Shakespeare* (Boston: Houghton Mifflin, 1997).

217 *"The reason we write":* M. Kundera, *The Book of Laughter and Forgetting* (New York: Penguin, 1981), 91, 92.

219 *Some literary critics:* J. Gold, *The Story Species* (Markham, Ontario: Fitzhenry and Whiteside, 2002); T. Deacon, *The Symbolic Species: The Co-Evolution of Language and the Brain* (New York: Norton, 1997).

220 *The interaction:* J.-J. Lecercle, *Philosophy Through the Looking Glass: Language, Nonsense, and Desire* (London: Hutchinson, 1985).

221 *The limbic sensation:* Z. Laskewicz, "Zaum," users.belgacom.net/nacht schimmen/zaumpaper.htm (1995).

222 *"I had not a dispute":* J. Keats, 1817 letter to his brothers, quoted in A. Phillips, *Promises, Promises* (New York: Basic Books, 2001), 23.

7. Metaphor, the Inner Voice, and the Muse

225 *The empiricist:* S. Parker, *Free and Impartial Censure of the Platonick Philosophy (1666),* quoted in G. Lakoff and M. Johnson, *Metaphors We Live By* (Chicago: University of Chicago Press, 1983).

When we think of metaphor: W. Shakespeare, *A Midsummer Night's Dream,* act 3, sc. 2; H. Pollio et al., *The Poetics of Growth: Figurative Language in Psychology, Psychotherapy, and Education* (Hillsdale, N.J.: Lawrence Erlbaum, 1977); www.cs.bham.ac.uk/~jab/ATT-Meta/Databank/table.html.

226 *Keats, who had medical:* A. Richardson, *British Romanticism and the Science of the Mind* (New York: Cambridge University Press, 2001).
My question: C. P. Snow, "The Two Cultures," *New Statesman and Nation,* Oct. 6, 1956, 413–414; E. O. Wilson, *Consilience* (New York: Knopf, 1998).

227 *the glimmering network:* W. V. Quine and J. S. Ullian, *The Web of Belief* (New York: Random House, 1978).

228 *When Newton first:* D. L. Carveth, "The Analyst's Metaphors: A Deconstructionist Perspective," *Psychoanalysis and Contemporary Thought* 7 (4) (1984):491–560.

229 *For creativity researcher:* C. Martindale, "Biological Bases of Creativity," in R. J. Sternberg, ed., *Handbook of Creativity* (New York: Cambridge University Press, 1999), 137.

230 *And when a book:* G. B. Murray, "Limbic Music," *Psychosomatics* 33 (1) (Winter 1992):16–23.

231 *In Yeats's poem:* W. B. Yeats, "For Anne Gregory," *The Collected Poems* (New York: Macmillan, 1965).

233 *"I shall behave"':* T. R. Hummer, "Against Metaphor," in J. Parini, ed., *Writers on Writing* (Middlebury, Vt: Middlebury College Press, 1991), 86–97.

236 *The notion of the muse:* R. J. Sternberg and T. I. Lubart, "The Concept of Creativity: Prospects and Paradigms," in Sternberg, *Creativity,* 3–15.

237 *"I call her up":* D. Justice, *New and Selected Poems* (New York: Knopf, 1995).
"A man cannot say": P. B. Shelley, "A Defense of Poetry," in H. E. Hugo, ed., *The Portable Romantic Reader* (New York: Viking, 1957), 536.
It has even been: M. A. Persinger and K. Makarec, "The Feeling of a Presence and Verbal Meaningfulness in Context of Temporal Lobe Function: Factor Analytic Verification of the Muses," *Brain and Cognition* 20 (1992):217–226.
Here is the painter: J. D. Flam, *Matisse on Art* (Berkeley: University of California Press, 1995).

238 *The psychologist:* M. Csikszentmihalyi, *Flow: The Psychology of Optimal Experience* (New York: HarperCollins, 1991).
Yet the sense: T. S. Eliot, "Virgil and the Christian World," in *On Poetry and Poets* (New York: Farrar, Straus and Cudahy, 1957); O. Paz, *Children of the Mire: Modern Poetry from Romanticism to the Avant-Garde* (Cambridge: Cambridge University Press, 1974), 160.

239 *Many sane people:* S. Freud, "An Early Paper on Aphasia," quoted in R. Dinnage, Introduction in D. P. Schreber, *Memoirs of My Nervous Illness* (Cambridge, Mass.: Harvard University Press, 1988); S. Freud, "Psychoanalytic Notes upon an Autobiographical Account of a Case of Paranoia," in *Three Case Histories,* ed. P. Rieff (New York: Collier, 1963).

240 *The most prominent theory:* P. A. Bick and M. Kinsbourne, "Auditory Hallucinations and Subvocal Speech in Schizophrenic Patients," *American Journal of Psychiatry* 144 (2) (Feb. 1987):222–225.
On this view: J. Jaynes, *The Origin of Consciousness in the Breakdown of the Bicameral Mind* (Boston: Houghton Mifflin, 2000).

243 *Perhaps the most:* Schreber, *Memoirs.*

244 *While hearing voices:* N. Zungu-Dirwayi et al., "Are Musical Obsessions a Temporal Lobe Phenomenon?" *Journal of Neuropsychiatry and Clinical Neurosciences* 11 (3) (1999):398–400.

245 *Schizophrenics, the chief:* B. Mohr et al., "Interhemispheric Cooperation During Word Processing: Evidence for Callosal Transfer Dysfunction in Schizophrenic Patients," *Schizophrenic Research* 46 (2–3) (Dec. 15, 2000):231–239; K. D. Hoppe, "Hemispheric Specialization and Creativity," *Psychiatric Clinics of North America* 11 (3) (Sept. 1988):303–315; M. G. Knyazeva and D. A. Farber, "Formation of Interhemispheric Interaction in Ontogeny: Electrophysiological Analysis," *Human Physiology* 17 (1) (Jan.-Feb. 1991):1–11.

246 *Initial evidence suggests:* B. Libet et al., "Time of Conscious Intention to Act in Relation to Onset of Cerebral Activity (Readiness-Potential): The Unconscious Initiation of a Freely Voluntary Act," *Brain* 106 (pt. 3) (Sept. 1983):623–642; D. Wegner, *The Illusion of Conscious Will* (Cambridge, Mass.: MIT Press, 2002).

248 *And Winston Churchill:* L. Havens, *A Safe Place* (New York: Ballantine, 1991).
Several lines of evidence: M. Stephane, S. Barton, and N. N. Boutros, "Auditory Verbal Hallucinations and Dysfunction of the Neural Substrates of Speech," *Schizophrenia Research* 50 (1–2) (May 30, 2001):61–78; S. S. Shergill et al., "Mapping Auditory Hallucinations in Schizophrenia Using Functional Magnetic Resonance Imaging," *Archives of General Psychiatry* 57 (11) (Nov. 2000):1033–38; K. Makarec and M. A. Persinger, "Temporal Lobe Signs: Electroencephalographic Validity and Enhanced Scores in Special Populations," *Perceptual and Motor Skills* 60 (1985):831–842.

250 *Congenitally deaf people:* J. G. Kyle, "Sign Language as Cognition for Deaf People: Pitfalls and Prospects," *Applied Cognitive Psychology* 3 (2) (Apr.-June 1989):109–125; J. McCrone, "How the Deaf Think in Sign Not Words," www.bt internet.com/~neuronaut/webtwo_features_deaf.htm (1993).

251 *Many mixed states:* A. Coppe, "A Second Fiery Flying Roule," in N. Smith, ed., *A Collection of Ranter Writings from the Seventeenth Century* (London: Junction Books, 1983), 92; Philo of Alexandria, quoted in A. Clissold, "The Prophetic Spirit," *Genius and Madness,* 1870, 67; A. Einstein, "Religion and Science," *The World as I See It* (New York: Philosophical Library, 1949), 24–28.

252 *"In an instant":* W. James, *The Varieties of Religious Experience* (New York: Modern Library, 1994).
The psychiatrist: M. Epstein, *Thoughts Without a Thinker* (New York: Basic Books, 1995).
Jean Cocteau attempted: G. Plimpton, ed., *The Writer's Chapbook: A Compendium of Fact, Opinion, Wit, and Advice from the Twentieth Century's Preeminent Writers* (New York: Viking, 1989), 68.

257 *Mystical and spiritual:* R. Joseph, *Neuropsychiatry, Neuropsychology, and Clinical Neuroscience* (Philadelphia: Lippincott Williams and Wilkins, 1996), 268; Gallup poll washingtonpost.com/wp-srv/politics/polls/wat/archive/wat042400.htm; A. Greeley, "Mysticism Goes Mainstream," *American Health* 6 (1987):47–49; V. S.

Ramachandran and S. Blakeslee, *Phantoms in the Brain* (New York: Morrow, 1998), 18.

258 *The first line:* Joseph, *Neuropsychiatry;* E. Rolls, *The Brain and Emotion* (New York: Oxford University Press, 1999); E. d'Aquili and A. B. Newberg, *The Mystical Mind* (Minneapolis: Fortress Press, 1999).
A second line: K. Dewhurst and A. W. Beard, "Sudden Religious Conversion in Temporal Lobe Epilepsy," *British Journal of Psychiatry* 117 (1970):496–507; D. M. Bear and P. Fedio, "Quantitative Analysis of Interictal Behavior in Temporal Lobe Epilepsy," *Archives of Neurology* 34 (1977):454–467.

259 *"There was always":* F. Dostoevsky, *The Idiot* (New York: Oxford University Press, 1998).
Epileptic religious behavior: Ramachandran and Blakeslee, *Phantoms,* 186.
Salzman himself: C. Lloyd, "A Conversation with Mark Salzman," *Salon,* Jan. 10, 2001, archive.salon.com/people/conv/2001/01/10/salzman/index.html.

261 *The psychologist:* M. A. Persinger, "Religious and Mystical Experiences as Artifacts of Temporal Lobe Function: A General Hypothesis," *Perceptual and Motor Skills* 57 (1983):1255–62.
Meditation seems to: M. A. Persinger, "Transcendental Meditation and General Meditation Are Associated with Enhanced Complex Partial Epileptic-Like Signs: Evidence for 'Cognitive' Kindling?" *Perceptual and Motor Skills* 76 (1) (Feb. 1993):80–82; R. E. Hoffman et al., "Transcranial Magnetic Stimulation of Left Temporoparietal Cortex in Three Patients Reporting Hallucinated 'Voices,'" *Biological Psychiatry* 46 (1) (July 1999):130–132; M. A. Persinger and K. Makarec, "The Feeling of a Presence and Verbal Meaningfulness in Context of Temporal Lobe Function: Factor Analytic Verification of the Muses?" *Brain Cognition* 20 (2) (Nov. 1992):217–226.

262 *One research group:* A. Newberg et al., "The Measurement of Regional Cerebral Blood Flow During the Complex Cognitive Task of Meditation: A Preliminary SPECT Study," *Psychiatry Research* 106 (2) (Apr. 10, 2001):113–122.

263 *"There is not":* James, *Religious Experience.*
"men ought to know": Hippocrates, "On the Sacred Disease," trans. F. Adams, classics.mit.edu/Hippocrates/sacred.html.

ILLUSTRATION CREDITS

" . . . and what is the use of a book," thought Alice, "without pictures or conversations?"

— Lewis Carroll, *Alice's Adventures in Wonderland*

Figure 1. Max Ernst, plate from *Maximiliana* (1964). © 2003 Artists Rights Society (ARS), New York/ADAGP, Paris.

Figure 2. Surface and cortical views of the brain, courtesy of the author.

Figure 3. The writing of a hypergraphic person. From "Manic-Depressive Insanity and Paranoia" by Emil Kraepelin.

Figure 4. Vesalius, illustration from *De Humani Corporis Fabrica* (1543).

Figure 5. Drawing from *Rebus Charivariques* (c. 1840).

Figure 6. Leonardo da Vinci, page from a notebook (c. 1490).

Figure 7. Max Ernst, "Le Musée de L'Homme" (1965). © Artists Rights Society (ARS), New York/ADAGP, Paris.

Figure 8. Frida Kahlo, "Frida 36" (1932). © 2003 Banco de México Diego Rivera & Frida Kahlo Museums Trust. Av. Cinco de Mayo No. 2, Col. Centro, Del. Cuauhtémoc 06059, México, D.F.

Figure 9. William Blake, frontispiece to *Europe: A Prophecy* (1794).

INDEX

Some men pretend to understand a Book
  by scouting thro' the Index:
as if a Traveller should go about to describe a Palace
  when he had seen nothing but the Privy.

— Jonathan Swift, *Mechanical Operation of the Spirit* (1784)

If you don't find it in the Index, look very carefully through the
entire catalog.

— Sears, Roebuck, *Consumer's Guide* (1897)